# Internet Retail Operations

## Integrating Theory and Practice for Managers

# SUPPLY CHAIN INTEGRATION
## Modeling, Optimization, and Applications

*Sameer Kumar, Series Advisor*
*University of St. Thomas, Minneapolis, MN*

**Internet Retail Operations: Integrating Theory and Practice for Managers**
Timothy M. Laseter and Elliot Rabinovich
ISBN: 978-1-4398-0091-1

**Human-Computer Etiquette: Cultural Expectations and the Design Implications They Place on Computers and Technology**
Caroline C. Hayes and Christopher A. Miller
ISBN: 978-1-4200-6945-7

**Closed-Loop Supply Chains: New Developments to Improve the Sustainability of Business Practices**
Mark E. Ferguson and Gilvan C. Souza
ISBN: 978-1-4200-9525-8

**Connective Technologies in the Supply Chain**
Sameer Kumar
ISBN: 978-1-4200-4349-5

**Financial Models and Tools for Managing Lean Manufacturing**
Sameer Kumar and David Meade
ISBN: 978-0-8493-9185-9

**Supply Chain Cost Control Using Activity-Based Management**
Sameer Kumar and Matthew Zander
ISBN: 978-0-8493-8215-4

# Internet Retail Operations

## Integrating Theory and Practice for Managers

Timothy M. Laseter ◆ Elliot Rabinovich

CRC Press
Taylor & Francis Group
Boca Raton   London   New York

CRC Press is an imprint of the
Taylor & Francis Group, an **Informa** business

CRC Press
Taylor & Francis Group
6000 Broken Sound Parkway NW, Suite 300
Boca Raton, FL 33487-2742

© 2012 by Taylor & Francis Group, LLC
CRC Press is an imprint of Taylor & Francis Group, an Informa business

No claim to original U.S. Government works

Version Date: 20110705

International Standard Book Number: 978-1-4398-0091-1 (Hardback)

**Visit the Taylor & Francis Web site at**
**http://www.taylorandfrancis.com**

**and the CRC Press Web site at**
**http://www.crcpress.com**

# Contents

# Preface

Internet retailing has endured many ups and downs over the course of its short existence. Like many innovations, it suffered from excessive hype followed by disillusionment; it deserved neither. Internet retailing does not fundamentally redefine the world of retailing. Though early advocates claimed it offered limitless shelf space and enabled consumers to find the lowest price at the click of a mouse, merchandisers still need to pick and price the right products and present them effectively to a significant body of consumers. An unlimited offering can be unbearably confusing and a low price may not be a bargain if the product shows up late or damaged (or not at all!).

Retail operations management has faced the most profound change, however. Most of the headcount in traditional retail operations resided in the physical stores now eliminated in the Internet model. Though traditional retailers had to master supply chain management and logistics, their distribution networks moved goods in pallet loads by common carriers—not in individual boxes destined for consumer homes. It is not a "new economy." The fundamentals still matter, but the answers have changed in the new business equations.

Despite the relatively short history of Internet retailing, many current practitioners, as well as hopeful entrepreneurs, lack a clear understanding of the history and the core principles of Internet retail operations. Accordingly, we have partnered to synthesize over a decade of our research and experience into this book. We hope it represents a complementary combination of both theory and practice as we merge our personal perspectives. The book provides chapters covering a range of topical areas we have examined over the years, as well as a variety of case studies.

As you will learn, many experiments did not succeed because they failed to appreciate the fundamentals—but others may have simply been before their time. Though Internet retailing represents a megatrend not to be ignored, it still represents a mere fraction of total retailing. Many years of experimentation and growth lie ahead. We hope our book will serve as a faithful guide to anyone on the journey of building their operations capability in the evolving world of Internet retailing. We will be watching!

**Tim Laseter**
*Charlottesville, Virginia*

**Elliot Rabinovich**
*Tempe, Arizona*

# Acknowledgments

Many people have proved instrumental in shaping this book, and we would like to acknowledge their gracious support. First, we must thank our students who serve as inspiration for our teaching and associated case writing. Your intellectual curiosity energizes us and often forces us to think more deeply about the issues of the day. More explicitly, a number of students wrote group papers that served as the foundation of many case study chapters or worked as research assistants to flesh them out.

Second, we must thank the many practitioners who have shared their real-life problems with us. Your passion for your business is infectious and keeps us grounded outside of the ivory towers of academia. Since most insisted that we disguise their names and never quote them, we assume calling them out by name would be unwelcome acclaim. But you know who you are.

The editors of *strategy+business*—Art Kleiner, and Randy Rothenberg before him—deserve special acknowledgment as well. They have allowed us access to the business-savvy readers of their award-winning journal. They have also pushed our thinking and encouraged us to more clearly articulate the issues according to the mantra of "telling the readers what to *think about*—not what to *think*." Like us, they abhor "best practices" but instead encourage thoughtful reflection. Much of the book owes its clarity to their guidance over the years.

Steve Momper of Darden Business Publishing graciously released the rights of our previously published teaching cases in exchange for the rights to several new cases developed as part of this project. We hope that this book will stimulate rather than cannibalize his sales.

Though the two of us have formed a strong research partnership over the years, we have also worked with a variety of world-class researchers who have contributed directly and indirectly to the contents of this book, including Joseph Bailey, Mary Jo Bitner, Sam Bodily, Ken Boyer, Steve Brown, Ed Davis, Philip Evers, Brent Goldfarb, Eric Johnson, David Kirsch, Michael Knemeyer, Arnold Maltz, Diane Mollenkopf, Charles Noble, Kamalini Ramdas, Eve Rosenzweig, Aleda Roth, Johnny Rungtusanatham, Rajiv Sinha, Elliot Weiss, and Ron Wilcox.

Of course, we need to acknowledge our institutions, the Darden Graduate School of Business at the University of Virginia and the W. P. Carey School of Business at Arizona State University. Both institutions have provided us steady support during the decadelong research culminating in this book. Though this represents an important personal milestone for each of us, we do promise to keep researching this fascinating topic for at least another decade.

Finally, we would like to thank our families for their ongoing support of this book and our careers in general. Academics and consultants are not always the best partners in life—and those of us aspiring to do both can be particularly difficult to stomach. Thank you, Jody and Rachel, for your life-long encouragement.

# Chapter 1

# Internet Retailing: From Experimentation to Execution*

The advent of the Internet as a tool to carry out purchases between buyers and sellers ushered in a significant evolutionary step in commerce that can be traced back to the nineteenth century and the use of catalogues by Sears–Roebuck to sell durable items to consumers in remote areas of the United States. A century later, Internet technology ushered in another radical transformation in commerce by further expanding individuals' options to buy products from businesses as well as other individuals. However, at the beginning of the twenty-first century, the bursting of the Internet bubble brought high-flying start-ups back to the ground with the recognition that profits mattered more than eyeballs, and good retailing still required having the right products at the right price. Further, though the shelves were now virtual, effective execution in the physical world still mattered.

In this book we argue that the most important functions and tasks needed to be successful in electronic commerce take place in the physical realm. After all, most customers choose to buy time and again on the web in order to have a wide

---

* With permission, this chapter draws upon the article *"Lessons of the Last Bubble"* by Tim Laseter, David Kirsch, and Brent Goldfarb published in *strategy+business*, issue 46, Spring 2007.

variety of products come to their doorsteps, as opposed to having to go to pick up the products where they are stored for sale and having to haul these items back home. The successful completion of Internet-based transactions between sellers and buyers requires a host of physical assets, including trucks, airplanes, fulfillment centers, and, of course, the physical package. Internet commerce does not take place exclusively in cyberspace.

From our experience of teaching the newest generation of managers in MBA programs, we have learned that much of the history of the developmental years of Internet retailing was lost to them and, accordingly, risks being repeated. As such, this chapter starts with a historical perspective on the Internet bubble at the turn of the century. It then reviews the progress of Internet retailing over the past decade before covering the remaining contents of the book.

## Lessons of the Last Bubble

On March 10, 2000, the NASDAQ peaked at 5132 before beginning a mind-blowing tumble that resulted in a 78% drop over the ensuing 2½ years that destroyed trillions in paper wealth. About half of the dot-com businesses went bust by 2004, but the survivors include a host of companies that are dramatically affecting the way business operates. The Internet may not have produced a fundamentally "New Economy," but it did unleash a transformation that continues through today. In the United States, Internet retailing has grown roughly 20% per year over the past decade—10 times faster than retailing overall. Of course, 8 of the 10 largest Internet retailers in 2010 are traditional ones; Amazon and Newegg are the only pure-play e-tailers in the top 10.

### Too Few Failures

The 50% failure rate of the dot-com era seems high until we put it into perspective. Compare the dot-coms to other business realms: From 1996 to 1998, for example, the survival rate for independent restaurants open for 3 years ran 39%. That is, a form of business with a very measurable market, using cooking technology that has existed for decades or more, failed 61% of the time. By comparison, the failure rate of Internet-based businesses tapping unknowable market opportunities with an unproven technology platform seems far more tame.

Perhaps this data simply suggest that the dot-com era was an overall success. Despite the trillions of dollars of market capitalization lost when the Internet bubble burst, maybe one should celebrate that the losses were not greater. But we disagree with this perspective. In fact, we bemoan the low failure rate.

To be clear, we do not wish that more start-ups had failed. Rather, to us, the low failure rate indicates that too few entrepreneurs were funded and too few new ventures launched. Had twice as many been launched, the short-term failure rate for individual businesses might have been higher, but a larger number of successful business models would probably have emerged, and these would have led to more enduring businesses in the long run. As Kenichi Ohmae suggested in *The Invisible Continent: Four Strategic Imperatives of the New Economy* (HarperBusiness, 2000), the dot-com era was like the exploration boom that launched the United States' westward movement in the eighteenth and nineteenth centuries. The Internet opened up an entirely new continent for colonization. Many venture pioneers sought to settle this new land. Upon reflection, that so many companies survived suggests that the first wave of the dot-com revolution suffered from too *little* entry, not too much. The hype-happy phase of the bubble created a land-grab mentality, with early entrants seeking to control the high ground rather than continue exploring. When the bubble burst, new explorers could not get the funding to start a new expedition of the remaining uncharted territory. Had the fall not been so dramatic, more firms could have sought to productively exploit the new terrain.

## Bigger Is Riskier

"Get big fast" served as the mantra of the era, but such a strategy offers both benefits and risks. On the one hand, scale economies certainly accrue to a big company. Wal-Mart can buy and then transport goods at a lower cost because it sells more than $400 billion in goods each year. In addition to having the resources to scour the world in search of the lowest-cost suppliers, Wal-Mart can invest in state-of-the-art radio frequency identification (RFID) technology to run its distribution network. The distribution network has enough density for economical cross-docking operations, which transfer goods between trucks without the extra cost of storing them for long periods of time. As a result, Wal-Mart turns its inventory eight times per year versus a median of four times for the industry as a whole.

However, a "get big fast" strategy in pursuit of scale economies has a dark side, especially in unpredictable markets. Webvan, for example, was founded in 1996, went public in 1999, and filed for bankruptcy protection in 2001. In the summer of 1999 it reported that revenues from the 6 months ending in June totaled $395,000, with net losses of $35.1 million. Despite those financial results, the company signed a $1 billion contract with Bechtel Corporation to build 26 distribution centers across the country, modeled on its unproven pilot operation in Oakland, California.

Webvan ultimately built three of the highly automated, large-scale distribution centers, and none of them reached break-even utilization levels. Each distribution center offered sales potential equivalent to 18 traditional grocery stores—a huge amount of capacity to bring online at one time in a mature industry. Webvan's projections had estimated costs based on high utilization rates, but at the 30% to 40% utilization rates actually achieved by the facilities, the company's costs were well above those of the traditional model, and its cash quickly dissipated.

By contrast, Wal-Mart achieved its scale over a very long time. Sam and Bud Walton opened the first Wal-Mart in 1962, but only after Sam had spent a dozen years running five-and-dime stores for the Ben Franklin chain. Eight years later, in 1970, Wal-Mart went public with $44 million in sales from 18 stores. It also opened its first distribution center that year. Sam Walton expanded much more slowly and only after proving the profitability of the small-town discount store strategy. Webvan tried to grow rapidly while struggling with the complexity of a highly automated business model and uncertain demand. Even though the model might have proven advantageous over time—with more experimentation—the "get big fast" thinking created a risk profile that was simply too extreme.

## First-Mover Fallacy

A key contributor to the land-rush mentality was the first-mover fallacy: a belief that the winners would be the ones who got there first and got big fast. Conventional wisdom argues that the first company to stake out a position will dominate its industry—especially during a rapid growth period like the early days of the Internet. However, history has proved that the opposite is often true: Commodore, Osborne, and Kaypro pioneered the personal computer industry in the early 1980s but did not establish dominant positions. Rigorous academic research has shown that early movers may achieve a market share advantage, but they do not systematically achieve greater profits or a higher survival rate.

A look at Internet retailing substantiates the idea that you do not have to be a first mover to succeed. Founded in 1994, Amazon is the clear leader in Internet retail sales, but it did not achieve full-year profitability until 2003 and did not achieve cumulatively positive net profits until 2008. It remains marginally profitable with net income of 3.4% in 2010. Another early "e-tailer," eToys, fared even worse. Founded in 1996, eToys went public in 1999 and declared bankruptcy in 2001 after its stock price plummeted from a high value of almost $85 registered in October 1999 (Figure 1.1). By contrast, Newegg, which sells new and used computer and electronic equipment, did not launch until 2001 and is now the second-largest pure-play Internet retailer, with 2009 sales of $2.3 billion.

Note: eToys went public on 20 May 1999.

**Figure 1.1    eToys stock price valuation in 1999 and 2000.**

First movers do not necessarily find the most fertile ground. Those who wait to explore later, or more patiently, benefit from the experiences of earlier settlers. They can bypass the hulking shells of unsustainable structures built by first-generation pioneers and salvage the best ideas buried in the wreckage. Consider FreshDirect, the online grocer in New York City with a delivery model similar to that of early mover Webvan. A privately held company with an estimated $240 million in annual sales in 2009, FreshDirect became profitable in 2009 and ranked 70th among American Internet retailers.

Unlike Webvan, which viewed the "last mile" as a golden opportunity and sought to be the first mover, FreshDirect took inspiration from Internet pioneer Dell. The founders sought to redesign the grocery supply chain using a rapid assembly "build-to-order" approach to provide fresher products at lower costs. They recognized that developing this capability would take time and focused experimentation. In 2008, a new CEO stopped the company from seeking new customers and turned attention to retaining the current ones by improving service quality. In 2010, the company expanded its business and now serves 600,000 customers in New York, New Jersey, and Connecticut from a central distribution center in Queens, just outside midtown Manhattan.

## *The Herd Instinct*

Why did so many companies try to be the first mover and pursue a "get big fast" strategy despite the questionable economic and strategic logic of that approach? Part of the blame clearly falls at the feet of the venture capitalists. Venture capitalists play a critical role in the economy by funding business ideas early in the life cycle when the risk of failure is high. By having a portfolio of such investments, venture-capital funds offer extraordinary returns even when only a small fraction of the businesses succeed. In normal times, venture-capital firms view thousands of ideas from passionate entrepreneurs but generally fund just a handful of businesses each year. Furthermore, they parcel out the money gradually as the companies prove the viability of their business models.

In contrast, during the heady days of the dot-com era, venture capitalists found themselves with a surfeit of money as more and more investors wanted a piece of the action. Although far more projects were chasing those funds than had been the case in past years, the venture-capital firms did not necessarily have the resources to screen all of those ideas with consistent rigor. Since investors could not maintain their formerly high levels of fundamental due diligence at the faster pace of the bubble years, they began to make investment decisions by looking to the decisions of other venture investors. As with the buffalo on the prairie, a few leading examples charging off with abandon can create a stampede, and when no one knows with confidence where to go, the safest path is to follow the herd.

Sociologists have a fancy name for this herd instinct: mimetic isomorphism. They have documented its prevalence in industries as varied as trucking and banking. That research has also demonstrated the rationality of copying others. Although copying rarely produces a breakthrough outcome, it does keep an organization from being left behind. Only a brave buffalo goes against the stampede, and unless that buffalo is extremely agile, it may well be crushed by the herd.

Unfortunately, once the process of mimetic isomorphism gets started, it is hard to stop. The only way to get funding during the dot-com heyday was to identify a new market and promise exponential growth. That exponential growth required huge funds that siphoned money away from potential late starters who could learn from the initial failures. The "get big fast" strategy produced more losses as companies focused on market share rather than profits. The venture capitalists—and then the capital markets—however, agreed to fund the massive investments and simultaneous losses. The only way to avoid the day of reckoning on profits was to continue promising more growth and seeking more money to fund it. Even before it went public, Webvan scored a $1 billion market capitalization by promising exponential growth from a mere $4 million in revenues— less than one-fourth of the annual sales of a single grocery store.

Although following the herd may appear rational in periods of high uncertainty whenever the herd dynamic is evident, there is reason to be wary that an opportunity has peaked. Jeffrey Immelt, CEO of GE, recently warned an auditorium of MBA students at the Darden Graduate School of Business to avoid the herd instinct; he cited his own experience upon exiting Harvard in 1982. He noted that he and only one other classmate joined the staid General Electric Company that year, just months after Jack Welch took the helm and launched what would become a phenomenal 20-year period of growth. What was the biggest employer of Harvard MBAs in 1982? A "hot" technology company called Atari, which hired 17 graduates. (By 2002, of course, when Welch retired, Atari was long dissolved, its brand name sold to Hasbro Interactive.)

The biggest risk of the herd instinct comes when the stampede turns and heads in the opposite direction with equal abandon. When the dot-com craze reversed itself, millions of investors lost a large proportion of their retirement accounts. More than 100,000 dot-com employees lost their jobs in the 10 months from October 2000 to July 2001. When bubbles pop, many people get hurt.

To avoid the bubble, we recommend lots of little experiments that send the herd in many different directions. Avoiding the "get big fast" strategy and the herd instinct allows for a more thorough investigation of the terrain. Many members of the herd will fall upon barren terrain and die, but in the long run, careful nurturing of the fruitful routes will produce a greater herd than over-grazing of the fertile patches discovered by the lucky few.

## Test All Assumptions

Karl Popper, a leading scientific philosopher of the twentieth century, argued for challenging conventional wisdom: "By criticizing our theories, we can let our theories die in our stead." A new business venture is a theory tested in the real world. We should test many such hypotheses, but we should also test our assumptions even before we let the market prove or disprove our business theory. In the dot-com heyday, smaller bets would have given more insight into how to bet more wisely the next time, and the munificent capital of that era might not have been squandered so much. Proving that something does not work—falsifying a hypothesis—can be even more valuable than finding supporting evidence. Popper also noted that "no matter how many instances of white swans we may have observed, this does not justify the conclusion that *all* swans are white."

During the dot-com bubble, large sums of money went toward big bets on first movers' intent on getting big fast. Observing some big successes in businesses with network effects or scale economies, investors concluded that all of the swans were white. In reality there were also black swans—and a fair number of geese, ducks, and egrets as well. The market results—and societal results—would have been better had the capital been more patient and had it gone into a more diverse range of exploratory investments. Although more businesses would have failed, the failures would have been smaller and would have provided less costly lessons. Multiple smaller experiments would have generated far more insight into the real drivers of value creation on the Internet and produced more exploration of the undiscovered terrain.

Uncertain times abound; despite Marx's claim of inevitability, business managers can avoid repeating the past. The dot-com era taught us that testing ideas with small bets and constantly challenging conventional wisdom offer the best path to finding the right market timing. Whatever the current uncertainties facing your company, do not allow your future to become tragic or farcical. History does not have to repeat itself.

## The Unfolding Story

Examining the heyday of the bubble provides context for understanding the current environment and the likely future. We can see the misperceptions that still linger and find hope that the gold rush mentality left many unexplored niches worth mining.

It is surprising that many business experts remained oblivious for years to the importance of mastering the execution of physical operations in Internet commerce ventures. Only those businesses who understood *why* they needed to increase their scale to yield profits and directed their efforts to appropriate growth were able to ride the highs of the dot-com boom of the 1990s and endure the dot-com bust.

Today, the surviving Internet retailers continue to thrive and have been joined by other competitors that have expanded the range of offers and sales. As shown in Figure 1.2, the industry has experienced sustained growth over the

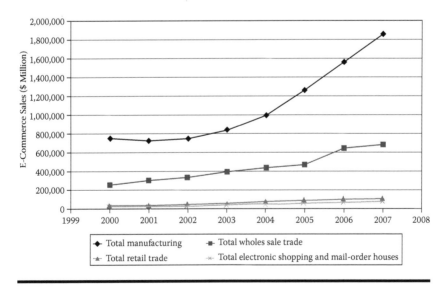

**Figure 1.2   E-Commerce Revenues from 2000 to 2007. According to the US Dept. of Commerce.**

first decade of the new millennium despite the crisis it went through when the dot-com bubble burst after 2000. Annual sales are about $100 billion, excluding revenue from web companies such as Google and Yahoo! and from travel sites and auction sites.

In the remainder of this book, we will expand on this overview and provide the reader with insights on the current state and inner workings of the Internet commerce industry. To that end, the book pursues an integration of theory and practice through a set of nine topical chapters. These rigorously grounded chapters offer an understanding of key theories and their practical application to Internet commerce. Each of these chapters provides insight into the drivers of the decisions rather than attempting to suggest a simple "best practice" model. Though "worst practices" certainly exist in Internet retailing, no universal solution applies in all of its varied contexts. For example, returns policies tend to be driven by product characteristics, customer behaviors, and competitive dynamics. The best policy must consider each of these factors and ultimately be viewed in light of the retailer's ability to make a profit. Our field-based research and anecdotes offer practical insights for managers.

Although the first section in the book is laced with case examples throughout, the second section offers a set of teaching cases written and tested in the classroom by the book's authors. These case studies provide an overview of various Internet retailers and place the reader in the position of the manager facing a strategic or tactical operations decision. Though obviously appealing in a classroom setting, these cases also appeal to practitioners looking for insight from companies facing similar challenges.

# Chapter 2

## The World Wide Web and Information Technology

The evolution in commerce brought about by the advent of the Internet is the result of many years of development in information technology. In this chapter we describe this development. We start by offering an overview of the Internet and the different mechanisms and technological advances that have contributed to its widespread adoption and success. Subsequently, we develop a framework that includes different Internet business models and juxtapose these models against commercial ventures in the offline world. This juxtaposition provides the basis to articulate different Internet sites' characteristics that have defined core areas of specialization across different online retailing ventures. These areas have been key to the success of these retailing ventures on the Internet. The chapter closes with a discussion regarding Internet commerce functionality and its potential to generate value and efficiencies and foster collaboration among consumers downstream in the supply chain.

## What Do We Mean by the Internet?

The Internet traces its origin, more than 30 years ago, to the INTERlinking of computer NETworks among scientists working under the auspices of the US Department of Defense's Advanced Research Projects Agency. Initially known as the ARPANET, the network evolved to use a standardized interface message processor that enabled each computer to treat the information it received from other terminals in the network as if they were coming from within its own hard drive. Another important aspect of this network was that it broke down the information transmitted among terminals into packets that could be transmitted indiscriminately through the best available links in the network and reassembled into the intended message to be delivered upon reaching their destination.*

The design of this system relied on protocols that regulated the transmission of information. These regulators were labeled Transmission Control Protocols/Internet Protocols or TCP/IP, and they shaped the Internet that we know today.

The design of this network of networks was also intended to allow for the future implementation and use of communication applications that did not exist at the time. Therefore, the network was intended to be ownerless and not controlled by anyone, and has continued to remain as such through today. This is a big departure from previous experiences with communication networks that have traditionally been owned and controlled by governments and private and regulated monopolies and oligopolies.

Moreover, the Internet was not optimized to run a particular application. In a sense, the Internet was meant to be "dumb" and would only take data packets from one end and deliver them to the other end. However, it was designed so that it did not need to know the contents of the data packets or need to have any influence on what the packets contained. Its goal was to simply convey the information sent through it. The intelligence in the Internet is meant to reside in its periphery, at the end points of the network where its users are. With these design principles, if a user has a great idea on an application that could be achieved by transmitting data packets, then the Internet could serve as the platform to execute it for them, no questions asked.

This simple but powerful structure led to a surge in innovations most significantly World Wide Web. The World Wide Web opened the Internet for commercial use because it enabled common individuals to easily access information in the network. Several advances in the World Wide Web contributed to this. As a whole, these advances (pioneered by Tim Berners-Lee at CERN) facilitated the process of locating and retrieving data on the Internet.

---

* For more information about the history of the Internet, see Vinton Cerf, "A Brief History of the Internet and Related Networks" at http://www.isoc.org/internet/history/cerf.shtml, and Richard Grifiths, "Internet for Historians, History of the Internet" at http://www.let.leidenuniv.nl/history/ivh/frame_theorie.html

## Technological Advances in the World Wide Web That Enabled the Commercial Adoption of the Internet

According to Saloner and Spence (2002), the first technological advance was the development of the hypertext transfer protocol (HTTP), which created a simple standard for assigning addresses to information residing on the Internet. These addresses facilitated the process of calling up information on the Internet through the use of applications commonly known as browsers.

The second advance was to have data residing in pages and the development of the hypertext markup language (HTML) embedded in the pages. Through the use of HTML in the pages, individuals could call up data in pages all over the Internet while reading other pages. HTML allowed the addresses for pages to be hidden in the text of other pages so that users could call them up by clicking with their mouse on the HTML code. This new development provided users with a more dynamic and fluid access to information on the Internet (Saloner and Spence 2002).

The advent of HTML spawned the development of user-friendly browsers that could run on MS Windows. The first of these browsers was Mosaic, which was developed by Mark Andreesen at the National Center for SuperComputing Applications at the University of Illinois. Mosaic and the browsers that followed it popularized the World Wide Web among less technical people because their Windows-based access made it easy for individuals to access content residing on the Internet through graphic interfaces. With such interfaces, nontechnical people could access information without the need to know where the data resided.

Initially, Mosaic and its successor, Netscape, allowed for only one-way communication on the web. Data in pages would be stored on a server while being displayed on each user's computer. Two-way communication on the web became feasible when Sun Microsystems developed Java.

Java is a programming language that can be used to write applets that run within a page being accessed by a user, regardless of the type of browser (e.g., MS Explorer, Firefox) reading the page. These applets can interact with the user, providing different data in response to input from the user and without having to call up the server where the page originated from for instructions. That way, users could seamlessly fill up order forms or place queries to or respond to queries from other users directly through the web.

Finally, the introduction of search engines offered users access to specific data on the web in response to specific queries based on individual needs and interests. In the early days, searching capabilities were available through portals, such as Yahoo!, that gave users access to the web by classifying pages under different categories that reflected broader interests (e.g., sports, shopping). This approach relied on the potentially flawed judgment of portal designers on how web pages should be categorized. The introduction of the page-rank algorithm by Altavista and Google addressed this deficiency. This algorithm relies on the number of links pointing to a particular page as well as the content in the page to respond to users' queries. Depending on the text in the queries, pages are listed starting from those that not only match the text in the queries but also have the largest number of links pointing to them, since this number is an indication of how relevant the page is according to the judgment of other web users (Battelle, 2005).

## Internet Business Models: A Framework

Since its inception, the Internet economy has been divided into three overarching segments (Figure 2.1). Building on the work of Mahadevan (2000), the first segment is made of portals and search engine sites that funnel traffic to other sites throughout the web. Companies such as Google and Yahoo! are part of this segment. The second segment is made of community and market makers that facilitate the exchange of information, product, and financial flows among Internet users. This segment includes organizations such as Facebook and eBay. These organizations broker the transmission and diffusion of information among networks of peers on the Internet through personalized contact and support in the form of security guarantees regarding the exchanges in the networks.

**Figure 2.1  Three segments in the Internet economy. (Adapted from Mahadevan, B. (2000). *California Management Review*, Vol. 42, No. 4.)**

The third segment comprises service and product providers offering Internet users the opportunity to buy services, products, and a combination of both. These organizations include retailers selling all kinds of products as well as firms selling financial, transportation, insurance, and other services to individuals. Among retailers, there are organizations such as iTunes selling digital products in the form of music and video downloads, for example. Furthermore, there are firms such as Amazon.com selling not only digital but also physical products (e.g., books) along with the delivery services necessary to distribute these physical goods to their customers.

It is important to underscore that these segments are highly interdependent. In particular, players in the service and product provider segment will benefit from being able to receive traffic funneled through the portals and search engine sites. Therefore, they must work with Google and other players in the portal and search engine segment to increase their chances of capturing this traffic.

Furthermore, the lines that separate these segments have continued to blur over time. For instance, firms that originally focused on selling products and services have also started to compete as market makers by facilitating commercial transactions between their customers and third-party firms. A case in point is Amazon.com. After initially selling only its own products on its site, it opened its doors to third-party vendors to sell their products to its customers under its brokerage.

These overlaps are not uniform across organizations. Some firms have been more active than others in expanding their functions to compete across the three different segments in the Internet economy. In doing so, these organizations have put together business models that exhibit different degrees of innovation and functional integration. Figure 2.2 presents a classification scheme of these business models, based on a framework developed by Timmers (1998). The classification identifies nine business models that are currently in existence and positions them along their dimensions of degree of innovation and functional integration.

Moreover, the business models adopted by retailers on the Internet share common points of emphasis that separate them from retail stores and traditional cataloguers. Table 2.1, developed by Spiller and Lohse (1997), summarizes these differences and shows clear distinctions in the variety and types of products offered and in the different pricing and promotional efforts and services.

## Characterizing Internet Retailing Models

From the work pioneered by Lindquist (1974), we expand on these distinctions by offering details on five key Internet retail site characteristics. These five characteristics were labeled by Spiller and Lohse (1997) as **Merchandise**, **Services**, **Promotions**, **Navigation**, and **User Interface**.

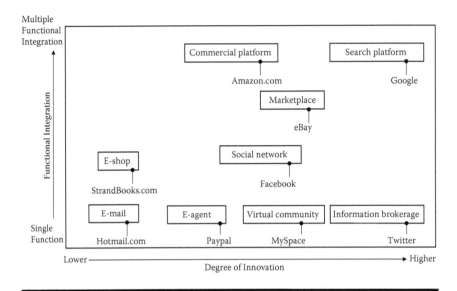

**Figure 2.2 Business models' innovation and functional integration. (Adapted from Timmers, P. (1998). *Electronic Markets*, Vol. 8, No. 2.)**

*Merchandise* characterizes the selection of products and variety of choices available at an Internet retail site. It can be reflected in the number of SKUs or the number of product categories available for sale. Identifying the number of product categories available at a retail site can be challenging because various types of products can be classified differently into separate groups. For instance, media products such as books come in different genres that can be further broken down into a number of subgenres, creating a deep classification array of hundreds of categories. On the other hand, clothing accessories such as handbags and shoes do not have a deep classification array and can be grouped into fewer categories without losing the richness in the description of the contents of each category.

*Services* characterize the value-adding assistance that Internet retailers offer customers in an effort to expand on the benefits that customers receive from buying from them. Some of these services include customer support functions to handle shoppers' questions and requests. Other services are less interactive—they center on providing information about products in the form of content descriptions, samples, and expert and customer reviews.

*Promotions* involve frequent-buyer schemes or subscription packages, such as Amazon.com's Prime, designed to foster loyalty among customers. However, they also involve giveaway schemes in the form of free shipping and handling offers designed to attract price-conscious shoppers who may

**Table 2.1  Analogies between Retail Stores, Traditional Paper Catalogs, and Internet Retailers**

| Retail Store | Paper Catalog | Internet Retailer |
|---|---|---|
| Sales clerk service | Product descriptions, sales clerk on the phone, information pages | Product descriptions, information pages, gift services, special search functions |
| Store promotion | Special offers, lotteries, sale catalogs | Special offers, online games and lotteries, links to other sites, or third-party vendors of interests, product sampling |
| Store window displays | Front and back cover | Home page |
| Store atmosphere | Copy quality, graphics, product arrangement, perceived image | Interface consistency, site organization, interface, and graphics quality |
| Aisle products | Products on first 2–4 spreads and middle spread | Featured products on each hierarchical level of the site |
| Store layout | Page and product arrangement | Screen depth, browse and search functions, indices, image maps |
| Number of floors in the store | Catalog organization | Hierarchical levels in the site |
| Number of store entrances and store outlets/branches | Frequency of mailings, number of unique catalogs mailed | Number of links to a particular site |
| Checkout cashier | Order form, toll-free phone number | Online shopping basket, one-click ordering |
| Visual presentation and feel of merchandise | Image quality and quantity, product description | Product description, reviews, image quality, contributed content by other customers |

*Source:* Spiller, P. and Lohse, G.L. (1997). *International Journal of Electronic Commerce*, Vol. 2, No. 2, pp. 29–56.

not return to buy again from the Internet retailer. Other schemes revolve around product returns. As part of these schemes, retailers relax their product return policies by waiving penalty charges for product returns, for example, in order to attract shoppers who may be reluctant to run the risk of buying items that are difficult to inspect and evaluate via the Internet.

*Navigation* characterizes the tools that Internet retailers provide to steer customers through the sites' hierarchy of pages until they find the products they are looking for. To excel at navigation, retailer sites must be organized in such a way that the hierarchy of pages at the sites is easily understood by customers as well as the organization of the individual pages. Navigation at retail sites should also be supported by search functions and by browsing capabilities that allow customers to find items through different attributes (e.g., brand, price).

*User Interface* brings attention to the need for Internet users to be exposed to a familiar format when exploring an Internet site while also receiving customized information about the products of greatest interest to them. Familiar formats include search boxes that are intuitive to use and also easy to find, usually at the very top of the Internet site. Providing customized information is an important component of the user interface because it filters out product offerings that may be irrelevant to customers, while directing the focus of the interface toward offerings that may carry greater importance in the eyes of customers.

## The Role of Merchandise, Services, Promotions, Navigation, and User Interfaces in the Success of Internet Retailing Ventures

The characterization of retail stores based on **Merchandise, Services, Promotions, Navigation,** and **User Interface** serves as a foundation to group Internet retailers according to the business models that they have adopted in order to compete in cyberspace. We considered different retailers: early entrants and latecomers, large and small retailers, and retailers that are narrowly versus widely focused on different products.

Table 2.2 presents the grouping of Internet retail sites. The first cluster, *Megasites*, includes stores with the broadest merchandise, the most comprehensive array of services and promotions, and the best navigation and user interface tools. The retailers that operate these sites tend to be those with the highest levels of sales and include quite a few firms that also operate brick-and-mortar storefronts to sell their products. Furthermore, these retailers have been in operation,

**Table 2.2   Grouping of Internet Retail Stores by Models**

| Group | Main Features | Examples |
|---|---|---|
| Megasites | Established firms with a comprehensive array of services and promotions and advanced navigation and user interface tools | Amazon.com Overstock.com Wal-Mart Buy.com |
| Focused sites | Established firms with a narrow merchandise scope but a rich array of services and promotions | Barnes & Noble Toys "R" Us Cooking.com Zappos.com |
| Basic sites | Firms competing based on aggressive promotional strategies and service arrangements to their customers. While these firms do not excel at providing customers with navigation and user interface tools, they offer compelling price points for the different products they have available as part of their existing merchandise | Costco Dollar Tree Woot.com Liquidation.com |
| Display sites | Firms with sites that showcase a narrow range of items but score high on their navigability and interface functionality. These sites only display and advertise products with the intent of directing customers to buy these goods at different brick-and-mortar stores | Zara Roche Bobois Century21 Toyota |

*Source:* Author classification based on Spiller and Lhose's (Adapted from Spiller, P. and Lohse, G.L. [1997]. *International Journal of Electronic Commerce*, Vol. 2, No. 2, pp. 29–56) framework.

on average, for longer periods of time than other firms. Amazon.com is the premier example of a web-only Megasite and Wal-Mart offers the best example of a brick-and-click Megasite.

The second group, ***Focused Sites***, includes those websites that offer a narrow merchandise scope and specialize on very few product categories such as Barnes & Noble and Cooking.com. Despite their narrow merchandise scope, there are many sites in this group that excel in their navigation and user interfaces. Moreover, because in some cases these sites are operated by retailers that also own brick-and-mortar stores, they offer a rich array of services and are very active in promotions, particularly in relation to shipping and handling and product returns.

The third group, ***Basic Sites***, clusters those sites that have chosen to compete based on aggressive promotional strategies and, thus, are active in offering unique pricing schemes and service arrangements to their customers. The retailers behind these sites do not excel in providing customers with navigation and user interface tools to enhance their experiences. Rather, they aim to offer compelling price points for the different products they have available as part of their existing merchandise. Some of these firms include large big-box retailers such as Costco that leverage their clout with their suppliers to compete in cyberspace. Other firms such as Liquidator.com are lesser-known retailers aiming to sell surplus or seasonal inventory to price-sensitive customers.

The fourth group, ***Display Sites***, incorporates those sites that showcase a narrow range of items but score high on their navigability and interface functionality. These sites only display and advertise products with the intent of directing customers to buy these goods at different brick-and-mortar outlets. Car manufacturer Toyota and apparel retailer Zara offer prime examples. Therefore, the sites are not designed to compete based on their merchandise richness and on their promotional activities. Moreover, because they specialize in the display and advertisement of products, these sites' services focus only on providing Internet users with information about the products they sell through brick-and-mortar outlets (e.g., apparel and furniture products) or through agents and dealers (e.g., cars and real estate).

The characterization based on **Merchandise, Services, Promotions, Navigation**, and **User Interface** also provides a point of reference to understand why some firms could not compete successfully in the Internet retailing industry. Some firms such as Value America chose a very broad merchandising approach to selling products via the Internet. Value America was founded in 1996. Its business model focused on connecting customers directly to consumer goods manufacturers via the Internet. The goal was to provide great product variety and convenience for customers who would be able to quickly buy and receive their orders at their homes while paying very low prices. Through Value America's website, customers could order a wide range of items (from grocery items to office supplies and electronics) and then have their orders transmitted directly to the manufacturers. The manufacturers would then process and ship the orders directly to the customers.

However, the execution of this business plan proved to be extremely complex. The sheer variety of merchandise offered by Value America created challenges in communicating with the manufacturers. Coordinating the processing and delivery of orders with so many manufacturers was also problematic. This resulted in extreme delays and frequent errors in delivering customers' orders and in processing product returns.

Also, customers could find in many brick-and-mortar stores most of the merchandise that Value America had for sale. This compelled Value America to compete based on the prices it charged not only for the products themselves but also for the shipping and handling fees it needed to collect to cover the delivery expenditures incurred by the manufacturers when fulfilling customers' orders. The end result of pursuing this price leadership strategy coupled with poor execution led to Value America declaring bankruptcy in 2000. In addition to being among the first-movers in Internet retailing, it became one of the first, high-visibility flameouts of the Internet bubble.

An aggressive reliance on promotional schemes also hampered Kozmo.com's chances of success in cyberspace. Kozmo.com's business model relied on aggressively promoting free one-hour delivery of all sorts of products (video rentals to coffee) in urban areas across the United States. This strategy proved to be extremely expensive to sustain without charging delivery fees. The company tried to gain scale economies in the distribution of products by aggressively using its promotions to expand on the traffic of orders processed and transported. However, it was not able to reach the volume needed to make its business model profitable, and had to shut down in 2001.

Poor interface functionalities were part of the reason behind the failure by eToys, a toy retailer founded in 1997. Since it opened its doors, eToys.com faced stiff competition from large retailers such as Toys "R" Us, which could offer customers great inventory variety and availability at discounted prices through their network of brick-and-mortar stores. To gain a foothold in the market, eToys .com started to aggressively court potential shoppers by advertising the convenience of ordering from their site, especially during the end-of-the-year holiday season. This strategy came to a head during the 1999 holiday season when eToys found itself overwhelmed by a large volume of orders. Its website was flooded with orders that eToys could not process and deliver on time to its eager clientele, and this lead to a deluge of inquiries from customers waiting for their gifts to be delivered.

In the end, a large portion of eToys' customers were left stranded waiting for orders that failed to arrive on time for Christmas. This resulted in a backlash against eToys, which caused a drastic decrease in sales and, ultimately, bankruptcy in 2001.

## Internet Commerce Functionality and Its Potential to Generate Value in the Supply Chain

The World Wide Web and its underlying technology have been instrumental in the rapid growth of data available on the Internet. However, has the World Wide Web been a useful application in making the Internet a good platform for commerce? The short answer is yes, but to a degree depending on the type of goods being transacted. Some products are better suited for Internet commerce than others because of the functionalities available for companies to sell their products through this new medium.

One of those functionalities is *scope*. The explosive growth of the World Wide Web has expanded the scope of this medium across individuals and firms. This vast scope has proved particularly valuable for individuals buying digital products such as music downloads, which can connect two parties independent of the physical distance separating them. Moreover, scope can be valuable for consumers to access and evaluate remotely a wide array of products that may not be otherwise available at nearby physical locations. Media products such as books are a good fit for these kinds of tasks (Shapiro and Vasian, 1998).

This is not to say that all products benefit from the vast scope of the web. Food products in general, and produce in particular, require that inventories be at close proximity to their markets. Otherwise, they will not be available for timely consumption prior to spoilage. Moreover, there are products such as apparel that are difficult to commercialize on the web because they are difficult for consumers to evaluate and inspect remotely through this medium. Oftentimes, the sale of these products on the web must be accompanied by fairly liberal return policies that lower consumer risk in purchasing them.

A second functionality is *customization*. The World Wide Web offers sellers a potentially vast range of uses for the Internet in the form of text, sound, pictures, and video that can be used to promote products directly to individual consumers. Moreover, because it allows for tracking buyer behavior, the World Wide Web can shape the information that customers receive via the Internet based on their previous search queries, purchases, and reviews.

Information that customers receive via the web can also be tailored through real-time interaction with shoppers. This interactivity allows individuals to provide cues to sellers so that the latter can offer more current information and target it to their customers' changing demand.

Consider the use of wish lists by Amazon.com's customers. This practice allows the seller to track changing tastes and update customers when changes in product prices occur or when a product has been updated with a new model.

Because of its design based on pages and HTML links, the web also allows for very efficient storage and search of information. Consequently, web users can have access to an increasingly large amount of product content at their fingertips. This content can take the form of product samples such as audio clips or even actual book pages. The content can also provide customers with references to what other shoppers have purchased.

Finally, a key functionality of the web is that it ***manages the transmission of information via the Internet in an asynchronous form***. Web users can log on at anytime and access product information and place orders 24 hours a day, 7 days a week, regardless of whether sellers on the other end are also logged on and available to receive or send information at the same time. This makes it efficient for customers to purchase at their convenience. Moreover, it allows sellers to process these purchases over time. That is, sellers can spread order-processing activities to reach a more uniform, continuous workload that would yield lower costs.

However, this assumes that all customers would be willing to experience delays in receiving the products they order. This is certainly not realistic. Sellers who are able to minimize these delays while keeping costs low will have a competitive edge. This is why sellers with a brick-and-mortar presence have a much more compelling advantage in this regard than their pure-play Internet competitors. However, the integration of multiple channels poses a series of challenges that need to be overcome prior to realizing this competitive strength. Many sellers have struggled to realize the advantages inherent in a multichannel setting due to an inability to control real-time inventory status at brick-and-mortar stores and picking and packing purchased items at these locations so that they are ready when customers arrive to pick them up.

Alternatively, trading off delays with greater product variety, superior level of quality in the service that buyers experience when purchasing on the web, or other customer benefits can help sellers compete in instances in which multichannel retailing or cost reductions are not feasible. The final part of this chapter discusses the web's influence in the creation of these cost efficiencies and customer benefits through the support of collaboration among consumers downstream in the supply chain.

## Web-Enabled Cost Efficiency and Customer Benefits

In its simplest form, a challenge that firms face when selling products via the web is that they need to ensure the timely delivery of these items to consumers. When shopping on the web, customers are not required to travel to stores to pick up their products. As a result, rather than being able to mass distribute products to stores for customer pickup, sellers need to engage in a distribution system downstream in the supply chain that is much more expensive because it requires the transportation of very small parcels to an enormous number of customer destinations.

Because these sellers can choose not to use physical retail stores to sell their products, these excess costs can be offset with savings on capital and operating expenditures associated with running those retail stores. However, these savings are generally available to all competitors in cyberspace and, thus, provide very limited competitive advantages. The key for sellers is to be able to develop the expertise to profitably manage the distribution of products to consumer destinations. Distribution costs along this last mile of the supply chain can account for a large portion of the operating expenses that sellers will incur. In some cases, sellers have opted to run this distribution at a loss by offering free shipping and handling fees to shoppers while making up for this deficit with higher product prices. In other cases, sellers such as those in the grocery industry have opted to manage this distribution in-house hoping to reap the highest possible cost efficiencies. These and other strategies point to different conditions that will shape the approach sellers take, and we will expand upon them later in the book.

Another relevant issue for sellers is the processing of purchased orders. Through the web, sellers have the ability to process simultaneously a virtually limitless number of information packets transmitted over the Internet. This allows for faster order throughput, minimal order-processing labor, a greater integrity in inventory records, and relatively inexpensive customer relationship management. A challenge for sellers is to authenticate buyers and provide the protections that are necessary to guarantee the absence of credit card fraud and fulfillment noncompliance. Another challenge lies in maintaining the integrity of inventory records in real time. With a large influx of orders coming in, sellers run the risk of losing track of exactly how much inventory they have available to respond to those orders. If inventory records are not updated in real time, as orders come in, it is likely that there will be unexpected stock-outs.

## Web-Enabled Collaboration among Individuals

The web has had an important effect in facilitating large-scale collaboration among individuals in the production of content-based goods such as music and books (including whole encyclopedias) that can be commercialized among customers. How is this possible? How can individuals engage in collaborative productive enterprises without being part of structured organizations and firms or without resorting to market payments for their work?

One reason for this lies in the web's support for the transmission and management of information across many different destinations in a decentralized fashion rather than making use of agents and property contracts that can generate losses in information. Through this decentralization, the web allows participants themselves to identify and allocate human creativity available to work on information very efficiently and at a large scale.

The formation of collaborative networks such as these is suitable for the production of content-intensive goods such as software and video because they are exclusively based on information that can be used by a contributor without diminishing its availability for use by another contributor. Moreover, these products are dependent on creative talent as another primary input. Creative talent, while generally available, is scattered among many different sources in the form of individual contributors. This poses the challenge of identifying and locating these sources, which the web has proved very effective in addressing through its decentralized architecture and its low-cost storage, communications, and processing capabilities.

Nevertheless, for this collaboration to work, participants need to have the motivation to decide for themselves the contribution they are willing to make. This motivation in the past has come from social/psychological rewards. Beyond this motivation, participants are assumed to have the best information about the contributions they can make. The web allows for the pooling of this information and its allocation based on judgments by other participants.

Moreover, it is important to allow participants to make contributions that are modular so that production can be carried out asynchronously and incrementally. Because the contributions are made in small pieces, it is possible to collect input from many individuals whose motivation levels will not sustain anything more than small efforts toward a bigger project. Also, there must be a low-cost integration that includes quality control over the modules and a mechanism for integrating the contributions into the finished product. This activity can be carried out by participants themselves by offering relevant control over what can be used and which can be accredited through the review/inspection of other participants.

Several activities in this area have led to the development of important products in the form of open software or in the form of apparel that is jointly designed and branded by consumers. Moreover, we have witnessed the application of collaborative networks to the development of business tools such as the recommender system adopted by Netflix.

There is a great deal of opportunity to advance further in the creation and commercialization of products through the use of collaborative networks. Those companies who will benefit the most will be the ones engaging the collective knowledge and talent in the creation of new products or the redesign of existing ones. This is especially true in markets where hobbyists play an important role in determining which products succeed in the marketplace. There are also opportunities to tap the wisdom of crowds to direct the growth of product catalogs offered to buyers as well as to develop product recommendations that would enable shoppers to bundle multiple products in their purchases. Amazon.com leads in this regard through its recommender system for a variety of products on its website. In so doing, it can generate sales for larger orders that are more economical to fulfill.

# References

Battelle, J. 2005. *The Search: How Google and Its Rivals Rewrote the Rules of Business and Transformed Our Culture*. Portfolio, New York.

Lindquist, J.D. 1974. Meaning of image. *Journal of Retailing* 50(4): 29–38.

Mahadevan, B. 2000. Business models for internet based e-commerce: An anatomy. *California Management Review* 42(4): 55–69.

Saloner, G. and Spence, A.M. 2002. *Creating and Capturing Value: Perspectives and Cases on Electronic Commerce*. John Wiley & Sons, New York.

Shapiro, C. and Varian, H.R. 1998. *Information Rules: A Strategic Guide to the Network Economy*. Harvard Business Press, Boston, MA.

Spiller, P. and Lohse, G.L. 1997. A classification of Internet retail stores. *International Journal of Electronic Commerce* 2(2): 29–56.

Timmers, P. 1998. Business models for electronic markets. *Electronic Markets* 8(2): 3–8.

# Chapter 3

# Scale Economies and the Network Effect in Internet Retailing*

As discussed in Chapter 1, the Internet bubble eliminated a host of early Internet retailers as companies mindlessly pursued the "Get Big Fast" strategy. While growth is desirable for any business, size alone does not guarantee success. As Webvan proved, scale that exceeds demand erodes profits and can bankrupt even the deepest coffers. At the same time, by focusing exclusively on profits, a company might miss the opportunity to become the dominant player. After all, it took Amazon 14 years to generate a positive cumulative profit. Had Bezos not invested to grow his business, Amazon could have ended up among the detritus in the flood that swamped so many of its competitors. The key to managing growth is to first understand the theories behind its advantages and then determine the importance to your business model. With that insight an Internet retailer can appropriately balance profits and growth.

Three different theories provide the justification for a strategy of rapid growth: economies of scale, network effects, and economies of scope.

---

* With permission, this chapter provides new material but draws upon the article "*The Big, the Bad, and the Beautiful*" by Tim Laseter, Martha Turner, and Ron Wilcox published in *strategy+business*, Issue 33, Winter 2003.

# Scale Economies

The theory of increasing returns to scale, or scale economies, dates to the beginning of the twentieth century, and a set of British economists, including Alfred Marshall, A.C. Pigou, and Nicholas Kaldor. Building upon Adam Smith's original observations, these economists reasoned that larger companies would achieve productivity advantages due to greater opportunities for division of labor.

Technically, a scale curve measures production costs as a function of facility capacity. Plotted on a logarithmic scale, the slope of the curve shows the fixed percentage reduction in cost for each doubling of capacity. Businesses with operations that offer significant economies of scale, such as wafer fabrication for integrated circuits, have steep scale curves where costs drop significantly when facility capacity increases—which is why the Intel Corporation and other chip makers regularly invest upward of a billion dollars in new higher-capacity facilities. Other businesses, such as apparel-producing plants, exhibit very limited scale economies. Since there is little opportunity to automate the process of sewing a dress or shirt, a larger apparel plant simply contains more sewing machines. A plant with 200 sewing machines run by individual operators does not produce shirts and dresses much more cheaply than one with only 100 machines. There is little value in having a bigger apparel factory.

Wal-Mart now ranks as the largest company on the planet. Although retailing, in general, has relatively limited opportunities to benefit from economies of scale, Wal-Mart has prospered by leveraging scale where it matters. For example, a Wal-Mart store building does not offer dramatic scale economies. A 100,000-square-foot store costs slightly less to build per square foot than a 50,000-square-foot store, but not enough less to provide a big competitive advantage. A retail distribution network, on the other hand, exhibits significant scale economies by enabling a business to exploit a lower-cost trade-off among facility costs, inventory costs, and transportation. Wal-Mart's distribution network dwarfs its smaller retail competitors' networks and produces a 1% to 2% margin advantage by our estimates. Given the thin margins in retail, this advantage is significant.

Amazon.com has sought, and in some cases achieved, scale economies. Its distribution network, although a fraction of the size of Wal-Mart's, ranks among the largest networks for fulfilling direct customer orders. Direct shipments of individual packages do not allow Amazon to gain the full-truckload advantages Wal-Mart captures through efficient cross-docking and shorter trips to its stores. Further, while the scale economies in fulfillment operations remain relatively marginal, Amazon does capture scale advantages relative to its online competitors (even Wal-Mart).

Outbound shipping represents a key cost element in Internet retailing. Shipping charges are levied upon each box shipped based upon a combination of package weight and size known as "dimweight" (derived from dimension and weight.) Amazon's massive scale offers the ability to aggregate multiple items into a single shipment, thereby reducing the cost per item.

Amazon's key source of scale, however, has come from its ability to amortize its massive investment in the web shopping engine across multiple categories. In the early days of Internet retailing, Amazon was able to subsidize the cost of its online interface through service contracts with partner companies like Toys "R" Us, Inc., the Target Corporation, and Circuit City Stores, Inc. Online retailing software that originally cost tens of millions to build from scratch can now be acquired for tens of thousands of dollars. However, no off-the-shelf software can match the user-friendly functionality of Amazon's online shopping interface.

Pursuing size under an assumption that you will gain scale economies in businesses with flat-scale curves offers no advantage and can in fact lead to decreasing margins if the incremental size is gained through lower prices. Even where a steep slope is possible, scale advantages do not just happen. A company must seek them out and exploit them. Examples like Wal-Mart and Amazon highlight the specific sources of scale and how companies have gained competitive advantage from it.

In fact, Hallowell has argued that there are inherent limits to scalability in Internet retailing. His scalability continuum starts with the highly scalable business of selling digital products such as music downloads or streaming video on one end to the difficult-to-scale unique and awkward products such as antiques and paintings. In between, he includes commodity products with standard handling such as books and toys left of the middle, and unique products with standard handling such as airline tickets to the right of the middle. The inherent scale limits have hampered the efforts of organizations such as Sotheby's from expanding effectively on the web, while at the other extreme the entire music industry undergoes a massive restructuring as digital delivery replaces the physical.

### SIDEBAR: Scale Curve Calculation

The term "economies of scale" has a precise meaning as well as a precise form of measurement—the scale curve. Technically, a scale curve measures the slope of the logarithmic curve plotted through a set of points representing cost per unit for various size facilities operating at the same level of "full" capacity utilization. In layman's terms, the slope defines the new cost base achievable by doubling the capacity.

Figure 3.1 below plots 90%, 80%, and 70% scale curves for a range of facility sizes, where a 90% scale curve indicates that the unit cost of a facility would be 10% lower for a facility twice the size, and an 80% scale curve indicates that unit costs drop by 20% for a facility of double the capacity, and so on. As can be seen from the chart, initially all three curves slope steeply and then eventually flatten out because of the logarithmic model. As noted on the horizontal

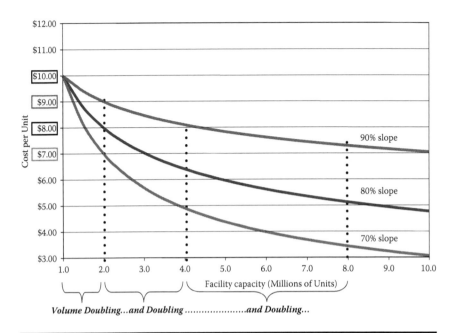

**Figure 3.1  Scale curves.**

axis, each successive "doubling" requires a greater increment of capacity, but the cost drops by a constant percentage.

The formula for calculating a scale curve can appear daunting but, in fact, contains only a few key variables:

$$Scale\,Effect\,(S) = 2^{\left(\frac{Ln(Cost_2 / Cost_1)}{Ln(Capacity_2 / Capacity_1)}\right)}$$

(3.1)

The formula applies where one facility provides a data point represented by $Cost_1$ and $Capacity_1$, indicating the unit cost at *full utilization* of that facility. A second facility provides a second data point as $Cost_2$ and $Capacity_2$. These four numbers provide an estimate of the slope of the scale curve (S) by solving the Equation 3.1.

Alternatively, the cost per unit ($Cost_2$) for a different scale facility (i.e., one with a different capacity level, $Capacity_2$) can be estimated given a known data point ($Cost_1$ and $Capacity_1$) and a known (or estimated) scale effect (S)*:

$$Cost_2 = Cost_1 \times \left(\frac{Capacity_2}{Capacity_1}\right)^{log_2(S)}$$

(3.2)

---

* In Microsoft Excel, log base 2 of the scale effect can be calculated using the LOG function. The syntax is LOG(number, base). For example, enter the formula =LOG(0.95, 2) to calculate the logarithm of 0.95 with base 2.

If you have data points for a number of facilities of different scale, you can also estimate the scale curve by performing a logarithmic regression and then observing the coefficient or simply calculating the slope from a pair of two points representing *an exact doubling of capacity* by the simple ratio of one cost to another.

As mentioned, scale curves assume full capacity utilization across all of the facilities under analysis. Unfortunately, few facilities run precisely at full capacity, so the cost per unit at full utilization must be estimated through an analysis of fixed and variable costs.

*Source: Competitive Cost Analysis: Scale and Utilization*, Heckel, Huang, and Laseter, Darden Business Publishing, OM-1256.

## Network Effects

Network effects came to the fore of business strategy during the height of the Internet boom to justify the phenomenal valuations of dot-com start-ups. Stock analysts applied the logic that the value of a network grows proportionately to the square of the number of users, a property of networks asserted by Bob Metcalfe, developer of Ethernet, a technology for connecting computers in a local area network, and the founder of the 3Com Corporation. Following what became known as Metcalfe's Law, a company's value quadrupled when the number of users doubled, or, if the number of users quadrupled, the value grew 16-fold. Given the exponential growth of the Internet population, the projected value gains were simply astronomical.

Unfortunately, even though a customer connects to a company's website via a computer network, the business itself does not necessarily exhibit network effects. To better understand why, we need to return to the economic arguments that predated the hype.

Economists noted the existence of "network externalities" in their research covering everything from ATMs to electricity to software. Formally, a network externality occurs when the value of participation in a network depends on how many other parties or which parties already belong to the network. Accordingly, a network effect is a demand-side argument for size versus the supply-side argument for scale economies.

Reflect on the early days of the telephone. In 1876, after participating in a demonstration call between Washington, DC, and Philadelphia, President Rutherford B. Hayes commented: "That's an amazing invention, but who would ever want to use one?" President Hayes failed to understand the network possibilities of the nascent tool. A phone connecting a central user in one city to another offered little advantage over the existing telegraph technology. However, unlike telegraphy, a telephone required no special training to use, and, accordingly, the network grew to encompass many individual users. Further, as more individuals acquired telephones, the value of having a phone increased for everyone connected to the network. More recently, the Internet has produced the same effect.

Economists argue that a market leader can gain a monopolistic position from the network effect by erecting "switching barriers." A competitor with a smaller network has trouble enticing customers to join its alternative network because it offers lower network value. Microsoft's dominance of the market for personal computer operating systems and ultimately PC application software offers an excellent example. Although alternative operating systems such as Unix, Linux, and Apple OS have challenged Microsoft's DOS and Windows systems, none have displaced them—even though some proponents claimed their alternatives offered superior functionality. Why? Because PC users value the ability to exchange files with other users without risk of compatibility problems. The largest network (in this case a virtual one) offers more value to the user. Similarly, the large base of Windows users drives application developers to tailor their products to Microsoft first. This also creates greater value for the users of the dominant network.

Among Internet-based companies, eBay exhibits the most powerful network effect. As more people list items for sale on eBay, the site attracts more buyers. The more buyers who bid on an item, the greater its value to the seller. This, in turn, attracts more sellers. For comparison, consider that Amazon.com has about the same number of customers as eBay, but its core retail business generates nominal network effects. Amazon customers benefit from the product ratings of other customers, and the acquisition of more customers improves Amazon's ability to mine its sales data to create customized purchasing recommendations, but the impact of this network effect is relatively small compared to eBay's. As Amazon shifts toward an online retail platform serving other sellers, network effects will become more important.

As the early leader in creating an auction community, eBay has leveraged network effects to dominate the market. Between 2002 and 2009, eBay grew from 28 million active customers to 90 million, while increasing the listings from 16 million to 118 million. Consider the story of uBid, Inc., the second-largest auction site in 2002. At that time, it claimed three million registered users bidding on its rotating stock of 12,000 branded products. By 2009, uBid had transitioned its business to focus on asset recovery—liquidating excess inventory for manufacturers, distributors, and retailers. By 2010, uBid's stock was trading for pennies, and public announcements explained that management had retained a restructuring firm, typically a step toward a bankruptcy filing.

Even though uBid and eBay both sell via auctions, uBid's original business model offered less of a network effect. eBay has well over one million sellers who claim eBay as their primary or secondary source of income, including a core group of Titanium PowerSellers who sell over $150,000 or 15,000 items *per month*. uBid auctioned new branded products from a small base of dedicated sellers originally and now a small base of customers seeking to liquidate goods. In such an asymmetric model, adding bidders benefits the small population of sellers but harms the disproportionately larger community of buyers because more customer-bidders drive up prices rather than attract more sellers.

In other words, sometimes a network, however large, produces little value. Many dot-coms focused on growth in customers as a key strategic tenet under the false assumption that size always translates into competitive advantage from scale economies and network effects. Such was the expectation of the ill-fated "last-mile delivery" companies Webvan, Kozmo, and UrbanFetch, but in reality their costs were largely variable and their customers did not get incremental value from an increase in the customer base. Here size added little advantage, and ill-advised pursuit of rapid growth led to their demise.

## Economies of Scope

The third theory supporting the size argument, economies of scope, concerns the benefits achieved by offering more than one product or service through the same organization. Economies of scope can affect both supply and demand.

General Electric captures demand-side benefits through its ability to bundle services from its financing unit with products from manufacturing units. For example, GE has long allowed its customers to finance the multimillion-dollar purchase of its jet engines via a leasing arrangement from GE Finance. More recently, GE has pursued a service strategy of selling "power by the hour" so that an airline does not buy a specific engine. Instead, a customer pays for access to a rotating stock of engines serviced and maintained by GE. On the supply side, GE Appliances combines with GE Motors and GE Aircraft Engines to purchase sheet steel in larger quantities for lower prices.

The most powerful economy of scope at General Electric, however, is probably the least tangible: its vaunted management development system. The company can provide a breadth of experience to its managers, who ultimately transfer best practices across disparate divisions. For example, Six Sigma, the analytical improvement process, was viewed largely as a tool for high-volume manufacturing operations until GE proved it could be applied across its wide range of businesses, including broadcast network NBC and finance arm GE Credit.

Amazon acquired or invested in a host of smaller players from pet food company Pets.com to the online grocer Webvan. Most proved ill-fated but did offer a hedge during the early "wild West" days of the Internet when few felt confident in their business models. Bezos had declared that Amazon might sell anything but firearms and livestock, and the company's heady stock prices provided fairly cheap currency for acquisition.

The more recent acquisition of online shoe retailer Zappos offers a better opportunity for economies of scope. With more than one billion in annual sells at the time of the acquisition, Zappos represented a fully matured business that Amazon agreed to run as a stand-alone entity. The Zappos management team had been adamant about this independence, and Bezos justified it by highlighting his desire to learn from the Zappos culture rather than impose Amazon's. Both have a customer-centric philosophy, but Amazon achieves that with a focus on prices and technology, while Zappos "delivers happiness" with a high-touch model. Bezos noted that Amazon was nearly 20 times bigger than Zappos so transferring talent and practices from Zappos to Amazon would have far more impact on the success of the combined entity than transfers from Amazon to Zappos.

Economies of scope can be negative as well as positive, however. Empirical research has demonstrated the value of "focused factories," which were first described by Harvard Business School professor Steven Wheelwright in the early 1970s. Amazon employs this philosophy in its fulfillment centers with different facilities focused by product types. Most facilities focus on the core media products of books, CDs, and DVDs. All of those products have relatively small dimensions, and benefit from highly automated sorting equipment. Lawn and Garden products, on the other hand, tend to have a much wider range of sizes and often lower volumes, thereby benefiting from a flexible, manual picking operation.

Arguments for focusing on core competencies, or more colloquially, "sticking to one's knitting," stem from a recognition that multiline businesses suffer from "costs of complexity." (Sometimes described by the misnomer *diseconomies of scale*, the disadvantages of size are more appropriately viewed as diseconomies of scope.) Amazon may face some risk of this as it experiments with groceries. That category adds sales volume but may require Amazon to expand its scope into delivery, clearly not a core competency. Worse yet, Amazon could suffer from what marketers call perceptual incongruity. Though consumers may be happy to get dry goods such as detergent and soup in the same shipment as a book or CD, they may not accept Amazon as a valid purveyor of fresh meat and produce.

Neither product line expansion nor business diversification automatically generates economies of scope. Economies of scope accrue only to companies that identify and capture synergies while simultaneously managing the risk of added complexity. Thus, scope expansion provides a powerful but double-edged sword. Broader scope can provide supply-side and demand-side advantage. However, increased complexity can confuse consumers and distract management from the core value proposition of a company. Although a multiline company should seek synergies across unrelated business units, beware of a company that tries to justify an expansion strategy purely on the basis of economies of scope.

## Defense versus Offense

Although the three distinct theories described so far propound solid arguments for the advantages of size, more often than not, success generates superior size, rather than vice versa. Although Wal-Mart posted $401 billion in revenues in 2009, its revenues in 1983 were a mere $4.7 billion, about one-eighth those of then-dominant retailer Sears. Not until 1990 and 1992, respectively, did Wal-Mart pass the Kmart Corporation and Sears in total revenues. Now those two leaders have merged in a feeble attempt to compete against Wal-Mart.

Wal-Mart grew to a dominant position because it offered a superior customer proposition. As it grows, it certainly leverages its size for further advantage—but it did not gain its dominance simply through the pursuit of size as a strategic objective. In fact, size may offer a more effective defense than offense.

At a mere 1% of total revenue, online sales remain a minor part of Wal-Mart's business model. However, thanks to its massive scale, that single percent ranks the company sixth among Internet retailers. While Wal-Mart's $3.5 billion in online sales pales in comparison to Amazon's $24.5 billion, the reverse is true when comparing the total sales of the two companies. Wal-Mart may never match the degree of online success of Amazon, but it can use its scale to defend its turf.

Size certainly offers benefits to the companies that understand and exploit it, but size alone offers a relatively weak basis for a corporate strategy. A small company that executes well offers far more potential than a large, feeble one. In the end, it is not the size that matters but how you use it.

# Chapter 4

## Operations Strategy
## for the Internet

Early hype over the Internet led to the somewhat overly simplistic strategy of picking a big market, followed by getting big fast and capturing eyeballs to lock in a first-mover advantage. Operations mattered little in most business plans. The Internet would enable a truly virtual model to handle the processing of orders; only technology and marketing mattered.

Value America was founded in 1996 and initiated operations in February 1998. It serves as the poster child. Serial entrepreneur Craig Winn envisioned a further evolution of the Price Club model that cut out the middlemen and allowed customers to leverage the stores' bulk purchases from manufacturers. However, in Winn's model, Value America even avoided the cost of buying and holding the inventory as the manufacturers would ship products directly to the customer. The company simply provided the technology to accept orders and pass them along to the manufacturers, and the marketing muscle to attract customers to the website. It regularly placed full-page advertisements in the national daily newspaper, *USA Today*, though detractors argued that, instead of customers, the ads targeted potential investors to hype its initial public offering (IPO).

The company's IPO, in April 1999—a mere 14 months after beginning operations—hit a high of $74 before closing at $55, which valued the profitless company at $2.4 billion. Eight months later, in December 1999, it cut 300 positions, nearly half its staff. By August 2000 the stock was selling for less than a dollar per share; the company filed for bankruptcy protection and laid off 185 people, about 60% of its remaining staff.

Maybe an operations strategy matters after all.

## Operations Strategy*

Before discussing the implications of operations strategy for Internet retailers, we need to first define what comprises an operations strategy. When pressed to articulate their own company's operations strategy, most executives will talk about efforts to reduce costs or improve quality, such as Lean or Six Sigma. Though important, such programs alone rarely produce a competitive advantage by aligning the physical assets and organizational resources in the operations domain to support the corporate strategy.

Michael Porter, creator of the famed "Five Forces" model of corporate strategy taught in every business school and applied by corporations worldwide, bemoaned this focus on efficiency displacing strategy. In a 1996, *Harvard Business Review* article with the provocative title "What Is Strategy?," Michael Porter argued that companies had lost sight of the importance of strategy altogether. A decade of unrelenting pursuit of operational effectiveness to close the cost-and-quality gap with an array of Japanese competitors, Porter argued, had set many industries on a path of competitive convergence. He feared that this single-minded pursuit of operational effectiveness would lead to mutual destruction, culminating in industry consolidations in which the survivors were companies that merely "outlasted others, not companies with real advantage."

Porter was so concerned about this trend that he opened his article with a bold-type heading intended to grab the attention of every operating executive: "Operational Effectiveness Is Not Strategy." He added sacrilege to provocation by including a sidebar titled "Japanese Companies Rarely Have Strategies." Though Porter never cited the Toyota Motor Corporation by name in the sidebar, it was pretty clear he was attacking the catalyst of the operations revival that institutionalized such vaunted concepts as total quality management, just-in-time production, and *kaizen* (continuous improvement). Could Porter really be so dismissive of the much-admired operations revolution inspired by this paragon of manufacturing excellence?

Yes, he could. Because Porter defined strategy in a way that reinforced its separation from operations, as if the quality of operations could simply be taken for granted in any effective company. Strategy was "the creation of a unique

---

* With permission, this chapter draws upon the article *"An Essential Step for Corporate Strategy"* by Tim Laseter published in *strategy+business*, issue 57, winter 2009.

and valuable position, involving a different set of activities." He also noted that "strategy is making trade-offs in competing"—including "choosing what *not* to do." Finally, he emphasized the importance of fit among a company's activities: "The success of a strategy depends on doing many things well—not just a few—and integrating among them."

Though operations practitioners and academics bristled at Porter's trivializing of operations, a closer examination of his arguments actually suggests that strategy and operations had more in common than either Porter or his critics were willing to admit. Effective overall strategy, by Porter's own definition, reinforces the critical need for an operations strategy. Porter dismissed the Japanese focus on cost and quality improvement, but he failed to appreciate the richness of the operations strategy of a company like Toyota in creating a differentiated position, the essence of strategy in Porter's model. Admittedly, Toyota's *product* positioning may not be distinctive from that of the rest of the industry. However, the Toyota production system stems from a revolutionary view of the function of a supply chain: It could produce the car a customer wanted "just in time" rather than "push" cars onto dealer lots and count on dealer financing and haggling to convince the customer to take it. That vision led to the series of operational innovations that allowed Toyota to easily respond to changing customer demands.

Instead of trivializing operational effectiveness and Japanese manufacturers like Toyota, Porter should have explained the critical need for an *operations* strategy in enabling the overall *corporate* strategy to succeed. After all, who designs and performs the bulk of a company's activities and seeks to (to quote Porter) *integrate among them*? Although Porter mapped the "activity systems" for leaders like Ikea, Vanguard, and Southwest Airlines, he offered little guidance about how to create these self-reinforcing systems that displayed good "strategic fit." That, however, is the essence of operations strategy.

## From Manufacturing to Operations Strategy

In fairness to Porter, he is not alone in trivializing operations. Strategists have been dismissing the function for decades. Another Harvard professor, Wickham Skinner, in a 1969 *Harvard Business Review* article, attempted to make business practitioners aware that the manufacturing function warranted more executive attention. Titled "Manufacturing—The Missing Link in Corporate Strategy," the article anticipated Porter's argument by more than 25 years, noting that "a production system inevitably involves trade-offs and compromises." However, rather than focusing on strategic positioning, Skinner highlighted a number of "decision areas" where the operations arena needed to resolve important trade-offs.

Other academics built upon Skinner's foundation as the concept of a manufacturing strategy evolved into a framework for a broader "operations strategy." In the late 1970s, Steven Wheelwright highlighted the importance of decisions involving the "manufacturing infrastructure," which led over time to the distinction between *structural* decisions, such as plant location and capacity, and *infrastructural* decisions, which involved increasingly pervasive computer systems such as manufacturing resource planning (MRP) used to manage the facilities.

Ultimately, this emerging focus on strategic decisions involving systems that support business processes found support in a competing strategy framework, the resource-based view (RBV) of a firm. Whereas Porter's industrial organization economics school considers the choice of industry to be paramount in determining success, the RBV school focuses on capabilities as the central precept of strategy. The resource-based view of strategy dates back 50 years to a provocative book titled *The Theory of the Growth of the Firm,* by Edith Penrose (Wiley, 1959). This strategy school, popularized by Jay Barney in the early 1990s, applies a bottom-up perspective that focuses on the firm rather than the industry. Its proponents highlight the need to build capabilities and note that "path dependencies" can limit a firm's options as it invests in different strategic activities over time.

Porter's argument that a company must choose a unique set of activities to support its competitive position pays short shrift to the difficulty of building capabilities. His perspective implies that a company need only select among a Chinese menu of activity options, just as a conglomerate can choose among a set of industries. Thus, the strategist thoughtfully selects the activities that will produce a competitive advantage; the operations leader merely executes. In reality, operations strategy must explicitly consider what capabilities to build and refine over time.

Merging Porter's positioning perspective, Skinner's manufacturing decision areas, and Barney's capabilities-based strategy offers a richer perspective on the appropriate definition of an operations strategy:

> *An operations strategy should guide the structural decisions and the evolution of operational capabilities needed to achieve the desired competitive position of the company as a whole.*

## Structural Decisions

Practitioners and academics alike admit that the operations strategy at most companies is generally determined on an ad hoc basis by the accumulated effect of many small and large operational decisions. Rarely does a company formally design and document its operations strategy in a deliberate fashion. At best, guidance on a few key operational choices might be found in an overall corporate strategy. Looking at a few cases of past decisions, however, can highlight the importance of well-designed operations strategies.

Structural decisions define the what, when, where, and how of investing in operations bricks and mortar. The original logic of operations strategy focused on manufacturing plants, but the same issues need to be addressed for the fulfillment facilities or call centers operated by Internet retailers. As the case study on Amazon.com that we include later in the book illustrates, four interrelated decision areas ultimately influence the size and scope of an Internet retailer's operational footprint, and they should be addressed explicitly and collectively in light of the company's competitive positioning.

## *Vertical Integration*

The logical starting point is to consider what "activities" (to use Porter's term) should be conducted in-house versus outsourced. Henry Ford's original River Rouge complex in Detroit was the epitome of vertical integration in the days when Ford revolutionized the automobile business with the Model T and Model A. Barge loads of raw iron ore fed the plant's steel mills, which supplied virtually all of the individual parts for the assembly plants. Ford's system used the new paradigm of mass production and scale economies to dominate the company's dozens of smaller rivals.

Internet retailers face a strategic decision in selecting the appropriate degree of vertical integration. At its formation in the mid-1990s, Amazon.com, Inc., went against the general trend of outsourcing and the dominant pattern among Internet retailing start-ups by building a vertically integrated network of fulfillment centers that would assemble and ship the orders customers submitted over the web. Amazon invented and continues to perfect the operating model for Internet fulfillment, and it knew that outsourcing would put its competitive advantage at risk. "We would be the teacher and then they would offer those services to our competitors," explained a senior operations executive in the early days.

As described earlier, Value America sought minimal vertical integration by employing a drop-shipping model where manufacturers shipped directly to the customers. However, Value America's failure does not mean that vertical integration should be maximized. eBags employs drop shipping for luggage quite effectively. Thereby Amazon has avoided forward integrating into delivery, a decision that was a critical part of the business model of its erstwhile competitor Webvan.

## Facility Capacity

Assuming a company envisions a sufficient competitive advantage from some degree of vertical integration, the specifications for the facility come to the forefront. Should a company aggressively build capacity ahead of demand or take a more conservative path of adding capacity only in smaller increments and only when market uncertainty subsides? Consider the example of Copeland, a division of Emerson Electric Company. In 1987, Copeland introduced the scroll compressor, a fundamentally new design concept for initial application in residential air conditioning. The company built capacity ahead of demand and even continued with a capacity expansion in 1989 despite initial demand that fell short of forecasts. Management was convinced—correctly, as history showed—that new regulatory efficiency standards would favor the scroll technology, and it built a competitive advantage that it still retains. Today, the scroll technology dominates the market; Copeland's design leads the industry, and Copeland maintains unmatched scale economies.

In the case of Internet retailing, Webvan bet big on capacity expansion by adding fulfillment centers costing $30 million apiece in a number of cities, even though the initial one in Oakland, California, was operating at marginal utilization levels. Emerson's confidence in the market demand forecast stemmed from a rigorous analysis of the impact of new energy-efficiency regulations on a well-known market. In contrast, Webvan was inventing a fundamentally new model for grocery shopping, one that required dramatic behavior change by inherently fickle consumers. A big bet in the face of reasonable certainty implies far different risk than a big bet in a formative market.

The degree of scale economies presents another consideration in setting capacity levels as described in Chapter 3. Though Webvan anticipated significant scale economies in fulfillment, competitors were entering the market with far smaller facilities with less exposure to utilization risk. In the end, Webvan's hoped-for scale economies were consumed by utilization shortfalls. In an ideal world, capacity can be added in small increments as demand develops, but rarely do businesses operate in an ideal world.

## Facility Location

Choosing where to site facilities also requires trade-offs in designing the operations footprint, regardless of whether the facility is in-house or outsourced. Inditex (the Spanish clothing company better known by its leading brand, Zara) maintains a scale-intensive pattern cutting operations in-house, and subcontracts the labor-intensive sewing to small mom-and-pop facilities in the surrounding region. Most fashion retailers outsource cut-and-sew operations to Asia to tap into low labor costs, but they face long supply chains requiring early design decisions and advanced volume commitments. Inditex's more responsive supply chain fits its strategy: In-house cutting offers enhanced control and helps offset some of the labor-cost disadvantage of the geographic location of its sewing plants.

Many Internet retailers have built fulfillment centers near their headquarters rather than logistic hubs. For example, the 34-person fulfillment center operation for 1-800-PetMeds, the leading pet pharmacy on the Web, is collocated with its executive offices in Pompano Beach, Florida, quite a distance from many of its customers spread throughout the United States.

By contrast, Zappos built its fulfillment center in Shepherdsville, Kentucky, separate from its Nevada headquarters. According to its website, Zappos chose the location "because its central location allows us to reach more customers more quickly." Sheperdsville sits less than 20 miles south of the United Parcel Service Worldport in Louisville, Kentucky, the 4-million-square-foot facility (equal to about 80 football fields) that serves as the world air hub for the shipping giant.

Locating call centers presents a daunting challenge to many Internet retailers. Given the importance of service, most Internet retailers operate domestic call centers despite potential cost savings of 50% or more if they located the centers outside the United States. *Internet Retailer* magazine described the story of Hayneedle.com that built a facility to house 140 customer service representatives in 2010. The new facility allowed the company to bring back to the United States the 25% of its contact operations that had been outsourced in Guatemala. The company attributed a 30% year-over-year revenue growth to the new facility that allows in-house staff to "better engage with customers and build brand loyalty."

## *Process Technology*

Finally, the structural footprint decision should address the process technology used in the facility. Again, consider the case of Copeland's scroll compressors. A dozen years after the introduction of its new design, Copeland felt compelled to add a Chinese plant to its operations footprint: Many competitors were producing in China by then, and the labor-cost advantage of the region could offset some of Copeland's scale advantage. Accordingly, Emerson opened a new scroll compressor plant in Suzhou in 2000. However, Copeland made distinctly different decisions regarding process technology at this new plant. Concerns over intellectual property protection, for example, led the company to exclude proprietary process technology and import the critical scroll plates from its US plants.

In Internet retailing, the degree of process automation varies widely across companies and across facilities for a single company. For example, Amazon's Wilmington, Delaware, facility uses sophisticated software to define picking routes, but the process remains largely manual from there. In Reno, Nevada, however, the company operates miles of conveyors to bring goods to a highly automated Crisplant sorter from operators using pick-to-light technology.

Kiva Systems offers a unique process technology option employing independent robots rather than conveyor belts, under the assumption that existing systems offer insufficient flexibility. Founded by Mick Mountz, a former member of the business process team responsible for designing the distribution strategy at Webvan, the technology can be found at leading players such as Diapers.com and Zappos. In a *Business Week* article in 2010, Mountz confidently asserted that Webvan would still be around had Kiva existed in 1999. Though clearly a creative approach to an age-old problem, it remains unclear whether the incremental flexibility justifies the incremental cost of the process technology.

# Operations Capabilities

Although the structure of a company's operations footprint represents a critical set of strategic decisions, management also needs to focus attention on the use of operations activities to build distinctive, strategically relevant capabilities. Porter properly dismissed the pursuit of operational effectiveness without a clear linkage to the company's competitive differentiation, but he underestimated the importance of building operational capabilities.

In Porter's defense, many operations executives also do not think about building unique capabilities but instead mindlessly pursue "best practices." In other words, they try to develop the capabilities that their fiercest competitors have already mastered. The concept of "best practices," in fact, reinforces the flawed mind-set that triggered Porter's attack on operational effectiveness. There are no universally superior methods that should be applied by all industry participants. Such a model yields competitive convergence and the often destructive model of pure cost-based competition. Instead, capabilities should be nurtured with a clear focus on the company's desired, differentiated position in the marketplace. However, where does one start?

To illustrate the concept, we will look at several Internet retailing operational processes that could be developed into competitively advantaged capabilities.

## *Customer Service Management*

Zappos built a billion-dollar business through a passionate commitment to customer service. The company displays the slogan "Powered by Service®" beneath the Zappos name on its website and starts its list of 10 core values with "Deliver WOW through service." CEO Tony Hsieh describes the company commitment in the title of his best-selling 2010 book *Delivering Happiness: A Path to Profits, Passion, and Purpose.*

However, simply proclaiming a commitment to customer service does not offer a competitive advantage. The capability has to be truly distinctive to provide the differentiated position that Porter demands. Stories of exceptional service from Zappos include arranging UPS pickup upon learning that the return had been held up due to the death of the customer's mother—and then following up with a flower arrangement offering condolences. Such thoughtfulness costs money, but the company contends that it reduces marketing costs: experts suggest that these costs to create a truly loyal customer pale in comparison to the cost of acquiring a new customer.

In addition to the out-of-pocket costs, Zappos invests in training its customer loyalty staff. After a week of initial training on the company culture, Zappos offers new employees $2000 to quit. Those who continue will spend three more weeks in training in order to become qualified to be assigned to one of the different positions at its customer loyalty team. Unlike most call center employees, Zappos customer loyalty team members do not have target times for calls but instead are instructed to spend as much time as necessary to ensure a WOW experience for the customer. The record in 2009 was a 4-hour call with a woman seeking a pair of shoes to address her health condition, peripheral neuropathy, where she could not feel her feet. Because of the condition, she was prone to losing ill-fitting shoes without realizing it while walking. The Zappos team member identified a pair of shoes with Velcro straps that solved the woman's problem.

## Operations Planning and Control

Zappos has clearly built a unique operational capability in customer service. In addition to propelling the company to over a billion in annual revenues in a decade, the capability was also a key factor in its acquisition by Amazon.com in 2009. While founder and CEO Jeff Bezos established a vision for his company to be "Earth's most customer-centric company," the Amazon approach shows marked differences to Zappos and hence offers the potential for synergy. Amazon employs technology to offer the broadest product range available anywhere and to consistently deliver on its promises at the lowest possible cost. Zappos uses "high touch" while Amazon uses "high tech": in fact, Amazon intentionally makes it difficult to contact a live service representative and instead focuses on preventing problems and using self-service technology to solve those that do occur.

Amazon does not seek to "WOW" the customer with unexpected shipping upgrades like Zappos but instead to deliver on very specific delivery promises through a different operations capability. As discussed earlier, Amazon.com made a strategic decision to vertically integrate into fulfillment. To leverage that structural investment, Amazon has invested in building a competitively advantaged capability under the generic banner of operations planning and control. For example, Amazon informs the customer of the precise cutoff time for ordering to receive a delivery the next day. No competitor manages such a broad product range with such precision.

To leverage its scale and strengthen its operational competitive advantage, Amazon continues to pursue some of the most daunting Internet retailing challenges. For example, Amazon launched its experiment with online groceries, Amazon Fresh, in 2007. Though well aware of the challenges faced by Webvan and other online grocers, Amazon seeks to be the world's largest store: the company knows that groceries represent a large portion of total retail sales and that the online channel will inevitably grow over time. In September 2009, Amazon's Vice President of Consumables, Doug Herrington, told Bloomberg: "We have a lot of confidence in the long-term economics. For a significant portion of the population, they're going to find that the convenience, selection, and pricing of online grocery shopping are going to be really compelling. . . . We want to be the place where you can discover and buy anything online."

Given the razor-thin margins in the grocery retailing market, Amazon's superior capability in Operations Planning and Control will prove critical to serving that market profitably. Groceries require special handling and tight controls to address the range of temperatures from ambient case goods to chilled produce to frozen ice cream. For example, bananas need to be maintained at temperatures within the narrow range of 56° to 58° Fahrenheit to forestall ripening or between 59° and 68° to induce it. Ice cream, similarly, needs tight temperature control to remain creamy; thawed and refrozen ice cream tends to be icy. Such challenges will push Amazon's current capabilities. But no pure-play Internet retailer is better positioned for the challenge of precise, cost-effective delivery at the lowest cost.

## Purchasing and Supplier Relationship Management

Over the past 20 years, manufacturers have invested heavily in developing their supply base through strategic purchasing and supplier development programs. Over time, these efforts have yielded huge benefits for the manufacturers, enabling them to increasingly rely on their suppliers in their continual pursuit of affordable, mass-produced goods in industries such as car manufacturing and semiconductors.

To our knowledge, no Internet retailer has achieved anything approaching an advantaged capability in this arena, but Zappos has the philosophic basis to build upon. In the book *Delivering Happiness*, Fred Mossler, head of merchandising (and other things within the scope of his current position as the "No Title" member of the three-person executive team quirkily described as "our monkeys" on Zappos' website), wrote the following comment on the traditional relationship model in retailing: "The typical industry approach is to treat vendors like the enemy. Don't show them any respect, don't return their phone calls, make them wait for scheduled appointments, and make them buy the meals."

Mossler explains that Zappos follows the golden rule with suppliers, and established collaborative relationships that shared risks and rewards. Rather than hoarding information in hopes of getting the upper hand in a negotiation, Zappos pursues "transparency" with suppliers just as it does with its employees. Suppliers can see inventory levels, sales, and profitability figures . . . the same information available to Zappos' buyers. The suppliers can also use Zappos' extranet to suggest orders and can even reach out to the Zappos' creative team and make changes to their brand boutique on the site.

## From Theory to Practice?

As Wickham Skinner highlighted 40 years ago, and the examples mentioned reinforce, the operations decision areas require trade-offs. Furthermore, even the best management has bandwidth limitations, forcing prioritization. This is especially true for Internet retailers commonly subject to resource constraints. As Michael Porter noted, strategy involves deciding what not to do as much as it does what to do. An operations strategy offers guidance for decisions related to structural investments as well as investments in capability building. The consistency, or "fit," among these structural decisions and operational capabilities will determine Internet retailers' effectiveness in achieving the desired positioning articulated by their overall corporate strategies.

Although it is true that most Internet retailers do not explicitly articulate an operations strategy, the decisions made by their operations staff will ultimately produce—or erode—competitive advantage. If you have not explicitly articulated an operations strategy, odds are you are on the dreaded treadmill described by the Red Queen in *Alice's Adventures in Wonderland*: "Now, here, I see, it takes all the running you can do, to keep in the same place. If you want to get somewhere else, you must run at least twice as fast as that!" Explicitly tie your operations strategy to your business strategy, and perhaps you can create competitive advantage instead.

# Chapter 5

# Supply Chain Management for a Virtual World

The management of supply chains necessary to support electronic commerce takes on unique challenges usually not found in other business settings. The Internet is a particularly powerful tool for consumers to access information about products. Through the web, customers can find a wide variety of merchandise without incurring onerous search costs. As a result, Internet retailers have increasingly found themselves in a position to offer their customers access to a long tail of products that can meet the most obscure of customer preferences. We will expand on these challenges and implications in the first part of this chapter.

Moreover, as we discuss in the second part of this chapter, the fulfillment of customers' demand for such a wide variety of products by Internet retailers involves the flow of small orders that may originate from, and may also be delivered to, a broad array of customer destinations. As a result, order processing and inventory management activities necessary to handle these orders are quite different in Internet-based supply chains than in other types of supply chains where bulk product shipments are the norm. In Internet retailing, orders may draw from inventory located at many different supply chain echelons and require their transfer across varying distances to their recipients. To respond to these challenges, Internet retailers must take into consideration a series of inventory management policies, which is also discussed in the second part of this chapter.

Finally, through the Internet channel, customers have the ability to customize different product attributes to meet their preferences. However, this customization is hampered by limitations that customers face in physically accessing and evaluating the products they buy. In the third part of this chapter, we offer research insights into how Internet retailers can use brick-and-mortar channels to overcome these limitations.

# Long Tails and Unlimited Shelf Space in Internet Retailing

Traditionally, product variety has played a central role in increasing inventory-carrying costs for retailers and expenditures caused by product returns. To control these costs, many retailers have maintained relatively few SKUs, yielding a pattern of concentration commonly known as the 80/20 rule and described by the Pareto principle. This pattern of concentration carries with it the risk of holding in inventory an extensive and inactive SKU variety. Accordingly, traditional brick-and-mortar retailers have been concerned with being able to balance additional sales from a wider SKU variety with their associated inventory-carrying costs.

MIT Professor Erik Brynjolfsson claims that the use of the Internet to carry out retail activities has broadened this concentrated pattern of sales by lowering consumer search costs. According to these arguments, Internet commerce has contributed to an expansion in the share of sales by niche products, thereby creating a longer tail in the distribution of SKU sales. This phenomenon may ultimately make it more attractive to carry a greater variety of SKUs without incurring excessive carrying and product return costs.

## *The Internet's Long Tail of Sales*

According to Chris Anderson, Editor of *Wired* magazine, retailers on the Internet can successfully accommodate a virtually limitless product variety because goods do not have to be displayed on actual shelves and thus their inventory is not limited by physical storage constraints. Moreover, search and recommendation tools can give customers easy access to this variety so that they can effortlessly buy the products that perfectly match their preferences (Anderson, 2006).

As a result, Internet retailers should be in a position to sell niche items that would prove to be unprofitable for sale in traditional retail environments. Figure 5.1 illustrates this issue. The x-axis ranks all products by their sales volume and identifies those obscure items that are ranked at the bottom and that

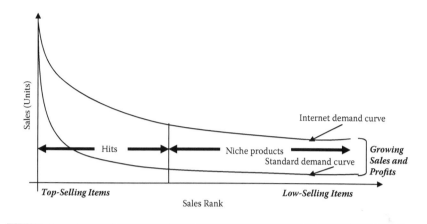

**Figure 5.1 Internet channels will fatten the long-tail, source. (Adapted from Anderson, C. 2006. *The Long Tail: Why the Future of Business Is Selling Less of More.* Hyperion, New York.)**

would be unprofitable for sale through brick-and-mortar outlets. Through the Internet, retailers will be able to sell higher volumes of a significant portion of these items. In essence, these higher volumes will fatten the long tail of the sales distribution across the products. As a result, Internet retailers will be able to offer these products with the expectation that they will attract enough sales to make these offerings profitable.

Anderson makes his case by using examples from media products like music, video, and books to argue that the future of business is to "sell less of more." The products he examines can be digitized, easily searched, and inspected by consumers on the Internet, and inventoried and distributed at fairly low cost. However, for other product categories, such as apparel, shoes, home appliances, and electronics, Internet retailers should be cautious in taking these claims at face value.

## Product Variety on the Internet: A Treasure Trove or a Source of Trouble?

While the Internet may improve customers' ability to search for and find items best suited to their needs among these product categories, retailers must ensure that they face a discernible market preference for product differentiation, as reflected in the distribution of actual sales across many different SKUs offered to consumers. It is unclear, for instance, whether such a preference would be hindered by limitations faced by consumers when purchasing remotely via the Internet nonmedia products in categories such as apparel, for example.

Difficulties such as these will inevitably translate into greater inventory-carrying costs. The challenges that customers face in evaluating and choosing items via the Internet can lead to having inventory sitting in shelves for very long periods of time or can result in inventory not being sold at all. These situations will ultimately require Internet retailers to absorb excessive expenditures of owning and holding this stock at their facilities.

Customers' preference for a wide variety of products may also be hindered by the limitations they face when sorting and choosing from a very large array of options or by Internet retailer failures in executing the operations necessary to complete their purchases. These problems will result in product returns that, in the end, will hamper the shift toward greater product variety in Internet sales.

The drawbacks that returns will generate for Internet retailers can be especially onerous if they rely exclusively on their own inventory. The Internet retailing industry includes many merchants that sell most of their products from stock they themselves own and carry at a facility. For these retailers, returns—which typically range from nearly 1% to well over 20% of sales depending on category (Brohan 2005)—can create product obsolescence risks and transportation and warehousing costs in excess of $20 per return, according to Gartner Research.

## Rising to the Challenge

To manage these returns, Internet retailing managers may reduce the scope of products they offer by eliminating items that are frequently returned. However, they may also consider whether these returns occur independently of these products and, instead, are caused by customers' difficulties in effectively searching, evaluating, and purchasing these products on the Internet.

However, through a detailed examination of the distribution of sales across SKUs in juxtaposition with the distribution of product returns across the same SKUs, Internet retailers can understand the preferences for product differentiation among their customers and define a more appropriate breadth of product assortment. Specifically, before embarking on an aggressive expansion of product portfolios, Internet retailers should evaluate customer preferences for product variety in relation to customer tendencies to rely on product returns after they have received their purchases.

If sales prove to be more broadly distributed than returns, it would suggest that a broad offering exposes the Internet retailer to a more manageable risk relative to the product breadth offered. On the other hand, a scenario where returns are widely dispersed, relative to sales, would represent a costly risk for Internet retailers. This scenario may reflect the widespread presence of "Devil

Customers," commonly found in Internet retailing apparel segments. These customers purposely buy multiple sizes and/or colors of the same product with an expectation of keeping only the one that fits or matches best while returning the others.

Customers would ideally like an assortment that provides sufficient choice but does not impose needless effort to identify the optimal selection during the shopping process. Should the process prove overwhelming or if the product cannot be adequately assessed in an online forum, the customer may simply buy the product with an expectation of returning it if it proves inadequate upon physical inspection.

To investigate the distribution of sales across SKUs in juxtaposition to the distribution of product returns, retailers should consider transactions that involve customer purchases (generating forward material flows) as well as purchases that are returned (triggering reverse material flows). Under this formulation, customers can expressly state their preferences for different SKUs by purchasing them once they have had a chance to evaluate, compare, and find those items that appear to satisfy their search criteria. However, under this formulation, customers will also have the chance to ratify or reverse their preferences by choosing whether to return those products that do not adequately meet their needs and expectations.

Moreover, product characteristics and product return motivations by customers should be considered in the process of understanding customer purchases and returns. Heim and Sinha of Texas A&M University and the University of Minnesota, respectively, have examined how product characteristics affect consumers' ability to find goods for purchase on the Internet. Boyer and Hult from Ohio State University and Michigan State University, respectively, have explored customers' motivations for returning products in the Internet retailing context. The effect of these factors on customer purchasing preferences and product return occurrences for product differentiation offers great potential for capturing Internet retailers' attention.

At the root of the long-tail challenges that Internet retailers may face is the fact that the limitless shelf space that the retailers have at their disposal to offer a broad range of SKUs does not necessarily reflect widespread preferences for an endless variety of SKUs by customers. These preferences will depend on whether customers will reverse their purchasing decisions by returning the various products they have bought on the web. The effectiveness of inventory variety as a competitive advantage for retail differentiation will depend on whether customer preferences are actually met, and this is reflected in the ratification or reversal of customer purchases through the occurrence of product returns.

One may assume that an expansion in product demand has no bearing on product return decisions. However, efforts to expand the scope of product sales carry the risk of attracting incremental demand by customers who on one hand may be more likely to experiment and buy a greater variety of SKUs but on the other hand are just as likely to indiscriminately return these SKUs without delay.

Could this phenomenon have equal applicability in an Internet commerce setting? Information Economics Theory points to the possibility that this may not be the case. It suggests that, through the use of the Internet, customers are in a position to make informed purchasing decisions about increasingly expansive arrays of products that should not generate a large scope of product returns.

However, if product diversity becomes too overwhelming, especially for items that are difficult to evaluate remotely via the Internet, a greater diversity in product sales may be accompanied by a greater scope in returns because it may become increasingly hard for customers to look for and find the products that best match their preferences. Furthermore, on the Internet, customers may find it more difficult to access increasingly rich, up-to-date, and accurate information about many products (not just the best-selling ones) as their variety increases. This is because purchasing decisions about individual products may be increasingly subject to incomplete and imprecise product information as well as other data imperfections that could degenerate into failed purchasing decisions and product returns.

Internet transactions also carry potential risks of failure for consumers, which could have additional implications for the occurrence of sales and returns. Customers' exposure to these risks depends on product characteristics and could alter the distribution of sales and returns across SKUs. In the following text, we present theoretical arguments on this role of risk in Internet retailing transactions. Our arguments build on two determinants of risk exposure (transaction expenditures and ambiguity) and the product characteristics that contribute to the importance of these determinants.

## Expenditures and Risk in Internet Retailing

Byron J. Finch of Miami University argues that customer expenditures in their online purchases will contribute directly to their exposure to risk in their transactions with Internet retailers. These expenditures will depend on the size and price of the products in these transactions.

Increases in the product size will increase transaction expenditures for online buyers because they will boost the shipping and handling (S&H) fees that buyers will pay for order delivery. Since Internet buyers are particularly averse to paying S&H fees, they will find it especially justifiable to buy large items and pay excessive S&H fees only for a narrow segment of popular SKUs that they know well. Customers are likely to avoid paying high S&H fees for little-known large items located at the tail end of the sales distribution in order to control their exposure to the risk of losing these expenditures if the products fail to meet their preferences. Consequently, we have found that increases in product size will skew the distribution of Internet sales toward best-selling SKUs.

Moreover, product prices will drive customers to search extensively for high-priced items in order to spend wisely and minimize their exposure to a risk of failure in their retail transactions on the web. Consequently, customers will not find it as advantageous to use the Internet in order to buy obscure products that carry relatively high prices. However, they will be more likely to return a poorly fitting product upon receipt when the price of the product is high. This is because customers will have a stronger motivation to recoup their expenditure after a purchase failure if the product they purchased carries a high value. Accordingly, higher-priced goods will exhibit a higher concentration in sales among best-selling items but a wider distribution of returns across SKUs than lower-priced goods.

## Ambiguity and Risk in Internet Retailing

Customers' exposure to the risk of making undesired purchases on the Internet is also a function of their ability to make more knowledgeable product assessments. The amount of time that products have accumulated on the web will lower this exposure.

As the amount of time a product has been available online increases, so will the amount of information about the product available to customers. This information will include data about different product attributes, as well as customer reviews and other user-generated content such as related product recommendations, pictures, and so forth. With this information, customers will be able to make more knowledgeable assessments of products located at the head end through the tail end of the sales distribution. Thus, the amount of time products have been available on the Internet will help customers gather more product information and make more effective and unambiguous purchasing decisions through the broader arrays of SKUs available on the Internet.

Furthermore, because the market will become more familiar with products as they accumulate more time on the Internet, returns for products with more time on the web will occur more sporadically across different SKUs. Product returns involving long-established items are not likely to spread out and occur indiscriminately across SKUs. Rather, they are likely to cluster around a few SKUs involved in purchase failures caused by systemic ambiguities, misrepresentations, or erroneous assessments by customers. Therefore, increases in the amount of time products have been available on the Internet will widen the distribution of Internet sales across more SKUs but skew the distribution of returns toward fewer SKUs.

## Demand Management

A conclusion from our previous discussion is that the success of retail ventures on the Internet is due in part to the ability of retailers to respond to changing demand without compromising the profitability of their sales. Managing customer demand on the Internet becomes critical in this endeavor.

These efforts include the direct fulfillment of consumer orders placed through Internet-retailing sites. As part of this consumer direct fulfillment service, also known as drop-shipping, wholesalers and other Internet retailer suppliers stock and own the items needed to fulfill orders. Furthermore, these suppliers make arrangements with third-party logistics (3PL) firms (e.g., UPS) to ship the orders, at the Internet retailers' request, to delivery destinations specified by consumers. The suppliers are generally responsible for managing and paying expenses incurred in these transportation operations and, in return, charge the Internet retailers an S&H fee for these services.

As summarized in Figure 5.2, drop shipping allows Internet retailers to focus mainly on marketing, customer acquisition, and order-processing functions. It enables retailers to transfer stock ownership and order-fulfillment responsibilities to suppliers who can leverage their advantages in warehousing and distribution operations to perform these activities more efficiently.

Retailers can benefit from drop shipping because they need not spend on inventory-carrying costs and warehousing assets. However, suppliers can also benefit because they can sell their products through the retailers' Internet sites and obtain access to a wider and more stable demand stream for their products.

| Internet Retailers | | Suppliers | |
|---|---|---|---|
| Focus on: | Marketing<br>Customer Acquisition<br>Order Processing | Focus on: | Stock Ownership and Holding<br>Warehousing Activities<br>Order Fulfillment |
| Benefits: | No Inventory Carrying Costs<br>No Warehousing Assets | Benefits: | Access to Wider Markets and More Stable, Easier to Forecast Demand |

**Figure 5.2 Responsibilities and benefits by Internet retailers and suppliers in drop-shipping arrangements.**

The profitability of drop-shipping arrangements depends on conditions that enable consumer orders to be fulfilled more quickly without raising stock levels. First, drop-shipping arrangements are more beneficial when few stocking locations are involved. Second, inventory policies favor performance in drop shipping when retailers are subject to increasing demand for their products due to changes in market share or popularity. Third, drop shipping contributes to shortening the time it takes to process consumer orders while lowering inventory-holding costs when a greater number of retailers set these arrangements with fewer suppliers or when the retailers face greater demand variability.

Drop shipping will also work for retailers and their suppliers when consumer demand is widely dispersed across a broad geographic area. This demand dispersion refers to the variance in the volume of orders across the markets served by each of the supplier facilities.

## The Role of Emergency Transshipments

The success of these arrangements also depends on the use of emergency transshipments. These occur when a supplier facility uses its inventory to satisfy demand originating at locations outside its own geographic market if stock is unexpectedly unavailable at facilities primarily in charge of fulfilling demand at those locations.

In drop shipping, emergency transshipments require that online retailers and suppliers share customer-order and inventory-status information. In return, emergency transshipments lower stock-out occurrences without expanding stocks at the supplier facilities. Fewer stock-outs, in turn, reduce unforeseen order-cycle delays and are likely to boost the fulfillment service afforded to consumers. Emergency transshipments yield additional performance benefits through scope economies, as they enable the clustering of multiorder shipments across multiple shipment origins. This effect lowers the time needed to group economical shipment load sizes and the cycle time spent in serving online consumers.

The reductions in stock-outs obtained from emergency transshipments in drop-shipping arrangements are maximized when supplier facilities fulfill demand that is uniformly balanced across markets primarily assigned to each facility. As demand across markets becomes less uniform, the benefits obtained from emergency transshipments in drop-shipping operations are mitigated. Therefore, in planning for emergency transshipments, Internet retailers and suppliers may wish to focus on SKUs for which demand involves a balanced distribution across market regions. Alternatively, Internet retailers that design their fulfillment operations to rely on drop shipping may decide to broaden their product offerings to achieve a balanced demand distribution across market regions.

Transportation costs should also be considered in the decision to carry out emergency transshipments as part of drop-shipping operations. Although emergency transshipments increase the costs necessary to transfer inventory from supplier facilities to consumer markets, these increases may be outweighed by gains in inventory performance. Nevertheless, drop-shipping participants must consider these added costs when evaluating performance gains obtained from emergency transshipments. Aversion by consumers to waiting for their orders to be fulfilled may compel Internet marketers to reduce the delays in fulfilling customer orders through emergency transshipments without much consideration for added transportation costs. However, suppliers, in particular, must consider whether these extra costs will erode the margins they obtain from the S&H fees they receive from Internet retailers.

It is also important to note that drop shipping can introduce a conflict between marketing at the retailers and operations at the suppliers. On one hand, retailers may find it necessary to limit their spending on promotional activities for different supplier products in order to comply with limitations in their financial resources. At the same time, suppliers may ration inventory available to the retailers in order to meet stocking limitations at their facilities.

How could retailers and suppliers address this conflict? An obvious course of action could involve increasing the prices retailers pay their suppliers in order to reward the latter for their inventory-carrying risks and also to ensure that retailers participating in drop-shipping arrangements are not rationed. Another option involves the subsidization of Internet retailers' customer acquisition by the supplier. Under this course of action, the supplier subsidizes the retailer's advertisement efforts in order to help rotate slow-moving inventory sitting at the wholesaler's facilities. Finally, retailers could also use bonuses to reward supplier inventory performance and fulfillment support.

Drop shipping can also introduce delays to the fulfillment of customer orders. This is because Internet retailers are exposed to holdups by their suppliers in these arrangements when unexpected excess demand for inventory occurs. Demand will increase unexpectedly when consumers shift their preferences among different products that either have been recently introduced or refashioned. Demand will also shift among products due to changes in customer preferences for particular attributes among those products. When such changes in demand occur, wholesalers will find themselves in a position where the inventory they have available to fulfill demand from Internet retailers will become insufficient and, as a result, they will resort to rationing the retailers' demand.

To protect themselves against these delays and to be responsive to customers' need for immediate gratification, retailers have increasingly opted to pair their Internet and brick-and-mortar channels. In the third and final section of this chapter, we expand on these strategies.

## Multichannel Retailing: Combining Internet and Brick-and-Mortar Channels

Multichannel retailing has historically involved the sale of products via brick-and-mortar stores and catalogs. Only recently, over the past two decades, has multichannel retailing expanded to include sales via the Internet. This type of sales has experienced a significant growth as consumers become increasingly familiar with the process of ordering online and picking up their products at retail stores. For customers, there are two benefits from this process. First, they can tap into a large variety of products from many locations and still be able to pick them up immediately at conveniently located outlets. Second, in buying these products, customers are not required to spend on shipping and handling fees, especially for products that are expensive to transport.

For retailers, there are some benefits that result from combining Internet and brick-and-mortar channels. Most notably, retailers can sell products through brick-and-mortar channels without having to incur distribution expenditures necessary to cover the last-mile delivery of orders to customers. In selling their products through brick-and-mortar outlets, retailers can rely on customers to pick and transport their products to their homes or other final destinations. Moreover, a greater reliance on brick-and-mortar channels can lower overall transportation costs in the supply chain. This is because, through this channel, retailers can adopt a multitiered distribution approach with full truckloads taking palletized inventory from nationwide distribution centers to regional and local distribution centers until it arrives all the way to the retail stores where consumers will retrieve the products.

Retailers that rely on multiple channels are also at an advantage when it comes to acquiring and retaining customers. Industry studies have reported that while customer acquisition costs for Internet-only retailers is $42 per customer, they are only $22 per customer for retailers that combine Internet and brick-and-mortar channels. This is one of the reasons why multichannel retailers spend heavily on customer retention (16% of their marketing and advertising budget) while Internet-only retailers spend only 3% on retention, devoting most of their resources to customer acquisition.

However, there are also important challenges for retailers that come from combining Internet channels with brick-and-mortar channels as an option for the sale of their products. Most notably, retailers will incur significant additional facility costs from their use of brick-and-mortar outlets to sell products bought in the Internet. This is the main reason why pure-play Internet retailers like Amazon.com or Overstock.com have chosen not to adopt multichannel strategies. Virtually all retailers that have adopted a multichannel strategy combining

Internet and brick-and-mortar channels are those that were originally operating brick-and-mortar stores.

Another immediate challenge involves the potential cannibalization of sales from one channel by the other. There is also an immediate need to design a fair distribution of incentives to be paid among employees across both channels. In setting up these incentives, retailers need to recognize the role that both channels play in the process of completing product sales, and distribute commissions and other sales incentives accordingly. Furthermore, retailers need to maintain uniform prices and promotions across both channels so that customers do not complain about paying more for the same product if they buy on one channel or the other.

Retailers also face other less apparent challenges when implementing multichannel strategies. Consider the issues involved in planning and managing inventory and storage capacity when a retailer combines Internet and brick-and-mortar channels to sell its products to consumers. The planning and management of inventories and storage capacity focus on decisions involving the timing and quantity of inventory replenishments for each SKU carried in stock at distribution centers and retail outlets. While inventory at distribution centers can be used to fulfill demand at the stores or to fulfill sales that involve direct-to-consumer delivery, inventory located at retail outlets can only be used to fulfill demand from consumers who wish to pick up the items at the stores and take them home (Agatz et al., 2008).

Therefore, the use of forecasts to determine appropriate stocking levels at distribution centers or at retail stores will vary depending on these differences in demand that the inventory at these locations is subject to. In particular, this includes setting safety stocks to buffer against demand uncertainty.

The opportunity costs of carrying safety stocks at retail outlets are higher than those for safety stocks at distribution centers because demand uncertainty is higher at retail outlets than at distribution centers. For one, demand at retail outlets originates from a much smaller demand pool located within a few miles of the outlets. Moreover, this demand is more sensitive to changes in the levels of inventory where products are sold. This is because customers at retail stores have direct visibility of inventories, and their purchase intentions will be affected by their perceptions of scarcity or abundance of inventories at the stores. The rate of depletion for inventories at retail stores will be exposed to hard-to-forecast swings in customer demand as a result of this phenomenon.

Furthermore, the opportunity costs of carrying safety stocks at retail outlets are higher than those for safety stocks at distribution centers because of both the higher facility cost of a conveniently located retail location as well as the opportunity cost of displaying another higher- value product to store customers. Moreover, because retailers have already invested in transporting and placing the inventory at retail

| Benefits | Challenges |
|---|---|
| • Greater availability of products at different locations<br><br>• More opportunity to give customers access to buying inventory without incurring last-mile delivery costs<br><br>• More products can be transported at full-truckload rates closer to markets<br><br>• Greater leverage to develop customer loyalty | • Added facility costs<br><br>• Cannibalization of sales from one channel by the other<br><br>• Higher complexity in inventory management plans and forecasts<br><br>• Greater carrying costs for safety stocks<br><br>• Need for a closer synchronization of inventory records across channels |

**Figure 5.3   Multichannel retailing: benefits and challenges.**

stores close to consumers, inventory at these stores is intrinsically more valuable than the inventory at distribution centers and, as such, it is more expensive to carry.

Multichannel retailing is also challenging due to the need to synchronize inventory records to ensure the availability of inventory shared across brick-and-mortar and Internet channels. This task can be critical when rates of sales for products are high or during promotional seasons because inventory levels across both channels will be subject to frequent changes during those times. Retailers have proved to be very competent in taking customer orders and keeping customers informed of the status of their orders. However, they can experience difficulties accessing timely and accurate updates of inventory records across channels to determine the amounts of inventory that have been allocated to customer orders and the inventory available to fulfill incoming demand.

We close this chapter with a summary of the benefits and challenges that retailers can encounter in their pursuit of combining Internet and brick-and-mortar channels. Figure 5.3 presents this summary.

# References

Agatz, N., M. Fleischmann, and J. van Nunen. 2008. E-Fulfillment and multichannel distribution—a review. *European Journal of Operational Research* 187: 339–356.

Anderson, C. 2006. *The Long Tail: Why the Future of Business Is Selling Less of More.* Hyperion, New York.

Anderson, E.T., K. Hansen, and D. Simester, 2009. The option value of returns: Theory and empirical evidence. *Marketing Science* 28(3): 405–423.

Anderson, E.T., K. Hansen, D. Simester, and L. Wang. 2009. How Price Affects Returns: The Perceived Value and Incremental Customer Effects. Working Paper, Northwestern University, Evanston, IL.

Andrew Petersen, J. and V. Kumar, 2009. Are product returns a necessary evil? Antecedents and consequences. *Journal of Marketing* 73(3): 35–51.

Baird, N. 2008. Rewiring retail: Lessons learned from the front lines of cross-channel retailing. The Cross Channel Retail Consortium White Paper. http://www .sterlingcommerce.com/PDF/Rewiring%20Retail.pdf.

Ballou, R. and A. Burnetas, 2003. Planning multiple location inventories. *Journal of Business Logistics* 24(2): 65–89.

Berman, B. and S. Thelen. 2004. A guide to developing and managing a well-integrated multi-channel retail strategy. *International Journal of Retail and Distribution Management* 32(3): 147–156.

Boyer, K.K. and G.T.M. Hult. 2006. Customer behavioral intentions for online purchases: An examination of fulfillment method and customer experience level. *Journal of Operations Management* 24(2): 124–147.

Brohan, M. 2005. Online retailers learn to live with that persistent problem of returns. *Internet Retailer* 7(4): 44–50.

Brynjolfsson, E., Y. (Jeffrey) Hu, and M.S. Rahman. 2009. Battle of the retail channels: How product selection and geography drive cross-channel competition. *Management Science* 55(11): 1755–1765.

Brynjolfsson, E., Y. Hu, and D. Simester. 2007. Goodbye Pareto Principle, hello long tail: The effect of search costs on the concentration of product sales. Working Paper, Sloan School of Management, Massachusetts Institute of Technology, Cambridge, MA.

Brynjolfsson, E., Y. Hu, and M.D. Smith. 2003. Consumer surplus in the digital economy: Estimating the value of increased product variety at online booksellers. *Management Science* 49(11): 1580–1596.

Chevalier, J. and D. Mayzlin. 2006. The effect of word-of-mouth on sales: Online book reviews. *Journal of Marketing Research* 43(3): 345.

Chong, J.K., T.H. Ho, and C.S. Tang. 2001. A modeling framework for category assortment planning. *Manufacturing and Service Operations Management* 3(3): 191–210.

Clemons, E., M. Gao, and L. Hitt. 2006. When online reviews meet hyperdifferentiation: A study of the craft beer industry. *Journal of Management Information Systems* 23(2): 149–171.

Coyle, J.J., E.J. Bardi, and C.J. Langley Jr. 2003. *The Management of Business Logistics*. South-Western, Mason, OH.

Del Franco, M. 2002. Managing the dropship process. *CatalogAge* 19(11): 37.

Evers, P.T. 2001. Heuristics for assessing emergency transshipments. *European Journal of Operational Research* 129(2): 311–316.

Finch, B. 2007. Customer expectations in online auction environments: An exploratory study of customer feedback and risk. *Journal of Operations Management* 25(5): 985–997.

Fisher, M., R. Raman, and A. McClelland. 2000. Rocket science retailing is almost here—are you ready? *Harvard Business Review* 78(4): 115–124.

Gardner, E. 2008. What now? Internet Retailer. http://www.internetretailer.com/article.asp?id=26595.

Glenn David, E. and S.F. Ellison. 2006. Internet Retail Demand: Taxes, Geography, and Online-Offline Competition (April 28, 2006). MIT Department of Economics Working Paper No. 06-14. Available at SSRN: http://ssrn.com/abstract=901852.

Grewal, D., M. Levy, and G.W. Marshall. 2002. Personal selling in retail settings: How does the Internet and related technologies enable and limit successful selling? *Journal of Marketing Management* 18(3–4): 301–316.

Hallowell, R. 2001. Scalability: The paradox of human resources in e-commerce. *International Journal of Service Industry Management* 12(1): 34–43.

Heim, G.R. and K. Sinha. 2001. Operational drivers of customer loyalty in electronic retailing: An empirical analysis of electronic food retailers. *Manufacturing and Service Operations Management* 3(3): 264–271.

Johnson, E.J., W. Moe, S. Bellman, J. Lohse, and P. Fader. 2004. On the depth and dynamics of online search behavior. *Management Science* 50(3): 299–308.

Laseter, T., E. Rabinovich, and A. Huang. 2006. The hidden cost of clicks. *strategy+business* 42: 26–30.

Metters, R. and S. Walton. 2007. Strategic supply chain choices for multi-channel Internet retailers. *Service Business* 1(4): 317–331.

Mollenkopf, D.A., E. Rabinovich, T.M. Laseter, and K.K. Boyer. 2007. Managing Internet product returns: A focus on effective service operations. *Decision Sciences* 38(2): 215–250.

Netessine, S. and N. Rudi. 2003. *Supply Chain Choice on the Internet.* Unpublished Manuscript, Wharton School of Business, University of Pennsylvania.

Piccoli, G., M.K. Brohman, R. Watson, and A. Parasuraman. 2004. Net-based customer service systems: Evolution and revolution in web site functionalities. *Decision Sciences* 25(3): 423–455.

Rabinovich, E., A.B. Maltz, and R.K. Sinha. 2008. Assessing markups, service quality, and product attributes in music CDs' Internet retailing. *Production and Operations Management* 17(3): 320–337.

Smith, M.D. and E. Brynjolfsson. 2001. Decision-making at an Internet shopbot: Brand still matters. *Journal of Industrial Economics* Vol. 49, No. 4, Symposium on E-Commerce, pp. 541–558.

Smith, S. and N. Agrawal. 2000. Management of multi-item retail inventory systems with demand substitution. *Operations Research* 48(1): 50–64.

Sousa, R. and C.A. Voss. 2006. Service quality in multichannel services employing virtual channels. *Journal of Service Research* 8(4): 356–371.

Thirumalai, S. and K.K. Sinha. 2005. Customer satisfaction with order fulfillment in retail supply chains: Implications of product type in electronic B2C transactions. *Journal of Operations Management* 23(3–4): 291–303.

Wood, S.L. 2001. Remote purchase environments: The influence of return policy leniency on two-stage decision processes. *Journal of Marketing Research* 38(May): 157–169.

# *Chapter 6*

# Defining the Value

In this chapter, we offer a discussion of the different services that Internet firms can provide in a supply chain setting. While there are many different business models built around services on the Internet, these services have commonalities that allow us to classify them into clearly defined groups with shared attributes. The first part of this chapter centers on this discussion.

Subsequently, in the second part of this chapter, we examine how these services' operations can contribute to the development of competitive advantages. To that end, we consider the impact that the deployment of Internet technology has had in the creation of economic value, competitive industry structures, and the realization of sustainable competencies. To the extent that these competencies are not easily mimicked by other firms and can contribute to the retention of customers, Internet organizations will be well positioned among their industry competitors.

## What Are the Main Internet Services That Exist in a Supply Chain Context?

Back on July 15th, 2002, in the wake of the dot-com bubble period, Jeff Bezos, founder and CEO of Amazon.com, explained during an interview with *Business Week*'s editor Doug Harbrecht that over the previous year the major change in the online retailing mode involved the integration of three "growth drivers": lower prices, convenience, and selection. These growth drivers that Mr. Bezos referred to define the main Internet services that can be commonly observed in a supply chain context (Figure 6.1).

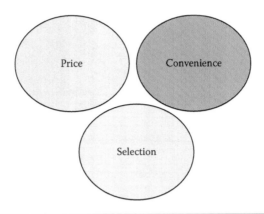

**Figure 6.1 Internet Services—drivers of growth in Internet retailing.**

Price setting offers the most fundamental and evident of all services a seller can provide on the Internet. Through the setting of prices, sellers interpret the market signals regarding the value and uniqueness of their product offering. Convenience captures customer perception around a number of factors ranging from the ease of online ordering to customer confidence in the sellers' ability to ensure prompt, accurate delivery, and, when needed, returns. Finally, the breadth of a seller's offering will depend on how effectively they can match product supply with demand.

## *Price Setting*

Most of the sellers on the web, especially those who weathered the dot-com bubble boom and bust, have experienced a drastic change in their price-setting decisions. They have transitioned from their early days when get-big-fast strategies compelled them to compete aggressively on prices to more recent times when the need to consolidate profits has driven them to design pricing schemes consistent with different customer segments in their markets.

Aggressive price competition among start-ups in the 1990s opened opportunities for the emergence of intermediaries like shopping agent mysimon .com. These intermediaries offered buyers a compilation of offers from different sellers in order to allow for an easy comparison of prices among them. This pushed retailers in the direction of a race to the bottom in which price leaders would dominate the market but would receive minimal profits in the process. Shopping agents would become indispensable in these markets by cataloging, searching, and compiling price information for customer use. Agents used their access to customers to capture some of the remaining profits of the retailers.

We can see an analogous scenario playing out in the news media and advertising businesses, where Google and other intermediaries have stepped in with their services and captured a significant proportion of profits. In the electronic commerce realm, where physical products and supply chain activities are involved, sellers have managed to transition away from a reliance on price competition. Internet retailers now charge buyers for the supply chain necessary for the delivery of their products to their buyers, as well as the products themselves. In pricing these activities, retailers have adopted a menu strategy, charging higher premiums for faster delivery. In doing so, online retailers separate their customers into different market segments by giving them the autonomy to choose among the delivery services they receive. Those customers who are price sensitive opt for the most basic, and cheapest, delivery option, while those customers who prefer a faster delivery willingly pay a premium for it.

## *Convenience*

Internet sellers should aim to retain those customers who care most about the quality of their shopping experience in order to capture the associated price premiums. Successful sellers have pursued four different approaches.

First, retailers have used branding to justify their premiums. There are at least two ways to use branding to support high margins. Being the "click" part of a brick-and-click operation offers higher profit margins. The online channel of a physical chain such as Wal-Mart.com certainly enjoys economies of scale. For pure Internet retailers, brand building and higher margins come at least partly from word of mouth and a lengthier "top of mind" tradition.

Second, retailers can use web-based services to support their premiums. Through these services, retailers may offer product attribute information, product reviews, and product previews (book samples), and their margins reflect that service. Firms like Amazon.com neutralize the physical advantages of brick-and-click retailers by going the extra mile in product information. Effectively managing product returns has also proven critical in competing with physical stores. Retailers that can offer customer-friendly return policies can lower perceived risks that shoppers may have when buying products that are difficult to evaluate online or require large expenditures.

Third, product mix can also influence premiums. Popular products do not command premium prices; if your favorite site does not have a product, another site will. High-premium sellers choose niches and establish their reputations by appealing to targeted audiences willing to pay for special access and expertise. As the largest online retailer, Amazon.com serves as an exception here since its scale allows the company to provide access to both popular and scarce items across many product categories beyond its core media products in books and videos.

## Selection

Because of the lack of constraints that the Internet imposes on the display of a large product variety, retailers could offer a large breadth of inventory that would save customers trips to brick-and-mortar stores. While this is a valuable service for customers, searching among a wide array of products has some cost, even on the Internet, so retailers should pay attention to the tools that they provide customers to identify and assess unfamiliar products. Retailers can charge premium prices when they save time-starved consumers by helping them find exactly what they seek. Savvy Internet retailers are wary of popular items that invite the price comparison that the Net makes easy. Choosing niches and catering to customers who need access to the unusual and unique minimizes price-based competition.

If all of this sounds familiar, it is because Internet retailing is still about selling the right stuff to customers who are willing to pay a fair price, and then taking care of these customers over time. Being on the Internet does not shield managers from bad product choices. Some retailers have struggled because their core products, for example, CDs, are being rendered obsolete by digital downloads via the Internet, the very medium they have based their business on.

However, buying physical products on the Internet continues to grow, and a smart product selection is important. This includes products across multiple channels operated by the seller. Brick-and-mortar channels should be put in synch with Internet channels to get the most out of the inventory across these channels.

Retailers like REI, for example, have gone through multiple stages in order to accomplish this goal. In the first stage, REI focused on addressing stock-out occurrences at its stores. If REI's customers could not find an item at one of the stores, REI offered them the option to order it through in-store kiosks and have it delivered to the store free of shipping and handling charges. REI would then order the item from its distribution centers and would have it delivered to the store with the next inventory replenishment shipment. Because replenishments occurred regularly, most items would arrive at the stores within a few days of the order.

In the second stage, REI offered customers the choice to make their purchases anywhere online and, instead of paying for home delivery for their orders, have products delivered at the nearest store free of shipping and handling charges. This service required a more proactive stance by REI in order to give each customer real-time information about the store where the order is to be delivered and an accurate estimation of when the order will be ready for pickup at the store.

In the third stage of the evolution, REI offered customers the option of buying online from the store's current stock and picking up the items at the nearest store, free of shipping and handling charges. To support this model, REI had to tackle the challenges of tracking inventory in real time at the stores. Moreover, REI had to build processes to ensure that items would be ready for pickup at the stores within minutes of receiving the online orders.

A smart product selection can also draw from inventory owned by the Internet sellers' suppliers and located at the suppliers' distribution centers. Under this arrangement, commonly known as *drop shipping*, Internet sellers manage the online catalog of products and customers' orders. In turn, the suppliers are responsible for holding the inventory and shipping it upon request by Internet sellers. For Internet sellers, this arrangement expands the scope of products they can offer. For the suppliers, it offers direct access to new markets for their products without having to establish physical stores or distribution centers for holding inventory in the markets prior to establishing demand.

Finally, the realization of greater variety in product selection can come from mixing and combining of other products carried in stock to more closely meet customer needs and wants. Such bundling can also generate incremental profits for the Internet seller. Consider the case of FreshDirect, an online grocer operating in the greater New York City metropolitan area. Among the variety of products FreshDirect offers, customers can buy 55 customized varieties of coffee, mixed from 22 different coffee beans, which are roasted and ground to order. While the cost of regular coffee beans average $0.70/lb, prices for the customized varieties of coffee average $4.62/lb plus delivery charges.

## How Can the Internet Be Used to Offer Services That Contribute to the Development of Competitive Advantages?

Services can contribute to the development of competitive advantages on the Internet. Deployment of services enabled by Internet technology can create economic value, depending on competitive industry structures, on how easily these services can be mimicked by other firms and how they can contribute to the retention of customers.

Because of its open architecture and standards, the Internet in itself does not provide a unique advantage to those who adopt it to conduct business. The Internet offers firms the opportunity to establish new competitive positions in relation to what was possible before the advent of this information technology tool. Only those organizations that deploy the Internet for competitive advantages can create sustainable economic value. This observation bodes well for small start-ups because they can draw benefits from innovative and hard-to-replicate uses of the Internet. However, this is also good news to more established firms that are able to use the Internet to complement their traditional ways of operating their businesses.

During the early days of the Internet's commercialization, revenues proved difficult to estimate because, in some cases, stock options drove a focus on revenues rather than assets. Costs were also difficult to estimate because Internet firms were paying suppliers for inventory and services with equity, warrants, or stock options rather than with cash. This practice led to the underestimation of the need for capital in the operation of Internet firms.

The Internet has reconfigured existing industries such as book retailing and music retailing by enhancing the supply chain participants' ability to communicate with consumers, to gather information about consumers' tastes, and to execute transactions through the offering of digital alternatives to physical products. However, these benefits also make it more difficult for sellers to capture profits because the barriers to competition are not very high.

Two aspects of Internet commerce have the potential for providing sellers with sustainable competitive advantages. The first one centers on the virtual services involved in executing transactions between sellers and buyers. For most products, Internet commerce requires accurate in-stock information, order-tracking capabilities, comparison tools, and effective product configuration mechanisms.

The second aspect revolves around physical services supported by the infrastructure and the fulfillment and logistics functions involved in completing the processing of orders from buyers. This aspect has the potential for generating returns, depending on the type of product involved. The implications for the commercialization of media products like books or music CDs on the Internet are more favorable for consumers than those for other products. Consumers can easily search, evaluate, and compare media products on the Internet, and it is relatively simple to stock and fulfill their orders. However, these advantages create a great deal of competitive pressure for sellers because they must compete in a setting where inputs and services are fairly homogenous across firms and in which wholesalers and other distributors are powerful enough to make it easy to foreclose and ration inventories for some Internet sellers at the expense of others.

Other goods are more challenging to commercialize on the Internet. For instance, shoes or apparel require the experiential assessment of consumers after their purchase, while groceries and other food items face perishability risks and need to be stored next to the markets where they will eventually be sold. These challenges create an opening in the competitive space for sellers to differentiate their offerings and realize sustainable advantages. Consider the case of Zappos .com, a shoe retailer that has used the web to sell its products to consumers by establishing itself as a service leader and, in doing so, promoted the kind of customer loyalty needed to generate frequent repurchases and larger orders. FreshDirect, the online grocer operating in the greater New York City metropolitan area, also has established itself as a leader in its segment through the design of an inventory policy that places its products in close proximity to its customers to guarantee the product freshness customers may find at their neighborhood stores, but with a broader product variety and reliable order delivery.

The sustainability of the competitive advantages that these strategies provide is evidenced over the long run as Internet retailers are able to attract and retain customers. Traditionally, firms have relied on low introductory pricing to build long-term market share. The problem with this strategy on the Internet is that it attracts mainly bargain hunters who are willing to buy at these low prices but are just as able and willing to switch when other sellers undercut these prices.

Because customers on the Internet can switch their loyalties from one seller to another at virtually no cost, businesses need to be smart about pricing their offers. As part of this approach, companies need to understand how to bundle under their offers products and services involved in completing the processing and fulfillment of their orders.

To receive services such as fulfillment, customers must pay for their orders first. These payments usually even include a separate charge (labeled shipping and handling fee) for the service. Since these services are experiential in nature, they offer sellers an opportunity to compete based on service quality differentiation. Other services (e.g., accurate in-stock information or back-ordering information) are provided free of charge and are only relevant to the seller offering them. A third group of services, such as those that give customers access to product sampling and comparisons, are also free, but customers can avail themselves of these services while buying from other sellers. Therefore, competitors can freeload these services when transactions with customers are discrete and are paid for on an individual basis, one at a time.

Sellers can best leverage this third category of services when customers pay for them as part of subscription packages rather than on a transaction basis. The use of subscription packages limits the transferability of these services for purchase at other sites because customers have made a commitment to use these services in advance. This does not mean, however, that customers will be unable to switch to other competitors, especially if their subscriptions have a short duration. Moreover, customer retention will depend not only on their satisfaction with the service they receive from their subscription but also on how heavily they take advantage of their subscriptions.

Customers must make an active choice to terminate or change their subscriptions. As long as the firm provides consistent, reasonable service, customers have a low probability of terminating their subscriptions. The firm must also design subscription packages with multiple levels of service and usage for customers to select the alternative that best fits their needs. A one-size-fits-all approach at designing subscription packages will generate a substantial amount of cancellations due to low usage by customers.

Consider the case of Netflix versus the traditional movie rental models such as those offered in the past by Blockbuster or those more recently offered by RedBox. The Netflix model is based on monthly subscriptions, so retention rates are relatively high compared to the rates in the traditional models. Netflix customers must make an active choice to end their monthly subscriptions or change them. On the other hand, in the traditional movie rental models, customers default immediately to an inactive state every time they return a title they rented, and must make an active choice to rent again in the future.

Under its model, Netflix must design subscription packages well suited to customers' needs and that also generate profits. Profits simply reflect the difference between the subscription fees and the costs customers generate based on the number and type of movies they rent per subscription period. The more movies customers rent, the greater the costs incurred by Netflix in mailing the titles to the customers and back. Furthermore, customers that rent newly released blockbusters more frequently generate greater copyright fees for Netflix relative to those who rent older, more obscure backlist titles.

To foster retention, Netflix emphasizes the convenience of its services by ensuring a fast and accurate delivery of titles and a speedy processing of returned DVDs. This allows customers to watch different titles more frequently during their monthly subscription periods. Netflix also excels at fulfilling customers' primary demand, as reflected in the percentage of demand they fulfill from the top of customers' movie wish lists, and in offering a virtually limitless variety of titles unmatched by any of the traditional movie rental companies.

Netflix will remain profitable as long as it succeeds in retaining those customers whose monthly subscriptions do not generate losses. In the long run, Netflix can improve profits by preventing customer desertion and upgrading subscribers to more profitable packages. Thus, for Netflix, profitability is not achieved exclusively by leveraging markups on discrete events or transactions. Rather, it is realized in the long run by capturing value over the lifetime of its customers.

Netflix's success also depends on being ahead of the technology curve. The company already disrupted the movie sales and rental industry and compelled Blockbuster to redefine how it rents movies to rely less on its brick-and-mortar stores. Moreover, because Netflix lets its customers hold on to rentals indefinitely, it provides customers with a cheaper, more convenient alternative to buying the films outright.

This industry will undoubtedly continue to evolve by increasingly using the Internet to stream all kinds of movie titles and other content to viewers. Those businesses that are able to offer customers access to the right content, at the right place, and at the fastest and cheapest way will win. Consumers, not networks, cable firms, and other providers, determine what they want to watch, when, where, and how.

Under this view of the future, the Internet gives viewers access to customized content rather than bundles of channels or preprogrammed shows, most of which offer little benefit in addressing viewers' tastes. This juxtaposition resembles what has happened in the music industry, where individuals have been able to use the Internet to consume only the content they want and not pay for packaged music that offers little utility to them.

# Chapter 7

# Outsourcing Internet Retail Operations

Outsourcing has traditionally focused on tactical, nonessential activities. However, the focus has changed recently. Firms in a range of industries, particularly in the technology areas, outsource core, strategic activities that could substantially affect their profitability if not performed well. While many Internet retailers, such as Amazon, have pursued vertical integration, others have actively pursued outsourcing to focus their scope along the value chain. In this chapter, we will explore the motivations for outsourcing and provide perspective on how to make what should be a key strategic decision.

The motivation to outsource for Internet retailers has driven organizations to look for different ways to shrink their scope along their supply chains while seeking opportunities to enhance effectiveness in their operations to provide great customer service. At the most basic level, Internet retailers, like many other organizations, outsource to achieve lower costs as part of their operations. These expenditures include labor and other resources that generate variable costs, but they also include the transfer of assets such as inventory and distribution facilities in an effort to lower their fixed costs (Maltz, Rabinovich, and Sinha, 2004).

Improving asset utilization provides a related but different motivation for outsourcing. Internet retailers are in a continuous struggle to avoid the underutilization of their inventory facilities and equipment, particularly during the slow-selling times of the year when demand rates are not very high. When a third-party organization takes over these facilities, it can add volume from other customers to improve utilization. By narrowing their efforts to a single function or discipline, third-party firms can also offer scale economies that may not be available to Internet retailers. These scale economies result from larger facilities as well as from broader and denser distribution networks available to the third-party providers of the outsourced activities.

## Internet Retailing Decisions to Outsource Their Distribution Facilities' Footprint*

The decisions by Internet retailers to outsource the ownership of their distribution facilities have led to different structures for their distribution networks, primarily as a function of strategic intent and scale. As illustrated by the two dimensions along the vertical and horizontal axes in Figure 7.1, some retailers have developed distribution competencies in-house, while others have chosen to depend heavily on outside service providers. Moreover, the number and geographic location of distribution centers vary, from a single location driven by happenstance to multifacility, global networks strategically designed to optimize cost and service.

As indicated in Figure 7.1, several different considerations can drive a company to move from a single facility to multiple sites. Large Internet retailers with a broad geographical focus and lots of financial resources will be able to afford multifacility, in-house networks, but most other companies lack the scale or the strategic commitment to invest in such a capital-intensive fulfillment competency. As a result, as an Internet retailer expands its geographic scope and pool of resources, the need to lower transportation costs and speed up delivery can drive it to open additional facilities that are closer to customers.

Less obviously, product characteristics can also influence the network structure. Small items can be shipped cheaply even over long distances, while large, bulky items cost more in outbound delivery. Complicating the decision making, however, large items are more likely to achieve good inbound shipping economies, even to multiple facilities. As pointed out by Boyer et al. (2004) all of these issues need to be examined by retailers in the context of their business, products, and demand characteristics. Overall, retailers handling standardized, small-sized items for which last-mile delivery does not need to be expedited to reach customers will tend to choose network structure design with fewer facilities, outsourced to external logistics specialists (Figure 7.1).

---

* With permission, this section draws in part from the previously published work by Laseter, Rabinovich, Boyer, and Rungtusanatham (2007). From Sloan Management Review. Copyright © 2010 by Massachusetts Institute of Technology. All rights reserved. Distributed by Tribune Media Services.

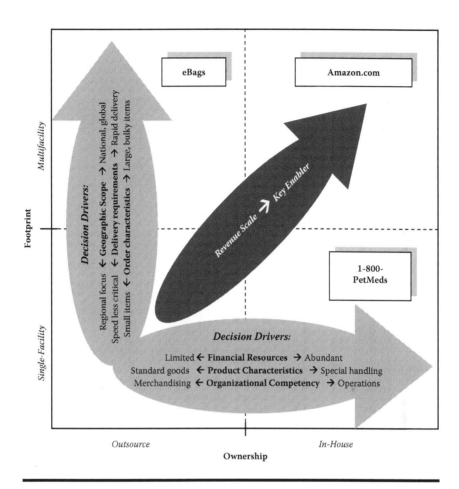

**Figure 7.1  Network structure design considerations. (From Laseter, T.M. et al. 2007. *MIT Sloan Management Review* 48(3): 58–64.)**

Other retailers will prefer to build their distribution networks in-house. Amazon.com, for example, made a strategic decision to build operations competencies to provide the service required of its customer-centric philosophy. While many early Internet retailers discounted the importance of operations to their detriment, others would have preferred to follow Amazon's lead but lacked the financial resources to do so. Without the funds to build their own networks, smaller firms have outsourced fulfillment, thereby converting significant fixed costs to a variable cost.

Finding a capable outsourcing provider can be difficult when the product requires specialized handling, however. For example, 1-800-PetMeds operates out of a single, in-house fulfillment center in Florida, far from most of the larger centers of population in the United States. Although such a location would produce a significant cost disadvantage in many retail categories, it works for PetMeds because most of its shipments are sent via U.S. Postal Service Priority Mail, which is priced at a flat rate regardless of the shipping destination. The special staffing and controls required for the handling of prescription medicines also pushed 1-800-PetMeds to keep fulfillment in-house. As PetMeds grows, adding another facility closer to the West Coast may become necessary to enable faster delivery times. But the need to maintain in-house control of prescription drugs will likely mean that such a facility will be operated by in-house staff rather than an outside provider.

The choices for a traditional retailer with a growing presence online prove no less daunting. Most retail distribution networks have been designed to efficiently handle full-truckload shipments of full-caseload goods. Wal-Mart has gone further, employing advanced technology and its scale to create a network of specialized high-volume distribution centers and cross-docks to deliver its breadth of products to its stores at greater velocity and lower cost than any retailer in history. However, that highly tuned network offers little advantage for the pick, pack, and ship fulfillment operations required to support online sales. The distinctly different operating characteristics of their existing networks have led many offline retailers to turn to Amazon.com for their online operations despite the depth of supply chain management expertise found in big-box retailers.

With such a wide variety of options, the appropriate network architecture is anything but obvious. Furthermore, the optimal answer changes over time as online retail sales grow in importance. Consider the example of Borders, the big-box retailer of books. In April 2001, Borders outsourced its website and fulfillment operations for Borders.com to Amazon. The difficulties of managing a separate online channel seemed disproportionate to the relatively small revenue it generated as an overall percentage of sales (less than 1% at the time of the agreement). However, strategic dynamics change over time. A couple of years ago, Borders increased the use of interactive marketing via the Internet and found the formerly logical outsourcing decision a constraint. Although still cost effective, the outsourcing model limited Borders' ability to capture the customer directly online. This led Borders to cancel its contract with Amazon and bring online fulfillment back in-house.

Clearly, no-one-size-fits all network structure applies to Internet retailers. What's more, the "right" answer will keep changing as Internet retail sales continue to grow. The decision to outsource distribution facilities ranks among the most critical of strategic issues, however, because of the capital implications of vertical integration and the "lock in" risks of picking the wrong network partners. The best Internet retailers will invest in a network architecture that fits their specific product characteristics and strategic competencies at a price they can afford.

## Logistics Outsourcing Decisions in the Broader Internet Retailing Context*

Our research shows that, in some cases, the supplementary benefits offered by external logistics outsourcing partners prove very attractive to Internet retailers. These benefits normally translate not only into broader fulfillment network footprints but also into more complete and reliable fulfillment services. For example, outdoor-gear retailer Recreational Equipment, Inc. (REI), has partnered with external providers to manage customers' requests and inquiries related to in-store pickups of online orders. This has allowed REI to improve its in-store inventory utilization by better matching stock availability with demand. Another large retailer, QVC, partnered with CommerceHub to monitor drop shipments that go directly to online customers from QVC vendors. CommerceHub provided a central communications point for monitoring all order shipments and inventory data, allowing QVC to avoid having to develop individual data standards and hardwired data connections for each supplier. The service shortened QVC's order-cycle times and simplified order packing and automated carrier tracking, thereby reducing QVC's late-delivery and stockout risks.

These services will be offered more effectively depending on their scalability, as defined by the number of additional customers that can be covered at extremely low incremental costs. Which types of services are more scalable? Why?

In general, services that can be delivered almost entirely through the web are more scalable than services that require human or infrastructure intervention. The former services include those offered to consumers by iTunes, YouTube, and Facebook, and those offered to QVC and other Internet retailers by providers such as CommerceHub. They are based mainly on the transfer of bits between supply chain partners. Because this transfer carries minimal marginal costs, the addition of individual users requires minimal expenditures. These businesses have taken advantage of this and have been able to grow exponentially as a result.

---

* With permission this section draws in part from the previously published work by Rabinovich and Knemeyer (2006) in *California Management Review*. Copyright © 2006 by The Regents of the University of California. Reprinted from *California Management Review*, Vol. 8, No. 4. By permission of The Regents.

On the other hand, services that require human or infrastructure intervention, such as the fulfillment of Internet customer orders, are subject to substantial marginal costs. This is because their expansion to cover additional customers requires substantial investments in fixed assets such as fulfillment centers and transportation equipment.

This phenomenon has made it difficult for Internet sellers of physical goods to easily scale up their businesses. Many of them have chosen to scale up their operations with the support of external intermediaries that have the available infrastructure and footprint to accommodate their increasing market demand. Just a few years ago, there was an expectation that these intermediaries would not be able to find a place to compete in this industry. The current trend appears to undermine this expectation. These intermediaries—often referred to as logistics service providers (LSPs)—have emerged to help Internet retailers leverage their networks of relationships with customers and other entities in their supply chains in order to fulfill their orders more effectively. They may take care of product returns, for instance, or work with their partner carriers on last-mile deliveries. Or their value may be in providing information—order confirmation, especially when products are being shipped directly from Internet sellers' suppliers to Internet sellers' customers.

## Barriers and Challenges to Adoption

A major barrier in the implementation of relationships with LSPs is the poor understanding that Internet retailers have about their relationships with these service providers. Many retailers set up these relationships to quickly solve deficiencies in specific logistics functions, with little thought about the long-term implications of these relationships

In other cases, retailers will work with the lowest bidders. This approach may invoke a "winner's curse" in which logistics providers will shore up their own profitability by boosting their prices or cutting costs soon after the contracts are signed. It is up to the retailers to prevent these situations from happening through a close monitoring of performance metrics and communication with LSPs and shoppers.

Other Internet retailers have chosen not to consider LSPs because their infrastructures favor in-house control. In the case of product returns, for instance, some sellers with brick-and-mortar stores will rely on their stores' footprint and will channel product returns to these sites. In doing so, these retailers can aggregate and send back in bulk the returned products to their regional or national distribution centers for restocking, refurbishing, or scrapping. While this approach provides low costs in transporting product returns, it may delay the restocking, refurbishing, and resale of items routed through those distribution centers. If the items are time sensitive (because they are seasonal or perishable), the loss in their value during the return process may very well offset the transportation cost savings obtained from this approach (Blackburn et al., 2004).

Retailers need to move beyond a simplistic understanding of how their relationships with other organizations will work in a networked environment such as the web. Otherwise, they may miss opportunities to improve their competitive positions in the industry. The web offers challenges that retailers need to consider as they establish their relationships. A critical issue is the nature of interorganizational transactions on the web and their implications for the development of links between retailers and service providers and beyond.

## Interorganizational Transactions on the Web

Because the web has simplified transactions between sellers and different parties in the supply chain, including customers, early observers came to believe that at some point the web would enable a new age of perfectly competitive markets. According to their forecast, these markets would eliminate many intermediaries, including logistics providers (The Economist, 1999).

However, this has not occurred because, in order to search and buy on the web, it is necessary to compare sellers' offers that are not truly homogeneous. Although the offers may involve seemingly identical products, they may comprise logistics services that carry different costs and quality. Also, these services cannot be assessed prior to purchasing by the average consumer because they are experimental in nature. To establish the true value of these services (as a function of price and quality), it is necessary to actually experience them. This has made it difficult for consumers to lock in the best logistics service quality at the lowest price.

Retailers that understand this phenomenon have leveraged relationships with LSPs to attract shoppers who seek first-rate logistics service quality. However these relationships are unique because they lie at the center of networks that include not only LSPs but also retailers' end consumers and suppliers.

## Toward the Development of Service Networks

Retailers on the web can use their service providers as *hubs* to expand and reinforce their reach to new and existing customers, access new resources and products offered by their suppliers, or broaden the quality of options available to complement compatible delivery services available through carriers. In this role, service providers perform different functionalities along different areas of their networks of relationships with suppliers, customers, and delivery carriers (e.g.,

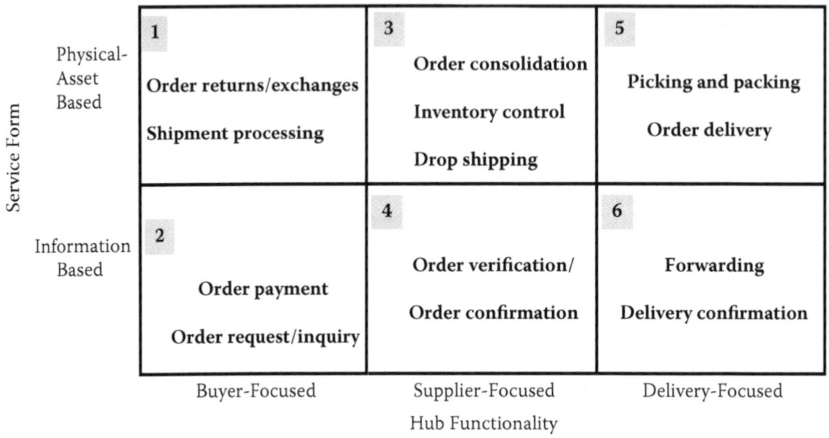

| Service Form | | Buyer-Focused | Supplier-Focused | Delivery-Focused |
|---|---|---|---|---|
| Physical-Asset Based | | **1**<br><br>Order returns/exchanges<br><br>Shipment processing | **3**<br><br>Order consolidation<br><br>Inventory control<br><br>Drop shipping | **5**<br><br>Picking and packing<br><br>Order delivery |
| Information Based | **2** | Order payment<br><br>Order request/inquiry | **4**<br><br>Order verification/<br><br>Order confirmation | **6**<br><br>Forwarding<br><br>Delivery confirmation |

Hub Functionality

**Figure 7.2** (From Rabinovich, E. and A.M. Knemeyer. 2006. *California Management Review* 48(4): 84–108.)

FedEx, USPS) to combine a diverse and dynamic set of resources available to sellers to become more responsive to changing market requirements (Figure 7.2).

LSPs can take over multiple functions simultaneously. Half of the categories in Figure 7.2 represent *physical-asset-based LSPs*—heavy users of transportation and inventory/warehousing assets. The other half of the categories covers *information-based LSPs*—providers that chiefly manage information.

The six categories are further defined by the LSPs' functionalities. Examples of LSP functionalities that fall into each category are provided in Figure 7.2. They include functions focused on Internet retailers' customers (buyer-focused functions), functions directed toward Internet retailers' product vendors (supplier-focused functions), and functions centered on the last-mile delivery of products to Internet retailers' customers (delivery-focused functions).

Internet retailers' interest in LSPs can also span bundles of functions offered by logistics providers, as opposed to discrete functions. This approach would allow retailers to streamline the set of physical assets and flow of data necessary to fulfill customers' orders. For instance, Internet retailers could rely on individual LSPs to perform clusters of functions that would yield improvements in customer service. These functions would involve *buyer-focused* categories in Figure 7.2, in which logistics providers would run information-based functions, such as order payment, and physical-asset-based functions, such as product returns and exchanges. In this case, retailers can establish relationships with logistics providers so they can expand their markets to include new products or extensions of existing products. They will also work with buyer-focused LSPs to cut the costs of handling inquiries from customers who want to track their orders or returns.

Internet retailers may also seek LSPs to perform multiple functions sharing complementary and even common physical assets and information in order to streamline the array of material goods and flow of data upstream in their supply chains. For example, a logistics provider could help Internet retailers to expand the use of warehousing assets devoted initially to carrying out functions involving inventory supplied by Internet retailer vendors to also receive and process customer-order returns and exchanges of products originally sourced from this very same inventory.

Also, consider categories 3 and 4 in Figure 7.2. Through these functions, LSPs can help Internet retailers tap into resources and inventory offered by their suppliers. These *supplier-focused* LSPs can help retailers so that they can drop ship and verify and confirm orders using a wide array of supplier-owned inventory. The relationships allow Internet retailers to expand their product offerings without investing in inventory or risking losses caused by inventory obsolescence and depreciation. Retailers may also use supplier-focused LSPs to more effectively control their own inventory, especially when it is necessary to replace obsolete inventory.

Furthermore, Internet retailers may seek individual LSPs to perform functions with common information in order to increase the integrity, accuracy, and promptness in their responses to customer requests. For instance, an Internet retailer may opt to rely on a single provider not only to handle customer order requests and inquiries but also to gather information to (1) verify that orders can be fulfilled on time with the existing inventory, (2) process customer payments, and (3) subsequently collect information verifying that orders are accurately and promptly delivered. These functions correspond to the categories under the purview of *delivery-focused* LSPs—providers that increase the scope and quality of options available to complement compatible delivery services available through last-mile carriers. Performing functions such as order-forwarding and delivery-focused LSPs are likely to provide benefits to Internet sellers that desire to expand quickly into well-established geographical markets and tap into low rates from last-mile carriers.

## *Creating Positive Network Effects*

Networks can have a positive effect on Internet retailers' bottom line if they can help expand the margins sellers obtain from their transactions with buyers. Margins will expand with price increases following the creation of links with LSPs that broaden the retailers' access to profitable customers and as those links broaden the range and quality of options available to complement retailers' logistics services or the products they receive from suppliers. Margins will also rise when LSPs contribute to reducing the cost of performing a particular logistics service externally. We expand on these two phenomena in the following text.

## Increasing Revenues

An LSP can help an Internet retailer raise prices not just when the retailer can serve more customers but when this expansion is accompanied by greater customer loyalty. The LSP can also enable the retailer to mark up its products by being able to promote to premium customers a wider range and higher quality of logistics services.

An expansion in market coverage will be sustainable when it lessens the uncertainty about the retailer's viability and value-adding capability in the eyes of customers. Only then will this expansion translate into greater customer loyalty (Keller 1999). Thus, the expansion must heighten trust and loyalty among customers to allow the retailer not only to increase its price premiums but also to sustain these increases in the long run. A shift in customer retention rates can make a difference in earnings, and this influence will accelerate over time. Loyal shoppers buy more, pay higher prices, and generate positive word-of-mouth, thus suggesting a strong link between loyalty and profitability.

Internet retailers will also develop sustainable competitive advantages from their use of providers if they can help customers overcome information gaps and lower their search costs in assessing particular logistics services received from their transactions with the retailers. By using the support of LSPs to help customers overcome these gaps, retailers will increase the probability of new and, most important, repeat business from customers. For instance, retailers may charge a premium if they can work with LSPs to offer a greater variety and quality of services in logistics. Internet merchants could mark up their offers and, in return, promise a more reliable fulfillment process by giving customers their money back if they do not receive their orders by a specific date. Also, they could charge a premium on their products to uphold expedited refunds when customers return items.

Sustainable competitive advantages will also result from Internet retailers' leveraging their relationships with providers to bridge dissimilar processes among new vendors. This expansion may widen opportunities for Internet retailers to adapt their transactions to the requirements of a greater number of suppliers and obtain more favorable sourcing conditions for the inventory that they sell. In addition, this expansion may allow retailers to preempt access to suppliers by their immediate competitors and, therefore, generate first-mover competitive advantages in their supply chains. By having more favorable sourcing conditions from suppliers and leveraging these conditions to tap into new inventory before their competitors, Internet retailers will be in a better position to offer broader, more innovative product selections that will help attract an increasingly large number of customers.

## Lowering Costs

Logistics operations make up a sizable portion of the total operating costs of Internet retailers. Industry experts have estimated that costs incurred in logistics services can account for up to 15% of revenue for an Internet retailer. These costs, as well as the attempts to lower them by working with LSPs, hinge on whether a retailer will choose to actually compete on low costs and do so by carrying out transactions where services are backed by third-party resources with unique value to customers involved in the transactions.

This decision will depend on the level of uncertainty faced by the Internet retailer in its relationship with an LSP. This uncertainty will be a function of the retailer's limited knowledge of the logistics provider's performance. It may also result from a lack of knowledge of the demand for products offered by the Internet retailer and of the logistics service that supports the marketing of those products. Hence, at the most general level, the sources of uncertainty can be grouped into two categories. One category concerns a lack of knowledge of the behavior of the other party, reflected in the logistics provider's performance. The other category pertains to a lack of knowledge of the environment surrounding the logistics service.

These sources of uncertainty will play a key role in Internet retailers' decisions to rely on LSPs. As uncertainty increases, retailers engaged in these relationships will incur greater *adaptation* costs, depending on the need by the retailers to fully specify in advance and continually adjust to unexpected or opportunistic changes in the conditions surrounding the logistics service exchange and in the performance of the LSPs. As these costs increase, retailers are likely to avoid relationships with LSPs because it will become more expensive for them to obtain services from these providers. For one thing, Internet retailers would need to devote resources to establishing a rigorous selection process that would involve checking references with industry sources, current LSP clients, and financial institutions. Retailers must also clearly articulate their expectations. That can be difficult to accomplish when LSP performance is uncertain.

Uncertainty about LSP performance can also make it difficult for an Internet retailer to target incentives to improve operations and productivity in collaboration with a logistics service provider. If LSP performance is hard to monitor and measure, a contract may need to spell out policies and procedures applicable to day-to-day activity, and that would typically make the LSP's services more expensive.

The role of uncertainty takes on a special significance when Internet retailers opt to carry out logistics services internally so that they can reach ill-defined markets. Some retailers have reported having faced this type of uncertainty in their logistics service environment when they tapped into obscure markets or decided to launch products for which no prior demand information was available. As a result, these retailers have decided to avoid relationships with LSPs for services whose functions involved significant demand unpredictability or where it was difficult to monitor demand for those services.

For example, at PetSmart, the multichannel retailer of pet products, LSP performance uncertainties and their associated costs have influenced the choice of not seeking LSPs' help with drop shipping for its online orders. Different conditions in PetSmart's business operations have made it costly for the retailer to gauge with certainty the performance that LSPs would bring to the table. For instance, drop shipping at PetSmart.com involves voluminous, high-value products, such as dog crates and horse saddles, and very few vendors—each with different drop-shipping policies and processes. These conditions have limited the scalability of drop shipping across products and vendors, and have required constant intervention and monitoring by PetSmart. As a result, it has been difficult for the merchant to confidently predict the level of performance it would obtain from an LSP carrying out the tasks necessary to source inventory owned and held by PetSmart's vendors and coordinate its direct shipments to online consumers.

What is surprising is that, in the past, Internet retailers attempted to reduce uncertainty in their operations by pursuing market expansions through joint ventures and acquisitions involving other sellers that offered expertise and knowledge about obscure markets. These kinds of joint ventures were common in the early days of electronic commerce, when getting big fast was an imperative to attract investment for many Internet retailers. Such moves, however, prevented Internet retailers from developing internally the resources and expertise needed to deal with the uncertainty from entering those markets. In the long run, these strategies also prevented them from lowering uncertainty through the forging of direct linkages with suppliers, customers, and other supply chain members participating in those markets.

PetSmart has experienced this firsthand. In the 1990s, the retailer, like other brick-and-mortar retailers, grew its online business through joint ventures and acquisitions so that by 2001 PetSmart.com had become an independent venture owned in association with IdeaLab. At that point, PetSmart decided to take ownership of PetSmart.com and bring it back under its corporate umbrella. This allowed PetSmart's online business to benefit from merchandising and fulfillment capabilities that PetSmart had available in-house for its physical-store channel. This move also enabled PetSmart to become self-reliant in how it handled product returns. To that end, PetSmart staffed and equipped a distribution center with the purpose of processing and exchanging product returns sent directly by online consumers. As a result, PetSmart was able to develop the efficiency and expertise necessary to handle returns and exchanges, most of which involve customer gifts, high-priced equestrian gear, apparel, and other SKUs that are highly seasonal in nature and for which demand is irregular.

We have also found that excessive complexity in the processes needed to perform a logistics function will increase uncertainty and compel an Internet retailer to handle the function internally. As this complexity grows, the Internet retailer will opt to keep logistics functions within its confines. On the other hand, having simple processes involved in the execution of a particular logistics function will facilitate a retailer's engaging an LSP even when there is ambiguity about the conditions surrounding the function.

Consider again PetSmart and its inventory control. Compared to its other logistics functions, the retailer's inventory control is surrounded by stable conditions. Only the sporadic introduction of new product suppliers or the infrequent entry of major retail competitors could alter the external parameters bounding PetSmart's inventory control policies. Nevertheless, despite the stability surrounding its inventory control, the retailer has chosen to run this service in-house because of the highly complex tasks necessary to place inventory replenishment orders and monitor the status of in-stock, out-of-stock, and in-transit inventory items. This complexity is the result of the high interdependence that exists among different units throughout PetSmart in carrying out inventory control objectives. For one, PetSmart's online unit needs to be in constant communication with the rest of the organization to determine its inventory location (e.g., in-transit, at a warehouse) and status (e.g., in-stock, back-ordered) in order to provide customers with real-time information about inventory availability. Moreover, the online unit must coordinate with the rest of the organization to leverage PetSmart's clout in engaging its vendors to get inventory replenishments where and when they are needed. Finally, the online unit must regularly interact with corporate customer service and information systems groups to follow up with online shoppers if their orders cannot be immediately fulfilled because purchased items became unexpectedly out of stock.

In addition, the conditions surrounding the shipping of online consumer orders at PetSmart are quite unique and offer different challenges than those surrounding its inventory control. The shipping of online consumer orders is shaped by variations in the geographical distribution of the orders' destinations. As a result, orders shipping to online consumers located close to PetSmart's inventory facilities involve flexible time windows to source and release inventory from its facilities in order to meet delivery schedules agreed upon by consumers prior to purchasing. However, when orders ship to shoppers located far away from PetSmart's inventory facilities, they require stringent time windows in sourcing and releasing inventory from the facilities in order to meet delivery schedules consistent with those available to nearby shoppers.

Shipping is also influenced by variability in the SKU composition of online orders. While some of PetSmart's customers may place orders, including regularly purchased staples, others may order slow-moving items for which demand is infrequent or urgent. The sourcing and release of inventory to fulfill the former type of orders can be scheduled periodically, in advance, and in coordination with customers so that the execution of these shipping activities can take place during time windows that are easily adaptable to PetSmart's overall shipping plans and without interfering in the delivery terms stipulated when shoppers place their orders. On the other hand, the latter type of orders involves erratic and nonadjustable time windows in sourcing and releasing inventory from the facilities in order to meet delivery schedules that are acceptable to shoppers prior to purchasing.

Despite the conditions surrounding the shipment of online orders at PetSmart, the retailer chose to rely on an LSP to run this service. This was possible because PetSmart agreed to streamline its shipping processes to allow the logistics provider (1) to source inventory out of a primary facility and (2) to interact with a unified shipping team at that facility to ensure that inventory items are released to the right carriers and delivery lanes. At the same time, PetSmart leveraged its corporate scale to allow the LSP to merge the sourcing and release activities involved in shipping online consumer orders with the sourcing and release of inventory replenishment orders shipped to its brick-and-mortar stores. The integration of these shipping activities has allowed PetSmart to be more effective in planning and controlling outbound transportation to the markets it serves. The integration of shipments to online consumers and brick-and-mortar stores has also eased the processing and transportation of online orders that would otherwise require inventory to be sourced and released during stringent and erratic time windows.

## Conclusions and Implications

Intermediaries will not disappear in an Internet setting. Rather, they will take on different roles to enable Internet retailers to tap a greater range of services and markets. Some services are information based and can be delivered directly through the web (order payment and order request/inquiry), while others are based on physical assets (order returns and exchanges and shipment processing). In the case of services that can be delivered entirely through the web, intermediaries will have a more limited role because these services are more easily scalable than those in which physical products are involved. Intermediaries in the former settings often become *infomediaries* that contribute to the level of trustworthiness in transactions between buyers and sellers or focus their services in helping buyers find products that best match their individual preferences.

Intermediaries in settings where physical infrastructure and products are involved will take on a variety of services that will contribute to the scalability of retailers' operations. Their services are in direct response to shoppers' increasing ability to find products through infomediaries: these services can help retailers offer the product variety needed to respond to this increased product accessibility by shoppers.

There are other services that these intermediaries provide that focus on upstream echelons in the supply chain to help organizations scale up the management of inventory and product sourcing. While some of these services (for instance, drop shipping) contribute toward expanding product variety, most other services help firms achieve scale and scope economies through the consolidation of orders and different inventory management practices.

Overall, the decision to rely on an intermediary to perform these functions will depend on whether greater product variety and scale and scope economies will translate into sustainable improvements in revenues and cost efficiencies. Moreover, these benefits will be, to a great extent, a function of the uncertainty that Internet retailers will face in relation to the conditions surrounding the functions outsourced.

# References

Blackburn, J.D., D.R. Guide, G.C. Souza, and L.N. Van Wassenhove. 2004. Reverse supply chains for commercial returns. *California Management Review* 46(2): 6–22.

Boyer, K.K., M.T. Frohlich, and G.T.M. Hult. 2004. *Extending the Supply Chain:* AMACOM, *How Cutting-Edge Companies Bridge the Critical Last Mile into Customers' Homes.* New York.

Chen, L.S. Hancy and A. Padzik 2003. Small business Internet commerce: A case study. *Information Resources Management* 16(3): 17–41.

Compton, J. 2001. The hub of a new universe. *Customer Relationship Management,* January 28, http://www.destinationcrm.com/print/default.asp?ArticleID=1056.

*The Economist.* 1999. Finance and economics: Frictions in cyberspace. *The Economist,* 353(8146): 94.

Gonsalves, A. 2001. E-retailers expected to outsource shipping. *TechWeb News,* February 9. <www.internetweek.com/story/INW20010209S0001>.

Keller, K.L., "Managing Brands for the Long-Run: Brand Reinforcement and Revitalization Strategies," *California Management Review,* vol. 41, no. 3 (1999): 102–124.

Laseter, T.M., E. Rabinovich, K.K. Boyer, and M. Rungtusanatham. 2007. The future of the web: Three critical issues in Internet retailing. *MIT Sloan Management Review* 48(3): 58–64.

Maltz, A.B., E. Rabinovich, and R.K. Sinha. 2004. Logistics: The key in e-retail success. *Supply Chain Management Review* 8(3): 56–63.

Rabinovich, E. and J.P. Bailey. 2004. Physical distribution service quality in Internet retailing: Service pricing, transaction attributes, and firm attributes. *Journal of Operations Management* 21(6): 651–672.

Rabinovich, E. and A.M. Knemeyer. 2006. Why do Internet sellers incorporate logistics service providers in their supply chains? The role of transaction costs and network strength. *California Management Review* 48(4): 84–108.

Smith, M.D., J.P. Bailey, and E. Brynjolfsson. 2000. Understanding digital markets: Review and assessment. In *Understanding the Digital Economy: Data, Tools, and Research*, E. Brynjolfsson and B. Kahin, eds. MIT Press, Cambridge, MA, pp. 99–135.

Soderlund, M., M. Vilgon, and J. Gunnarsson. 2001. Predicting purchasing behavior on business-to-business markets. *European Journal of Marketing* 35(1/2): 168–181.

# Chapter 8

# Understanding the Drivers of Cost-to-Serve[*]

Analysis of data on e-commerce sales, which the U.S. Census Bureau began tracking in 1998, highlights an inexorable trend. In the first reported year, e-commerce sales totaled a mere $5 billion, a negligible share at only 0.2%. Over 80% of the online sales came from nonstore retailers, that is, mail-order houses and the new web-only companies like Amazon. A decade later, however, sales had exploded 25-fold to $127 billion due to three major shifts. First, the traditional mail-order business more than doubled in size from $80 billion to nearly $200 billion. Second, virtually all of that growth came from the shift from catalog-driven sales to online sales as the mix changed from 95/5 to 55/45. Third, the traditional retailers expanded into the new channel from a mere $1 billion in 1998 to $34 billion a decade later.

The average consumer, particularly young adults who have grown up with the Internet, generally assumes that online sales represent an even larger share. The assumption likely comes from a mental bias regarding certain types of goods. For example, examining the sales of online and traditional retailers of sporting goods, hobby, book, and music stores shows that 14% of the sales in that broad category come from online transactions. On the other hand, less that 1% of sales by food and beverage retailers come from e-commerce.

---

[*] With permission, this chapter draws upon the article "Hidden Cost of Clicks" by Tim Laseter, Elliot Rabinovich, and Angela Huang published in *strategy+business*, issue 42, Spring 2006, but updated.

Many factors, ranging from consumer preferences to industry structure, influence the penetration rate of online commerce. However, the cost-to-serve via the Internet versus traditional retailing ranks as the most critical from an operations perspective. By 2010, roughly 75% of U.S. households had access to the Internet, and nearly 2 billion people worldwide claimed Internet access through some means. All retailers—online and traditional—need to understand the cost drivers for accessing the online shopper. This chapter examines the drivers that make a given category or specific product more or less attractive for an Internet retailer.

## The eBags Story

eBags.com ranks as one of the more notable successes among Internet retailers. The leading online purveyor of luggage, eBags generates more than $130 million in revenue a year and has been consistently profitable since its founding in 1998, in the heyday of the Internet bubble. Thanks to direct "drop shipments" from manufacturers to end customers, eBags operates with minimal inventory and fewer than 100 employees, seemingly the archetype of the virtual company.

However, not everything has worked out as planned. In 2004, the online retailer, based in Greenwood Village, Colorado, acquired Shoedini.com, a seller of dress shoes for men and women, and renamed it 6pm.com. Having expanded from its original focus on luggage into backpacks, handbags, and other accessories, eBags considered shoes the next logical category for marketing synergies. Yet, despite the clear marketing logic, selling shoes online turned out to be more complicated than selling the other product lines.

The issue, as eBags discovered and as many online vendors have yet to understand, highlights the fundamental operational challenges of Internet retailing. It centers on a concept common in the business-to-business realm but rarely employed in a business-to-consumer context: cost-to-serve. Defined as the total supply chain cost from origin to destination, cost-to-serve incorporates such factors as inventory stocking, packaging, shipping, and returns processing. This metric also helps to explain why some of the early high-flying "e-tailers," such as eToys and Webvan, failed miserably.

In the eBags example, the cost of serving shoe customers is far higher than the cost of serving luggage customers. The 2004 Shoedini acquisition more than doubled the number of SKUs that eBags handled, and the complexity of managing the inventory exploded. Most bags come in two variations, usually different colors, but a shoe style comes in several colors and many sizes; there can be 30 or more variations of a single model.

Bags, furthermore, come in boxes that manufacturers use for shipping via small-package delivery to a fragmented base of mostly mom-and-pop retail customers. Shoes, on the other hand, ship to retailers in bulk packaging rather than in individual boxes. When 6pm.com sells a pair of dress loafers direct to a consumer, the manufacturer thus has to incur extra shipping and handling costs to repackage and ship the shoes.

Most important, shoes have a short product life cycle—typically 3 to 6 months—and suffer from a high return rate. (Some customers order two pairs at a time, planning to return the pair that does not fit.) Luggage life cycles can last 6 years, and return rates are minimal. eBags learned that, although shoes and luggage command similar gross margins, shoes carry a much higher cost-to-serve, and selling them online thus requires a different business model. In 2007 eBags sold 6pm.com to shoe specialist Zappos.

When launched in 1999, Zappos started with a drop-ship model, but the manufacturers of many desirable shoe brands would not support drop shipping. Accessing these brands forced Zappos to have a fulfillment center so it could buy in bulk and then ship individual orders to customers from its own inventory. Zappos initially sought to outsource the fulfillment center to eLogistics, but ultimately concluded that managing this critical aspect of the customer experience warranted the investment to own and manage the fulfillment operation directly.

Understanding the drivers of cost-to-serve at the level of individual items and individual customers allows an Internet retailer to unlock the full value-creating potential of the online channel as an alternative to—and complement of—traditional retailing.

## Trial and Error

Back at the dawn of online retailing, highflyers like Value America (an online "department store") and Webvan (an Internet-based delivery service that focused its offerings on grocery items) did not comprehend the operational cost implications of their business models. Value America started with a virtual inventory model supposedly applicable to any branded product. Although its initial offering, computer hardware, sold well, shipping and handling costs for lower-value goods proved prohibitive, and an unmanageable flood of returns ultimately sank the company in August 2000. Less than a year later, in July 2001, Webvan declared bankruptcy after concluding that it would never turn a profit despite its state-of-the art supply chain with a hub-and-spoke network of delivery cross-docks and highly automated distribution centers. (Chapter 9, which follows, provides further details on the challenges of "The Last Mile.")

Even Amazon.com did not fully appreciate all the factors driving its cost-to-serve. When Jeff Bezos opened his Internet store in 1995, he started with books, reasoning that it would be easier to offer the millions of titles in print online than through a traditional mail-order catalog. Although Bezos may not have fully grasped all of the inefficiencies inherent in the book industry, he saw that his model could minimize inventory risk—a significant problem in book retailing. Unlike other manufacturers, publishers take back all unsold copies of their product. Up to 30% of trade books ship back to the publisher at enormous cost to everyone: to the publisher, who refunds the payment to the retailer; to the retailer, who pays for shipping and restocking; and indirectly to the consumer. Amazon's online model minimizes the inherent inefficiency of placing potentially unsellable titles on thousands of retail bookshelves by relying instead on a relatively small inventory to support a "virtual bookshelf." If Amazon returns fewer books than a bricks-and-mortar retailer, it should be able to negotiate lower prices from the publishers (reflecting its lower cost-to-serve as a customer of the publisher). Amazon can then pass along those savings through lower prices to the consumer.

Although books worked for Amazon, toys were a different matter. As Jeff Bezos learned, the toy supply chain comes with a much higher cost-to-serve. Toys are more seasonal than books, and demand for them is far less predictable. Magnifying those challenges, most toys are made in Asia, and the replenishment cycle can easily outlast the actual selling season. That means merchandisers must accurately predict which toys will be hits and then buy enough inventory for the whole season; Amazon therefore gained no benefit from its "virtual shelves." Guessing too conservatively results in missed sales, and guessing too optimistically leads to write-offs because toy manufacturers do not typically accept returns of unsold goods. Without any toy merchandising expertise, Amazon guessed wrong for the 1999 holiday season and wrote off $39 million in excess toy inventory in early 2000, having sold only $95 million worth of toys.

Furthermore, conventional toy retailers enjoy advantages that traditional booksellers do not. Unlike Barnes & Noble, Wal-Mart and Toys "R" Us ship multiple truckloads of goods to each store weekly, which puts their transportation costs far below the cost of shipping individual toys to consumers. Recognizing these differences, Amazon gladly partnered with Toys "R" Us in 2000, shifting the inventory risk to the experts but leveraging the additional product lines to lower its own shipping cost for multiitem orders.

Nonetheless, the two partners had a falling out in 2004, with dueling lawsuits in the New Jersey court system. This denouement suggests that the cost-to-serve for online toy retailing produced a financial model that would not support the two parties' aspirations adequately.

Although successful online retailing depends on a variety of factors, the cost-to-serve of a particular product category can explain much of the variance in the penetration rates of Internet sales. Certainly, tech-savvy computer buyers are more likely than the general population to shop online. But equally important, the high value-to-weight ratio of computers—especially as laptops become more popular—minimizes the importance of transportation costs and makes the category a low cost-to-serve option over the Internet.

Cost-to-serve factors like inventory, packaging, shipping, and returns help explain why online sales of books outstrip online sales of other kinds of merchandise. Table 8.1 provides a conceptual framework for assessing the cost-to-serve across 10 categories. On the supply side, the costs vary, depending on whether the retailer can readily predict a stable level of sales to minimize inventory-carrying cost. The level of demand and size of the product affects the replenishment frequency and shipping mode, two other important cost drivers. Less obvious characteristics such as the shipping package, shelf life, and handling

**Table 8.1   Online Retail Cost-to-Serve Dimensions**

| | | Cost-to-Serve | | |
|---|---|---|---|---|
| | | *Low* | *Medium* | *High* |
| Supply | Demand pattern | Level | Seasonal | Erratic |
| | Replenishment | Daily | Weekly | EOQ/as needed |
| | Shipping mode | Full truckload | Consolidated LTL | Small package |
| Storage | Ship package | Shippable pack | Single SKU case | Mixed SKU cases |
| | Shelf life | Stable/ returnable | | Perishable |
| Picking | Picking method | Sortable | Nonsort, conveyable | Non-conveyable |
| | Item multiples | High multiples | | Single items |
| | Order aggregation | Single category | | Multiple categories |
| Delivery | Carrier | Postal service | Package delivery | Courier |
| | Customer scheduling | Unattended | Random attended | Scheduled attended |

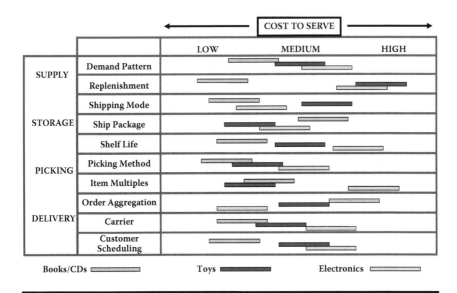

**Figure 8.1   Online retail cost-to-serve category comparisons.**

constraints affect the costs inside the fulfillment center. Whether it is paid for separately or hidden in a price proclaiming "free shipping," outbound shipping cost represents a significant factor for all online sales. With most shipped via package delivery at a charge based on the weight and dimensions of the package, aggregating orders into a single box offers significant savings. The degree of scheduling coordination with the customer also influences shipping cost. Using this simple framework, Figure 8.1 illustrates why Amazon's core business of books and CDs have lower cost-to-serve than toys and electronics.

# Future Growth

Future growth in e-commerce will come from continued modification of existing supply chains rather than wholesale replacement. For example, despite the generally low level of Internet sales in furniture and housewares, Williams-Sonoma has achieved great success online. The company, which operates a mix of retail, catalog, and Internet channels under its eponymous store brand as well as the Pottery Barn and Hold Everything brands (among others), sold $3.1 billion in fiscal 2010—61% through its traditional retail stores and 39% through its two direct-to-consumer channels. At $3.1 million in annual sales for its average kitchenware store, Williams-Sonoma does not gain any significant transportation economies in shipping to its stores rather than directly to its customers.

Ultimately, the company can maximize profits by assigning items to channels and brands to reach consumers at the lowest cost-to-serve.

Rather than minimizing the cost-to-serve across channels, traditional retailers often put their most popular items on their website. Although such an approach sounds logical, the reverse would typically work better. Traditional store-based retailing requires turning inventory quickly to justify expensive floor space. Slow-moving inventory—especially products with a high risk of obsolescence—can benefit from the centralized inventory pooling of online retailing. And if the product commands a high value-to-weight ratio, the cost penalty from direct-to-consumer shipping is minimal.

Best Buy, the big box consumer electronics, home office, and small appliances retailer, offers an interesting case example of how the retailing supply chain will evolve to offer the most cost-effective channel to serve customer needs. Best Buy's $2.5 billion in online sales placed it 10th in online sales in the United States for 2009, but web sales represents only 5% of the company's total sales of nearly $50 billion. By making smart use of its many service options—in-store shopping, in-store or online ordering with delivery from the store, online ordering with store pickup, and online ordering with direct home delivery—Best Buy can continue growing its online presence profitably. Finding the optimal cost-to-serve for each product and customer category would give Best Buy a competitive advantage over pure-play online retailers or less aggressive traditional competitors.

Best Buy operates a network of nine major distribution centers located across the country from Suwanee, Georgia, to Kent, Washington. The domestic distribution network serves more than 1000 stores with average weekly sales of more than $600,000 per store, which provides significant transportation scale economies compared with a pure-play competitor such as Newegg.com.

Founded in 2001, Newegg chose a name connoting a new birth at a time when most Internet retailers were struggling to survive the bursting of the bubble. With $2.3 billion in 2009 sales, all online, Newegg.com ranks second only to Amazon among pure-play online retailers and 12th overall, just behind Best Buy. Significantly, around 5% of Newegg's sales come from freight charges to ship products directly to consumers. Its smaller scale also means it can only justify three domestic distribution centers (in Southern California, New Jersey, and Tennessee) with average throughput of $700 million per year versus the nine distribution centers of Best Buy, which still process five times as much volume a year. Though Best Buy can save on transportation costs by using lower-cost full-truckload shipments, the relative importance of this bulk shipping network varies by product.

Consider the Samsung 63-inch plasma HDTV display recently offered by both companies at a suggested retail price of $2600. It comes in a 5 × 3-foot box, weighing 100 pounds. Shipment of such a bulky item through Best Buy's full-truckload distribution network offers significant savings over a small-package shipment directly to a consumer's home via UPS. Though Newegg's rates likely run lower, the cost for a consumer to ship such a box from Southern California to Denver would run between $80 and $500, depending on the required delivery. Best Buy has a distribution center in Aurora, Colorado, a suburb of Denver.

However, with relatively low unit sales for such an expensive product and a short product life cycle for consumer electronics, inventory held at the store represents a high cost and a big risk. Best Buy might benefit from keeping a minimum inventory of this item at the store—even just a display model—and having customers order it online for in-store pickup after the next delivery from the regional distribution network.

A pure online offering might work best for a high-end digital SLR camera like the EOS-1Ds Mark III, 21.1 megapixel model from Canon. With a suggested retail price of $7000, it is the most expensive model among the 50-plus digital SLR cameras that Best Buy sells, and it costs more than nine times the price of the most popular model, a Nikon 12.3 megapixel model at $750. As with the Samsung HDTV, low unit sales of the Sony HDV camcorder may not justify stocking the item at a store because of the high inventory-carrying cost and risk of obsolescence, and accordingly, Best Buy offers this as an online-only item. Unlike the Samsung HDTV, the digital camera weighs very little—less than 2 pounds—and, accordingly, Best Buy's distribution network provides little transportation cost savings. Rather than stocking it at each of the nine regional distribution centers, much less the 1000 different stores, Best Buy can gain more savings by pooling the inventory in a single national distribution center and shipping directly to customers' homes, minimizing the cost-to-serve for Best Buy as well as for the customer. Though it garners no transportation cost advantage by this approach, with more than 20 times the annual revenue of Newegg, Best Buy still has a purchasing and inventory advantage over its pure-play competitor, which sells the same model among its similar offering of 50-plus models.

For each combination of customer and merchandise, there is an optimal cost-to-serve option among the different delivery choices: store inventory, store delivery, in-store pickup, and direct delivery. For customers living far from a store, for example, even for bulky products like the Plasma HDTV, the benefits of routing the goods through a regional distribution center (such as that maintained by Best Buy) may be offset by the extra costs of a two-step distribution cycle, compared to the simplicity of direct home delivery. Finding the optimal cost-to-serve at the levels of customer and item is challenging but rewarding.

Even pure-play online retailers should consider the cost-to-serve in their pricing. Despite having the ability to customize web pages to each individual, few companies fully leverage the potential to price products to reflect the different underlying costs. For example, eBags offers special pricing for bulk purchases for corporate sales, but it does not attempt to adjust shipping costs on the basis of a customer's geographic location. Such fine-tuned pricing could potentially increase the company's profitability. That is the kind of detail that retailers will have to consider as they grow their online businesses.

## Accounting for Intangibles

Cost-to-serve in online retailing includes such factors as the expenses associated with inventory, transportation, and replication of the existing offerings of traditional retailers. To get a truer sense of cost-to-serve, however, it should also take into account intangible costs to the customer. Consider the current approach to furniture retailing, one of the least customer-friendly supply chains in retailing.

Because there are so many manufacturers offering so many styles in so many woods, finishes, and fabrics, most furniture retailers display a limited selection of goods. Customers place their orders and then wait for the couch, table, or chair to be manufactured, shipped to the retailer, and finally delivered to their homes. The whole process regularly takes 12 or more weeks—a cost in "pain and suffering" that falls squarely on the customers.

Early attempts to improve on the furniture retailing process via the Internet proved daunting. Living.com and Furniture.com focused on the "consumer experience" by investing in technology to allow shoppers to visualize the furniture in virtual mockups of their home. Both companies attempted to employ a drop-ship model to avoid the cost of holding inventory but ultimately found the challenge of ensuring product availability and scheduling precisely timed home deliveries untenable. Even when in stock and delivered on time, the product often arrived damaged or unacceptable for some other reason, resulting in return rates of up to 35% of sales. Despite good efforts, the "virtual" model failed for both of these early entrants in the furniture category.

After 18 months of bankruptcy proceedings, Furniture.com reopened under new management and with a new business model in 2002 in partnership with two of the country's largest retailers, Seaman's Furniture and Levitz Home Furnishings. The company ranked 200 among Internet retailers in 2009 and first among pure-play online furniture purveyors. However, its sales ran at only $59 million despite having hit a peak of $20 million per quarter before its bankruptcy.

While the current business model for Furniture.com appears more sustainable than the original, it might be better to emulate the automotive industry efforts at lead-time reduction. The big opportunity online for furniture retailers may lie not in eliminating storefronts but in dramatically reducing the lead times in the order-to-delivery cycle. Car dealers resolve the choice challenge by sharing inventory information among dealerships and exchanging vehicles to better meet a particular customer's desires. Roughly half of the vehicles sold by a typical dealership come from such an exchange; the other half come from the dealer's own inventory on the lot. Similarly, with furniture, customers could check the "look and feel" of a display model, and the retailer would then locate the desired inventory at another store or at a centralized stock pool with delivery in days, not weeks. Such a business model would leverage the Internet's information-sharing power to lower the "cost" of long-lead times without incurring an undue level of inventory investment.

In the end, future success for retailers of furniture, electronics, luggage—any sort of retailers—will not be a matter of expanding standard offerings to the burgeoning Internet channel or replicating existing online models. Despite the obvious marketing synergies, toys present different challenges from books, and shoes different challenges from luggage. Smart retailers take a close look at the costs of bringing each item to each consumer—the cost-to-serve—to decide how to merchandise their offerings and ultimately grow their business by applying the right retail model at the right time.

# Chapter 9

# The Last-Mile Challenge*

As we have discussed in this book, the advent of Internet retailing produced a fundamentally new value proposition to the consumer: easy access to convenient ordering with seemingly infinite selection. For example, rather than dropping by the local Barnes & Noble superstore and physically sifting through the 150,000 titles on the shelves, Amazon's online shopper browses more than 4 million titles from a personal computer using a search engine and the collective insight of millions of other consumers to inform the decision.

Unfortunately, the online advantage is undermined by a benefit only bricks-and-mortar retailers can offer: the ability to walk out of a local store with product in hand. Accordingly, Internet retailers have struggled with the trade-off between product variety and delivery speed, in a battleground known as "The Last Mile."

This chapter offers a historical perspective on the early skirmishes over the last mile during the days of the Internet bubble in the late 1990s and early 2000s, describing the fundamental challenges that led to the demise of many first movers. The first section describes the early players who attempted to forward-integrate in order to capture direct access to the consumer with same-day delivery. Next, the chapter reviews the story of the intermediaries who chose not to operate their own retail operations but to serve as facilitators over the

---

* With permission, this chapter provides new material but draws upon two articles originally published in *strategy+business*: "The Last Mile to Nowhere," *strategy+business*, third quarter 2000, issue 20 and "Oasis in a Dot-Com Delivery Desert," *strategy+business*, third quarter 2001, issue 24, copyright 2010 by Booz & Company, Inc.

last mile's rough terrain. Finally, we close with a current perspective on the challenges and the companies seeking to find a profitable model for the future.

## First-Mover Delivery Models

As documented in the article "The Last Mile to Nowhere" prereleased to the media in early 2000, a number of Internet retailers believed that same-day delivery would hold the key to success in Internet retailing. George Shaheen, the CEO of Webvan Group, Inc.—one of the most spectacular failures in Internet commerce—famously declared: "One or two companies will legitimately earn the right to cross into a person's home. We intend to be one of those. I don't believe there will be a multiplicity of companies doing this successfully." As it turns out, Shaheen was prescient as none of the initial players proved successful due to four major issues: limited online sales potential (despite the hype of the time), high cost of delivery, a selection–variety trade-off, and existing, entrenched competition.

As shown in Table 9.1, the first movers offering same-day delivery tended to focus on a mix of two broad product categories: immediate gratification/impulse items (e.g., videos, music, books, magazines, snacks) and routine necessities like grocery and household items, for which many consumers seek to minimize shopping time and effort. All offered thousands of items, but order sizes varied dramatically. Not surprisingly, the companies focused on instant gratification/impulse items tended to have the smallest orders.

All offered extended delivery hours and 24/7 ordering, but the distribution/fulfillment centers ranged from simple 4500-square-feet spaces filled with rack shelving, to highly automated, multimillion-dollar, 300,000-square-feet facilities. Delivery vehicles ranged from bikes to scooters to small cars to vans—often sporting striking colors and images to market the brand. Although most offered free delivery, some priced their offerings to discourage small orders. Also, to ensure that consumers received great value, they even discouraged tipping.

Although each company offered a slightly different business proposition, all offered the convenience of online ordering and same-day delivery, thus addressing the time lag problem encountered in the category-killer e-tailing model pioneered by Amazon. These local deliverers hoped that gaining control of the last mile would ensure success. Despite raising hundreds of millions of dollars to fund their visions, all of them failed—except Pink Dot, which actually began prior to the Internet era.

## Limited Online Sales

During the early days of Internet retailing, analysts focused on spectacular growth rates and assumed that the Internet represented a "new economy" that would quickly make obsolete the current retail paradigm. Internet retailing sales in the market-leading United States produced an impressive growth from $5 billion in 1998 to $15 billion in 1999, and the most frequently cited forecast from Forrester Research predicted sales of $184 billion by 2004. Though these were impressively large numbers and rates of growth, the analyst failed to put the numbers in context. Annual sales for $5 billion represented only less than two tenths of 1% of the U.S. retail market of $2.6 trillion. Even a simple comparison with traditional mail-order shopping—a model dating back to the Sears, Roebuck and Co. catalog introduced in 1893—highlighted that the Internet would not provided enough volume to fundamentally alter the economics of home delivery. At an estimated $57 billion in 1999, mail-order sales more than tripled e-commerce sales.

Additionally, much of the Forrester forecast included "digitally delivered goods," such as airline and event tickets, online brokerage and banking services, plus "researched goods" like automobiles, which have a separate delivery network. Ultimately, Forrester proved overly optimistic since 2004 Internet retailing totaled only $71 billion, or roughly 2%, of the total retail of $3.5 trillion. Though this represented a 10-fold increase in the penetration rate of the online channel, it proved less than earth shattering.

## The Role of Delivery Economics

Even more critical in these projections was Forrester's failure to consider the huge geographic expanse of the United States. Ultimately, delivery economics depend on two key drivers: sales concentration and population density. As shown in Figure 9.1, once the billions in sales were divided among the population—even just considering the major cities identified in the expansion plans of the first movers—the lack of sales becomes more obvious. Among U.S. cities, only New York suggested a sufficient level of sales density to support a dedicated Internet-based delivery business.

For those not familiar with the consultant's perennial favorite information graphic—the bubble chart—Figure 9.1 warrants more explanation. The horizontal axis indicates the number of Internet users per square mile in each city on a logarithmic scale. (Note that the logarithmic scale represents a *10-fold* increase in user density for each increment along the scale, rather than the more typical increase of a fixed linear amount.)

**Table 9.1  Local Delivery Overviews Circa 2000**

| Company | Kozmo | Pink Dot | SameDay | Urbanfetch | Webvan |
|---|---|---|---|---|---|
| **Started** | 1997 | 1987 | 1999 | 1999 | 1996 |
| **Coverage** | Atlanta, Boston, Chicago, Houston, Los Angeles, New York, Portland, San Francisco, Seattle, Washington, D.C. | Los Angeles, Orange County | Atlanta,[a] Chicago,[a] Dallas,[a] Memphis,[a] New York,[a] Los Angeles, San Francisco, Seattle,[a] Washington, D.C.[a] | New York, London | Atlanta,[a] Chicago,[a] Dallas,[a] Denver,[a] Newark,[a] Philadelphia,[a] Sacramento, San Francisco, Seattle,[a] Washington, D.C.[a] |
| **Offering** | | | | | |
| Videos/DVDs | ● | | ● | ● | |
| Games/toys | ● | | ● | ● | |
| Music | ● | | ● | ● | |
| Electronics | ● | | ● | ● | |
| Books/magazines | ● | | ● | ● | |
| Snacks/food | ● | ● | | ● | ● |
| Grocery items | | | | | ● |
| Health body | ● | | | ● | ● |

| | | | | | |
|---|---|---|---|---|---|
| Household items | • | • | | • | |
| Gifts | • | • | | | • |
| **Stocked items** | 15,000+ | ~2000 | Not published | 50,000 | 15,000+ |
| **Average order size** | $15 | Not published | Not published | $40–50 | $90 |
| **Hours of delivery**[b] | 10 a.m. to 1 a.m. | 6 a.m. to 3 a.m. | 6 a.m. to 3 p.m. | 24 hours a day | 7 a.m. to 10 p.m. |
| **Fulfillment centers** | 13 distribution centers in six markets | 12 fulfillment locations (4,500 sq ft) | 4 distribution centers with an average size of 100,000 sq ft | 1 distribution center plus "several fulfillment centers" | 1 distribution center of 336,000 sq ft plus 12 small transfer hubs (SF) |
| **Delivery response time** | Under an hour: can specify delivery time | Under 30 minutes | Same day (within 2 hours) & next day | Under an hour: can specify delivery time | 30-minute window specified by the shopper |
| **Delivery method** | Van, car, scooter, bicycle, and foot | Blue VW bug with pink dots | Not published | Van, scooter, bicycle, and foot | Beige-and-white van |
| **Delivery charge** | Free | $2.95 flat, no minimum order | Free >$50 order; $6.95 <$50 order (within zone) | Free, $10 minimum order | Free >$50 order; $4.95 <$50 order |
| **Tipping policy** | Optional | Optional | No tipping | No tipping | No tipping |

a Announced expansion.
b All offer delivery 7 days a week, 365 days a year, and 24/7 ordering.

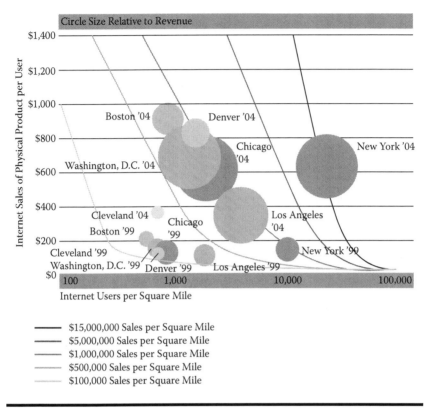

Circle Size Relative to Revenue

Internet Sales of Physical Product per User

$1,400
$1,200
$1,000
$800
$600
$400
$200
$0

Boston '04    Denver '04
Chicago '04    New York '04
Washington, D.C. '04
Cleveland '04    Chicago '99    Los Angeles '04
Boston '99
Cleveland '99    New York '99
Washington, D.C. '99    Denver '99    Los Angeles '99

100    1,000    10,000    100,000

Internet Users per Square Mile

——— $15,000,000 Sales per Square Mile
‒‒‒‒‒ $5,000,000 Sales per Square Mile
········· $1,000,000 Sales per Square Mile
——— $500,000 Sales per Square Mile
——— $100,000 Sales per Square Mile

**Figure 9.1    Internet sales density analysis.**

Population growth (and, in some cases, decline) and Internet penetration rates drove the migration to the right between 1999 and 2004. For example, in 1999 an estimated 60% of the 4.4 million inhabitants of the Washington, D.C., greater metropolitan area had Internet access—the highest penetration of any U.S. city. Since the Washington, D.C., area covers nearly 3500 square miles, those 2.6 million users produced a user density of about 750 per square mile. The forecast suggested that by 2004, increasing Internet penetration and population growth would drive the user density to more than 1300 users per square mile.

The vertical axis estimated the Internet purchases of those users. Using Washington, D.C., as the example, again, and the forecast for 2004 yielded a projection of annual online physical-product sales of nearly $700 per user—well above the overall 1999 U.S. average of around $125.

The size of the circles captures an important third variable: market size. Although high user density and high sales per user drive sales density, the overall market size also played an important role. For example, Denver, with a user density of nearly 1300 per square mile and projected 2004 sales per user of $800, was forecast to have $1.3 million of sales per square mile per year. Washington, D.C., fared worse, with sales per square mile of only $900,000—but offered a bigger prize due to the greater total population.

The curved lines on the chart highlight different combinations of sales levels and user density that yield the critical value of sales per square mile. The $14 million in sales per square mile in New York City suggested an attractive market; even dividing by 365 days per year for the 24/7 Internet economy, the revenue potential totaled more than $39,000 per day per square mile.

Unfortunately, after New York, the potential to deliver goods economically in cities fell off quickly. Most major cities offered a forecast of approximately $1 million per square mile in sales each year—equal to less than $3000 per day. And that was the forecasted total for *all* online sales of physical goods, not just the fraction that people wanted delivered instantaneously. Worse yet, that fraction would have to be shared by several local deliverers.

## High Last-Mile Costs

Not only are the sales spread across lots of "last miles," it costs a lot of money to get there. Extracting from publicly available information at the time, the New York City–based Kozmo.com, Inc., spent about $10 to make a delivery—even ignoring overhead costs such as advertising. That was in Manhattan—the densest delivery area in the country—and thus probably its lowest-cost market. With an average order size of about $15, it should not have been a surprise that Kozmo was bleeding money.

However, in the heady days of the New Economy, investors and entrepreneurs assumed that profitability was simply a matter of gaining the inevitable economies of scale garnered with the exponential growth rates. Unfortunately, physical delivery does not benefit from the network effect that supports other types of information economy businesses. This was an issue we discussed in Chapter 3. As shown in Figure 9.2, variable labor costs undergird local-deliverer economics, with the drivers who deliver packages composing the bulk of the cost. A van-based deliverer gets some advantage by fully utilizing the vehicle space, but a bicycle courier can carry only a limited number of items. More customers simply mean more bicycle trips.

## New Trade-Off: Speed versus Variety

More fundamentally, a vertically integrated local deliverer, such as Kozmo.com, could only address the issue of instant gratification at the expense of limitless

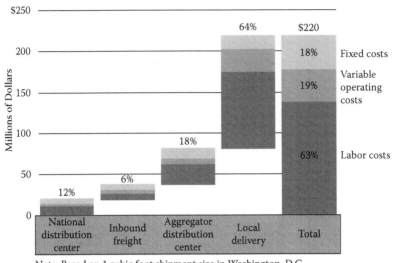

Note: Based on 1 cubic foot shipment size in Washington, D.C.

**Figure 9.2    Breakdown of total distribution costs.**

offerings. To achieve fast response, the local deliverer has to hold product locally, rather than in large national distribution centers, as category killers and large catalog retailers do. So the speed advantage gained by Kozmo.com and Urbanfetch.com, Inc. meant a variety loss. Kozmo, for example, offered about 15,000 items in total, versus more than 10 million total items at Amazon.

Even applying the Pareto principle (that 80% of the sales dollars come from 20% of the items stocked), the local deliverer could steal only a fraction of the total sales volume from a category killer, that represented by high-volume items. Typically, though, high-volume items provide the least profit per unit because of heavy price competition. So, even though the local deliverer model addresses the instant gratification need, it presents a new trade-off of a limited selection. Nothing comes free.

## Entrenched Competitors

The ability to redefine the local delivery model simply on the basis of Internet retailing was clearly suspect. It also ignored the presence of entrenched competitors with existing assets and significant scale economies—the traditional package delivery businesses of the US Postal Service (USPS) and United Parcel Service, Inc. (UPS), as well as bricks-and-mortar retailers like grocery stores.

Existing bricks-and-mortar retailers were not going to concede the online market to the "pure-play" start-ups. Leading grocery chains, such as North-Carolina–based Lowe's Food Stores, Inc., began offering online ordering with curbside pickup at the local grocery store in 2000. The consumer gained the advantages of efficient 24/7 online ordering with no checkout lines, and the grocer avoided the high investment requirements of a home-delivery network. Nongrocery clicks-and-mortar players also entered the game. In May 2000, Barnes & Noble, Inc., launched same-day delivery in Manhattan of books ordered online, matching the capability of Kozmo and Urbanfetch, and finally linked its physical stores and online presence, thereby leaping ahead of the still-virtual Amazon.com.

UPS, FedEx, and USPS had the most to lose if local deliverers found a way to make a business out of same-day service. Most of the $57 billion in mail-order products were shipped via the three providers; a little more than half of consumer catalog shipments went through USPS alone. The established players, notably FedEx and UPS, however, also found home delivery challenging despite well-oiled operations and a business-to-business (B2B) baseload to amortize the costs. The last-mile costs for a rural home delivery run about four times the cost of an urban business delivery. As such, a new set of intermediaries sought to gain the high ground in the last mile.

## The New Intermediaries

Rather than seeking to cross the rough terrain of the last mile, many new providers have attempted to fill a more modest need, playing an intermediary role between shippers and consumers to help them connect more cost-effectively and conveniently. The models have ranged from the simple to the sophisticated to, quite frankly, the silly.

We classify the players along two dimensions: the location of their proposed solution and the technological sophistication of their business model. Along the first dimension, some companies aimed to facilitate deliveries straight to the home; others created delivery mechanisms at select suburban locations accessible to the consumer, and yet others developed drop-off/pickup sites in urban buildings where multiple consumers live or work. The technology these companies employed ranged from simple, staffed pickup sites to high-tech automation with Internet connectivity.

Whatever their model, all the new intermediaries defended the need for their last-mile solution by citing the striking growth in direct shipments to the home. Their business plans highlighted the fact that, traditionally, 20% to 30% of home deliveries required multiple delivery attempts, which increased shipper costs and simultaneously disappointed the consumer who received the infamous "sticky note" explaining that the package could not be delivered.

Shippers historically left another 30% of packages unattended at their destination, even though no one was available to receive them, potentially inviting theft and risking weather damage—a hassle and cost to both the consumer and the shipper. While all these intermediaries were attacking a very real problem— billions of packages and potentially billions of dollars in waste—the last mile remained tough to conquer.

Consider Brivo Systems, Inc., one of the earliest entrants into the intermediary game. Founded in May 1999 by two management consultants intent on cashing in on the Internet revolution, Brivo, headquartered in Arlington, Virginia, offered a sophisticated "smart box" to enable secure delivery of packages to unattended households. Designed and partially funded by IDEO Product Development, the Palo Alto–based industrial design firm famous for creating the original Apple mouse and the Palm V, the 2½-foot-tall steel-and-plastic box (sized, according to Brivo, to accept 96% of all packages shipped in the United States) contained a two-way wireless modem and an embedded Intel 386 processor connected to a numeric keypad. When a consumer placed an order for home delivery, the system generated a unique key code for accessing the Brivo Box, which was printed on the shipping label. The delivery person, whether from UPS, FedEx, or USPS, entered the code from the package and placed the item in the box. The box then sent an e-mail or pager message to its owner announcing that the package had arrived. When home, the owner entered his or her standard personal code to open the box and retrieve the goodies. Piloted in Northern Virginia and Silicon Valley, the Brivo Box worked, but not enough customers could justify the $10 to $20 per month Brivo wanted to charge the owner to install and operate the boxes at their homes.

Brivo's most publicized competitor, zBox Company (founded in October 1999 in San Francisco) believed that consumers would not accept such a price level, so they designed a less-sophisticated, lower-cost solution. The zBox smartbox offering did not have the Internet messaging capability but did have a proprietary system powered by a 5-year battery that generated a new access code for each package delivery. As with the Brivo solution, the unique code was added to the shipping label so the delivery person could access the box only once, whereas the consumer could access it repeatedly with a single personal identification number. Citing market research that consumer acceptance dropped off significantly when a monthly fee exceeded $10, zBox offered its solution for an "introductory price" of $5 per month, plus a $60 security deposit for the box. At 24 inches high × 21 inches deep ×3 2 inches wide, the zBox was smaller than the Brivo product, but it still could accept 80% of single-package deliveries and 70% of two-package deliveries, according to the company.

The most impressive part of the zBox story was the company's high-profile strategic partners. The company partnered with GE/Fitch, a joint venture between General Electric Plastics and Fitch, Inc., to design and manufacture the boxes; ran a pilot test with USPS in the San Francisco Bay area that was supported by 30 online retailers; and captured a major investment from the Whirlpool Corporation. Having independently uncovered a significant consumer need for various delivery appliances as part of its Integrated Home Solutions Initiative, Whirlpool viewed zBox as a strategic investment.

Unfortunately, neither company captured sufficient consumer demand. Brivo ultimately changed its focus to security monitoring over the web. Whirlpool absorbed the product line and the management team of zBox, and now the name "ZBox" refers to a guitar pickup impedance adapter and not a delivery receptacle.

## Store and Office Solutions

A second pocket of companies—offering what we call the "retail-aggregator" solution—bet on a decidedly low-tech answer. Their model simply collected deliveries at a retail outlet, typically a convenience store, for eventual pickup by the consumer. Unlike the smart box, which addressed only the unattended home-delivery problem, retail aggregation tackled two last-mile challenges: unanswered doorbells and the high cost of delivery to multiple locations.

In Japan, for example, a very different delivery model evolved. Thanks to extremely high delivery density over relatively small landmass, *takuhai-bin* services can offer same- or next-day delivery to most Japanese consumers. Also, Japanese convenience stores provide an optional link in last-mile delivery, offering convenient neighborhood pickup and the option to pay cash.

Announced in September 2000, a joint venture between UPS and Texaco proposed a similar model. Consumers could choose to ship a package to a Texaco station rather than to their home, and the station attendant would secure it behind the counter until the consumer came to claim it. Neither UPS nor Texaco charged extra for the service because both saw a benefit from the proposition: UPS would save money by more packages to a single stop, and Texaco could gain additional traffic to its gas station/convenience stores. The mighty duo decided to pilot the concept in the Benelux countries because both companies had their European headquarters in Brussels. Unfortunately, the Benelux region had a low volume of online sales, and the pilot failed to prove the concept.

An independent startup, Pax-Zone, Inc., introduced a similar model to the United States in October 1999. Starting in Chicago with an eclectic mix of retail partners, the company established the concept sufficiently to extend its initial 60-store network through a partnership with Circle K, a convenience-store chain with 2200 sites nationwide. PaxZone also charged nothing extra to the consumer because it effectively converted a higher-cost, lower-margin consumer delivery into a lower-cost, higher-margin business delivery.

Another staffed model aggregated the deliveries in office buildings rather than suburban convenience stores. Consider the Toronto-based Inplex, Inc., started in 1996 as an outsourced mailroom service for multitenant office buildings. Over time, the company added a website that allowed building tenants also to acquire office supplies, order courier service, and eventually to have packages accepted for personal delivery.

More recently, in the fall of 2010, Wal-Mart has extended its "site to store" model to locations operated by FedEx Office (previously known as FedEx Kinko's) in Boston and Los Angeles. The original model allowed consumers to place orders on Wal-Mart's website and avoid shipping charges by picking up the goods at the store. The FedEx partnership extends Wal-Mart's reach into in urban areas where it has limited penetration—for example, only two stores in Los Angeles and none in Boston at the time of the announcement. Now Wal-Mart customers will have the choice among 26 pickup locations in Los Angeles and 18 in Boston.

## Labor-Saving Models

Another type of solution provider—the automated aggregator—spans suburban and urban locations and offered a high-tech version of the more labor-intensive aggregator model. Two examples of automated aggregators illustrate the challenge in striking the right balance between cost and sophistication.

In July 2000, a UK shopping center developer/owner, Brendan Flood, announced a breakthrough idea to profit from the otherwise debilitating growth of online retailing. His concept, dubbed "e-stop," would solve the last-mile problem with a highly automated drive-through pickup location, conveniently located along major thoroughfares. After ordering the goods online, customers would drive into the e-stop and swipe a membership card to notify a customer service officer of their arrival. Proceeding to a loading area, customers would remain in their cars while the service person loaded the ordered goods into the trunk. Since e-stop's 5000-square-foot "mini warehouses" would offer refrigerator and freezer storage space, the facilities could even hold online grocery orders. Initially targeting 35 sites by the year 2002, Flood estimated that the United Kingdom could eventually support up to 500 e-stops. In this model, the consumer would gain a convenient, free service, while the e-tailer avoided the expense of a dedicated fleet of vans for direct home delivery—a model of e-tailing not uncommon in the United Kingdom—by aggregating orders into 40-foot trucks to deliver goods to the e-stop.

Unfortunately, the envisioned scale proved to be quite a stretch. Flood was unable to obtain funding for the substantial investment for and operating costs of 2.5 million square feet (500 e-stops at 5000 square feet each) of prime retail space. Frankly, anyone with a logistics background realized that a single 40-foot truckload would likely fill the entire storage capacity of a 5000-square-foot facility—implying a degree of operational perfection that would make Toyota's just-in-time system look like child's play.

Another automated aggregator offered a model with a more modest mix of technology and investment. In September 1999, a team of Israeli entrepreneurs launched a U.S.-based company, eShip-4u, Inc., to develop a network of "automated delivery machines," or ADMs. Designed with an internal carousel and variably retractable doors, the ADM had a variety of slot sizes to hold packages ranging in size from a jewelry box to a computer monitor. Like the Brivo box, eShip-4u's ADMs employed wireless technology to inform the consumer of the arrival of a package by e-mail or pager. Like ATMs (which were originally designed to reduce costs for banks), the ADM drew the greatest initial interest from delivery companies hoping to eliminate the cost of redelivery. Deutsche Post and FedEx piloted the machines in locations ranging from gas station tarmacs to rail stations to shopping centers. The ADMs could hold packages for consumer pickup that could not be delivered to their homes on the first attempt (see Figure 9.3a,b).

**Figure 9.3a    eShip-4U Automatic delivery machine (ADM) for Deutsche Post. (continued)**

**Figure 9.3b (continued) eShip-4U Automatic delivery machine (ADM) for Deutsche Post.**

Though consumer acceptance of the technology was high, Deutsche Post chose a lower-tech "locker box" for its "Packstations" from an alternative provider, KEBA, an Austrian technology company (see Figure 9.4). Deutsche Post currently has more than 900 Packstations throughout Germany.

Despite a successful pilot with FedEx, eShip also ran aground in the United States; FedEx's decision to acquire Kinko's shelved a plan to deploy thousands of "Ship 'N Get" machines across the United States. Siemens absorbed the management team and eShip's assets, and the only remaining operational ADM can be found in Israel.

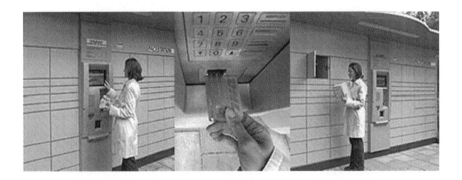

**Figure 9.4   KEBA locker box Packstation for Deutsche Post.**

## Continued Experimentation

Though many experiments for tackling the last-mile challenges have failed, new experiments continue. Sears Holdings operates MyGofer.com as an online storefront for Sears and K-Mart stores for same-day curbside pickup or delivery. In 2009, Sears Holdings opened a drive-through warehouse under the MyGofer .com brand in an old K-Mart in Joliet, Illinois. The pilot operates exclusively for online customers rather than a blend of both online and traditional brick-and-mortar store shoppers.

Pure-play companies continue to experiment as well. As discussed in a case study we present in this book, the start-up RelayFoods.com, based in Charlottesville, Virginia, employs a model involving partnerships with local retailers and farms, coupled with mobile pickup locations. A customer orders groceries before midnight from a selection of more than 15,000 items from 50-plus providers. The following day, the company aggregates the items from the supplier partners and then parks their trucks in popular neighborhoods or along major commuter arteries to allow customers to pickup the order during the afternoon.

Winning in a dynamic economy requires a commitment to refine and adapt the business model continuously to navigate the ever-changing competitive landscape. Eventually, someone will find a value proposition that works—but many others will fail along the way.

# Chapter 10

# Managing Product Returns*

Internet retailers tend to have a lot higher return rates than their brick-and-mortar counterparts. This is because their customers cannot directly inspect products offered on the Internet in order to thoroughly evaluate them before actually buying them. This makes the management of product returns a critical issue in Internet retailing, particularly when specialty items such as apparel and shoes are involved.

In this chapter, we provide an overview of product returns and their managerial challenges for Internet retailers. It starts with product returns and their volumes and costs. Then the chapter focuses on managerial issues involved in the handling of product returns. It then covers the different considerations that retailers should have regarding alternative product return policies. The chapter also addresses the role of third-party specialists in managing product returns and introduces four principles that will contribute to improving the management of product returns and the product return experience for customers. Finally, the chapter closes with a discussion of the process involved in refurbishing, remarketing, and reselling products that have been returned.

---

* With permission, this chapter draws in part from the previously published work by Laseter, Rabinovich, Boyer, and Rungtusanatham (2007). From *Sloan Management Review*. Copyright © 2010 by Massachusetts Institute of Technology. All rights reserved. Distributed by Tribune Media Services.

**117**

# The Magnitude of Product Returns in Internet Retailing

Data show that while overall product returns are estimated at about 8.7% of sales for the entire retail industry in the United States, they are significantly higher for Internet retailers, ranging up to 35%, depending on the category. As Table 10.1 shows, return rates are not uniform across the Internet retailing industry. These rates, which were obtained directly from industry sources, can vary dramatically from one Internet retailing segment to another. This table reveals that return rates are particularly high for Internet retailers competing in product categories where close inspection and testing is necessary as part of the purchasing decisions made by customers. In particular, product returns are more likely to occur for categories that involve furniture and home decor products for which it is difficult to judge textures and aesthetic appeal remotely via a computer screen. The same is true for apparel, jewelry, and shoes. In such categories, many relevant attributes for consumer decision-making cannot be conveyed easily via a digital medium such as the Internet. Moreover, unlike digital products such as music, it is difficult for Internet retailers to communicate accurately the relevance of these kinds of products to consumers through the use of samples or models via the web.

The occurrence of product returns can impose substantial costs on retailers. In all, it is estimated that managing product returns costs US companies well over $200 billion annually. In the case of Internet retailers, they must not only arrange for the collection of unwanted products from customers but also either dispose of the products or, alternatively, refurbish, restock, and resell them

**Table 10.1   Product Return Rates in the Internet Retailing Industry**

| Internet Retailing Segment | Average Return Rate |
|---|---|
| Shoes | 35% |
| Women's apparel | 25% |
| Men's apparel | 20% |
| Children's apparel | 18% |
| Home goods | 7% |
| Electronics | 4% |
| Books, music, and other media products | 2% |

*Source:* Authors' correspondence with industry executives in 2010.

through their own channels or through an inventory liquidator. Typically, retailers recoup only 10–20% of the returned products' original value (Stock, Speh, and Shear, 2006).

Product return costs can result from the amount of value products lost from the time they are sold until they are sent back by customers and remarketed or liquidated by Internet retailers. Costs also result from warehousing and transportation operations necessary to process the returns as well as from customer service activities necessary to keep customers abreast of the status of their returns (Guide, Souza, Van Wassenhove, and Blackburn, 2006).

However, the cost of returns is only one aspect of the problem. Returning merchandise can be expensive for customers as well. According to Ofek, Katona, and Sarvary, researchers at the Harvard Business School, there are several contributors to customers' costs. First, there is the opportunity cost of time associated with the return process. Second, there is the disutility associated with not having a matching product for the duration of time from the initial purchase until the return is processed and customers are compensated or their items are exchanged. Third, not all Internet retailers offer lenient return policies. In some cases, a restocking fee is imposed on the customer, often ranging from 10% to 25% of the purchase price. Moreover, waiting periods are sometimes required before issuing cash refunds, and, increasingly, retailers only offer exchanges or store credit.

## Tackling Product Returns

In some cases, Internet retailers have tried to manage returns by instituting stringent return policies and focus all their efforts in communicating these policies in order to set expectations among customers. Through this approach, retailers can limit product return occurrences to instances when items are defective, for example, thereby lowering product return rates dramatically. Retailers can also use these policies to limit the amount of time buyers can have their products in their possession before returning them. By instituting these time limits, retailers selling items with short life cycles (e.g., seasonal, perishable, or high-tech products) can collect back their products from customers and still be able to sell them before their value is completely depleted.

Return policies carrying conditions that are too stringent can negatively affect sales in unintentional ways. Customers wary of buying from Internet retailers in the first place may never place an order. This can be especially relevant when retailers are selling products that require a close and detailed inspection by customers prior to purchasing them. Since such a prepurchase evaluation is not feasible through the Internet, customers will prefer not to take their chances and will choose not to buy from an Internet retailer with return policies that are not very accommodating of potential selection errors in their purchases.

In other cases, retailers have tackled product returns by identifying those customers who tend to abuse the returns policies they have in place. In the eyes of the retailers, these are "devil customers" who engage in frequent product returns or who return products for no specific reason. There are more egregious cases as well. One company had regular customers who would order $10 worth of products they wanted, plus another $40 of undesired products so they could obtain free delivery for a $50 order. Those customers would then return the $40 of unwanted products. Moreover, "devil customers" will take advantage of promotions and low-price deals but will be fairly insensitive to the time needed for refunds or replacements. So, even when approving returns from these customers, savvy Internet retailers can better manage cash flow and profits by giving priority to the customers who contribute to higher margins and show greater loyalty.

Because the vast majority of customers behave fairly and reasonably, companies can structure return policies to allow their customer service representatives to go the extra mile for honest customers while stopping such egregious abuses. But not all retailers choose to do this. Rather, they focus on identifying these "devil customers" to simply stop selling to them in the first place and thus eliminate any possibility of receiving excessive product returns later on. While this strategy can be very effective in addressing a number of product return problems at their root, its execution is not without risks. Customers with legitimate product returns can be identified as "devil customers" and be unfairly penalized. When these types of incidents occur, they can generate negative word of mouth that can, in turn, result in the loss of valuable customers for the Internet retailer.

## The Role of Third-Party Specialists

A number of retailers have outsourced the management of their product returns to third-party specialists. More often than not, these retailers make this decision after being overwhelmed by their product returns problems. Third-party firms that specialize in managing product returns for Internet retailers include Newgistics, Inc., headquartered in Austin, Texas, and customer support specialists Global Response, headquartered in Margate, Florida. These third-party firms are uniquely equipped to offer Internet retailers faster execution and economies of scale because they already have in place large networks of facilities and a specialized infrastructure to handle the shipment of goods from end customers back to the retailers. Moreover, because they use their facilities and resources to process large volumes of product returns from multiple retailers, these third-party specialists are able to not only process returns at very low costs per unit but also sustain a high level of utilization in the capacity of their facilities and resources throughout the year that will make it possible for them to be very price competitive over time.

Third-party specialists, however, may not be equally effective for all retailers. Online sellers that also have brick-and-mortar storefronts, such as the electronics retailer Best Buy Co., Inc., may not benefit as much from relying on these specialists. Best Buy can leverage its existing infrastructure to offer customers the potentially more convenient option of returning online purchases to the brick-and-mortar stores. Accordingly, it has the option to restock to the store or to aggregate returns and send them back in bulk to regional or national distribution centers for restocking, refurbishing, or scrapping.

## Key Principles for Internet Retailers to Follow

Internet retailers can obtain important benefits from taking a more hands-on approach at managing returns and improving the product return experience for customers. As summarized in Figure 10.1, our research points to four principles that will contribute to these aspects. First, retailers should keep the interaction simple to minimize customer effort when returning a product. Customer effort is

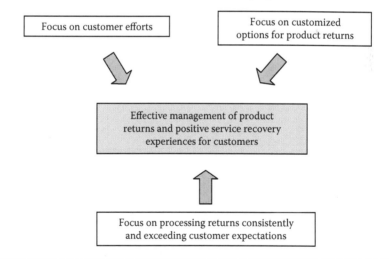

**Figure 10.1 Contributors to the effective management of product returns and positive service recovery experiences for customers. (Adapted from Mollenkopf, D.A. et al., 2007. Managing Internet product returns: A focus on effective service operations.** *Decision Sciences,* **Vol. 38, No. 2, The Next Frontier in Services Research Special Topic Forum, pp. 215–250.)**

one of the most important drivers of returns satisfaction. Second, retailers need to not only process all product returns consistently and treat customers fairly but also strive to offer them a product return service that exceeds their expectations. Third, retailers should strive to offer customized options for returns where possible. Some customers are happy to perform the transaction completely online, while others want to talk to a human operator or return the items at brick-and-mortar stores when the retailer operates multiple channels. Moreover, not all product returns are the same. They require different types of responses, depending on the motivations and reasons customers want to send back the items they bought.

In the next section, we expand on these principles. Product returns can be the basis of a service recovery opportunity for Internet retailers to redress problems experienced by their customers. This can be true even if there are no flaws in the execution of their transactions with customers (Andreassen, 2000). For example, Zappos generally delivers exactly what a customer orders, often faster than the customer expected. However, because of the uncertainty regarding the precise fit of footwear, some customers order multiple sizes of the same style and simply return the shoes that do not fit. In those instances, returns reflect an inherent problem with the medium of Internet retailing rather than execution failures. Regardless, the way Zappos handles returns can actually build customer loyalty. In short, returns will be evaluated from the consumer's perspective as part of the ongoing service the customer receives during a particular purchase experience and accordingly require the same attention as the initial delivery.

## Managing Internet Product Returns: A Focus on Effective Service Operations

A well-handled service recovery can have a positive influence on customer satisfaction and both trust and commitment toward the Internet retailer. This influence also carries value over time, such that positive recovery experiences can mitigate negative perceptions previously caused by a poorly executed transaction that lead to a product return. Service recoveries help build ongoing relationships with customers dissatisfied with their initial encounters (Maxham, 2001). Thus, the satisfaction customers have regarding an Internet retailer will be continually updated based on their most recent recovery service encounters.

### *Customer Effort*

Internet retailers need to make it easy for customers to make the transition from shopping offline to shopping online. A significant part of that transition rests on the customers' ability to navigate and buy on the Internet. This requires taking a proactive approach to prevent returns through a focus on providing easy-to-download and easy-to-use navigational tools and effective search capabilities that will allow customers to easily find what they are looking for. If, however, the consumer already faces a potentially negative situation in making a return to the Internet retailer, offering a user-friendly interaction will go a long way toward minimizing the negative impact of the return, and thus it will enhance both satisfaction with the return process and the perceived value of the returns offering for the consumer.

Another factor that can have potentially negative consequences for Internet retailers involves the effort that customers must go through to physically carry out their returns. Such situations are an example of the theoretical construct known as "procedural justice," in which customers are deeply sensitive about the fairness in the processes that resolve disputes and allocate resources to address problems with the services that they receive.

Within a returns context, procedural justice issues include ease of access to the recovery process, some level of control over the process, and a perception that the process occurs in a fair amount of time and/or at a fair speed and is adaptable to the customer's needs. Along these dimensions, Internet retailers must focus on the level of effort the customer must expend to prepare products for return and physically enter them into the Internet retailer's return system. Increasing levels of customer effort to carry out returns will result in lower perceptions of value and lower levels of satisfaction with the return process.

It is important to note that customers do not assign equal importance to the efforts they must allocate to the different components of their product return processes. Our research of shoppers across five different Internet retailers selling diverse products, such as pet supplies, office products, shoes, and handbags, has shown that customer satisfaction with product return services received from Internet retailers is intimately linked with the amount of time customers must spend preparing their product returns for shipment back to the Internet retailers. This is summarized in Figure 10.2. In this figure, we present our results from a study of more than 400 customers across the five retailers. According to these results, less time needed to process a return is directly correlated with higher customer satisfaction, according to survey measures of satisfaction.

Another way for Internet retailers to maintain procedural justice involves making certain that customers are promptly credited for their returned products. The quick processing of returns and updating of customer accounts is critical to the return process. While these efforts may not reduce operating expenses for Internet retailers, we would argue that they will improve customer satisfaction with the return transaction. This makes them as important as other elements

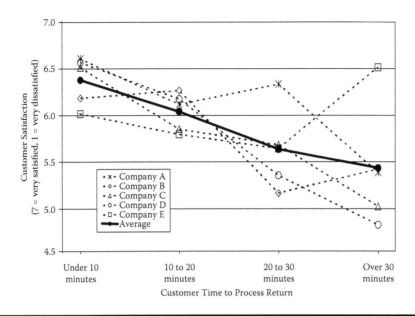

**Figure 10.2 The relationship between customer time to process a return and satisfaction. (From Laseter, T.M. et al., 2007. *MIT Sloan Management Review* 48(3): 58–64.)**

because of the significant impact by satisfaction on loyalty intentions, and thus future purchasing behavior.

## Processing Returns Consistently and Exceeding Customer Expectations

Responsiveness beyond customers' expectations during the product returns' recovery process may also contribute to generating a positive affinity toward the Internet retailer. Responding promptly and appropriately to a customer's return situation, compensating customers for problems, and providing customers access to knowledgeable customer service representatives (live or through online chats) during the return process all have a strong influence on a customer's perceived value of the returns offering.

However, to be successful in the long run, Internet retailers must strive to maintain consistency in their returns' service quality in order to create a loyal market base. Not only do historical service experiences have a strong direct effect upon loyalty intentions but they also indirectly affect customers' loyalty intentions through their satisfaction with, and the value they perceive from, the returns offerings. Customers' previous experiences with product return services shade—either positively or negatively—their perceptions of the current transaction. Therefore, managerial decisions that ensure a consistently superior service experience are likely to directly generate sustained loyalty intentions as well as to indirectly contribute to the reinforcement of those intentions through improvements in customer satisfaction with and value perceived from the returns offerings.

## *Customized Options for Product Returns*

Product returns involve different scenarios that require unique managerial requirements and practices. An Internet retailer can experience product returns triggered by buyers' remorse or customers' dissatisfaction because the products did not meet their preferences. This latter case can occur when customers receive unwanted gifts, for example.

These types of returns are considered to be false returns because they occur without a particularly valid reason, but they occur so frequently that practitioners refer to them as standard returns. To lower the risk for customers as they explore and buy different types of products in inventory, many retailers have tried to make it easy for them to return purchased goods. To that end, they provide "no questions asked" open-ended return policies, where customers can return for any reason and receive full credit for their purchase.

This treatment of product returns requires not only communicating clear return policies to customers but also providing effective ways to track returns to individual customers. An effective means is to provide easy access to prepaid return labels, as well as online self-service for spare labels. Tracking and personalized customer confirmations and credit also support a user-friendly returns model

Product exchanges are also a common issue for Internet retailers. Customers often perceive merchandise exchanges as a failure in their purchase experience. Accordingly, the most responsive Internet retailers send product replacements to their customers prior to receiving the returns being exchanged in order to ensure a positive customer experience.

This process often requires the implementation of a communication mechanism between the Internet retailer and its customers. Customers can then send in information about the returns before the returned products are delivered back to the Internet retailer. This process is often used for electronics repairs and upgrades. It is also commonly used to support Internet retailers' addressing warranty claims from customers with broken or damaged items.

The most advanced retailers want to make sure that they can recover the returned merchandise at a low cost while providing customer replacements in an expedited fashion. Consequently, such retailers use expedited outbound shipping service for the new item and a ground service for the returned item in order to offer customers the fastest recovery service.

A third situation for product returns handled by Internet retailers like Best Buy involves end-of-contract scenarios for products such as cell phones. These transactions must also ensure rapid recovery and possible replacement of valuable assets. They also entail uncertainty over whether devices can be refurbished and placed back in inventory. Crediting the customer and recovering the goods remains an important priority in these scenarios, but this still leaves open the question of whether to return the goods to stock or to dispose of them through alternative discount channels. The most effective retailers offer an intelligent tracking of products being sent back through which automatic notifications are triggered to inform customers of the progress of their returns. These systems also enable automatic reporting and reconciliation of the status of products in the retailer's inventory.

The customization of different processing options for these scenarios will not be complete without the implementation of policies that help Internet retailers decide how to make use of products once they have been returned. These policies will carry a great deal of importance for products that have been subject to false returns, are still in good condition, and can be remarketed to customers. In the last section of this chapter, we elaborate on these policies.

# Challenges and Opportunities in Remarketing Product Returns

The recovery of products returned by customers to an Internet retailer is a multistep process that generally starts with the retailer's capturing the returned items from customers through the U.S. Postal Service (USPS), United Parcel Service (UPS), or other third-party logistics (3PL) organizations. In the next step, items are transported back to a facility for inspection, classification, and disposition. This facility may be a centralized warehouse or a regional distribution center and may be owned and operated by the Internet retailer itself or a third-party specialist such as Newgistics. At the end of this step, it will be possible to assess the condition of the returns and make the most profitable decision for their future use. Some items may be liquidated or disposed of, but others may be refurbished and remarketed. For this latter group of merchandise returns, the Internet retailer will need to have in place policies that will support a fast, cost-efficient resale of products in the market.

The key is to ensure that products are quickly available for resale to avoid excessive depreciation in their value. At the same time, Internet retailers should strive to maintain efficient operations, especially in warehousing and transportation, in order to limit the costs necessary to perform the previously outlined steps in the recovery of the returned products.

Figure 10.3 is adapted from the work by Blackburn, Guide, Souza, and Van Wassenhove (2004) to illustrate how delays in recovering returns can downgrade the value of products involved in this process. The top line in Figure 10.3 illustrates the depreciation in value that a product that has been subject to a false return goes through during its recovery by an Internet retailer. The lower line represents the declining value of the product had it been subject to refurbishment as part of the return process.

The slopes in these lines reflect the sensitivity that the value of products has with respect to the timing of their sale to customers. High gradients will correspond to products that have short life cycles due to technological changes (such as computers and other electronic items) or changes in customer tastes (such as apparel and other high-fashion merchandise). High gradients may also correspond to products subject to expiration dates due to perishability concerns (such as dairy and other food items).

Internet retailers must be proactive in quickly recovering these kinds of items when they are returned, especially if they are high-value products. Under these conditions, it may be beneficial for Internet retailers to ensure that products are quickly available for resale to avoid excessive depreciation in their value, rather than aggressively pursuing cost savings through the execution of efficient operations in warehousing and transportation during the recovery of the returned products. For these products, Internet retailers should consider the design of responsive return policies that expedite their recovery. As part of these policies, they could set up decentralized facilities for the collection and evaluation of returns in order to ensure a fast capture, processing, and preparation of merchandise for resale.

The low-sloping lines in Figure 10.3 would correspond to products with values that are relatively independent of their time of resale. These are durable goods with long life cycles that are not exposed to changing technologies or customer tastes or that can be resold independently of expiration dates. Products such as furniture fall in this category.

Relative to other products, furniture does not require very proactive recovery in order to stave off loss of value due to depreciation. As such, an Internet retailer like eFurnitureShowroom should focus on efficient operations, especially in warehousing and transportation rather than speed, to limit the costs necessary to perform the different steps in the recovery. As an example, as part of their efforts, eFurntitureShowroom could centralize the collection and evaluation of

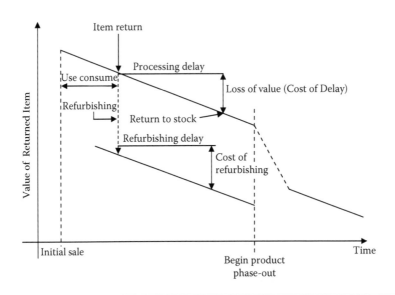

**Figure 10.3  Time value of product returns in Internet retailing. (Adapted from Blackburn, J.D. et al., 2004. *California Management Review* 46(2): 6–22.)**

returns in order to ensure that recovered items are transported in large loads at low, full-truckload rates.

In the end, the strategy best suited to process product returns will depend on the type of products being recovered and whether it maximizes the difference between the item value recovered and the cost of processing the returns. On the one hand, Internet retailers may consider designing a strategy focused on the efficient processing of returns by leveraging scale economies and lowering fixed costs through the use of centralized facilities for the capture and processing of returned merchandise. However, product returns under this strategy will be subject to processing delays that can cut dramatically into the values of items involved, especially if those products have high values and compressed life cycles. In the case of these products, responsive strategies may be best suited for the processing of returns. Minimal delays will reduce loss in item value chains. In short, there is no "one size fits all" solution to returns processing for Internet retailing. Instead, each retailer must design a process that balances cost and speed, depending on the characteristics of the product sold.

# References

Anderson, E.T., K. Hansen, and D. Simester. 2009. The option value of returns: Theory and empirical evidence. *Marketing Science* 28(3): 405–423.

Andreassen, T.W. 2000. Antecedents to satisfaction with service recovery. *European Journal of Marketing* 34(1/2): 156–175.

Blackburn, J.D., V.D.R. Guide, G. Souza, and L.N. Van Wassenhove 2004. Reverse supply chains for commercial returns. *California Management Review* 46(2): 6–22.

Boyer, K.K. and G.T.M. Hult. 2005a. Extending the supply chain: Integrating operations and marketing in the online grocery industry. *Journal of Operations Management* 23(6): 642–661.

Boyer, K.K. and J.R. Olson. 2002. Drivers of Internet purchasing success. *Production and Operations Management* 11(4): 480–498.

Grimaldi, P. 2008. Day of rejects: Store clerks gear up for gift exchanges. *Tribune Business News*. Washington, DC, December 26.

Guide, V.D.R., G.C. Souza, L.N. Van Wassenhove, and J.D. Blackburn. 2006. Time value of commercial product returns. *Management Science* 52(8): 1200–1214.

Laseter, T.M., E. Rabinovich, K.K. Boyer, and M. Rungtusanatham. 2007. The future of the Web: Three critical issues in Internet retailing. *MIT Sloan Management Review* 48(3): 58–64.

Maxham, J.G. 2001. Service recovery's influence on consumer satisfaction, positive word-of-mouth, and purchase intentions. *Journal of Business Research* 54(1): 11–24.

Mollenkopf, D.A., E. Rabinovich, T.M. Laseter, and K.K. Boyer. 2007. Managing Internet product returns: A Focus on effective service operations. *Decision Sciences*. 38, No. 2, The Next Frontier in Services Research Special Topic Forum, pp. 215–250.

Ofek, E., Z. Katona, and M. Sarvary. 2009. *Bricks and Clicks: The Impact of Product Returns on the Strategies of Multi-Channel Retailers*. Unpublished Manuscript, Harvard Business School, Cambridge, MA.

Spencer, J. 2002. The point of no return. *The Wall Street Journal*, May 14, D1.

Stock, J., T. Speh, and H. Shear. 2006. Managing product returns for competitive advantage. *MIT Sloan Management Review* 48(1): 57–62.

## Chapter 11

# Amazon: Supply Chain Strategy and Innovation

Jeff Bezos founded Amazon.com in 1994 and launched it on the Internet in mid-1995. Since its inception, Bezos has thought of Amazon as a consumer-centric organization and has defined the company's mission as delighting its customers. To that end, Amazon has set three overall performance goals. First, Amazon has sought to offer its customers the greatest product selection anywhere. Second, Amazon has taken on the challenge of providing the best service to its customers by offering them rich product information and abundant customer and expert reviews, a fast and timely fulfillment of their orders, and hassle-free returns. Third, Amazon has aimed to offer its customers the lowest prices for all of the products it sells.

Today, Amazon is striving to become a place where people can come to find and discover anything they might want to buy online. Its key pillars of abundant selection, great service, and low prices are interrelated in what the company calls a *virtuous cycle*, and together constitute the foundation of Amazon's growth. As Figure 11.1 illustrates, through this virtuous cycle, Amazon has been able to realize important synergies that have contributed to sustaining and expanding its business model.

Starting with an expanding product selection, at the top of the cycle, Amazon has been able to offer customers a compelling shopping experience relative to what is available elsewhere on and off the Internet. It offers customers top-quality service. The product selection and customer service combination has led to continuous gains in traffic at Amazon's website from new and returning customers. As Amazon has expanded its volume of sales, it has been able to

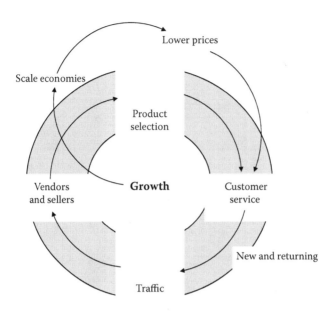

**Figure 11.1   Amazon's "virtuous cycle." (Adapted from Amazon.com.)**

gain scale economies in inventory management and transportation to support its objective of giving customers increasingly lower prices. Moreover, its gains in sales have helped Amazon attract more merchandise suppliers interested in selling their products through its website. In turn, the availability of merchandise from more suppliers has continued helping Amazon in its quest to broaden its product selection.

This virtuous cycle has led to annual sales at Amazon.com that exceed $25 billion in 2009. This is 15 times higher than the net sales in 1999 when they were $1.64 billion. To make its virtuous cycle turn in its favor, Amazon has developed a supply chain strategy based on cumulative trade-offs among a number of structural and operational decisions. A look at these decisions can provide insights into how the trade-offs involved in these decisions have contributed to Amazon' success.

## Amazon's Structural Decisions

Amazon's structural decisions have defined the what, when, where, and how of its investment in the facilities it uses to run its operations. The backbone of these facilities is its fulfillment centers, where Amazon stocks the inventory for many of the products it sells. At its founding, Amazon.com went against the general trend among Internet retailers and decided not to outsource its fulfillment centers. Instead, it built a vertically integrated network of facilities that would hold its inventory and use it to assemble and ship the orders that customers submitted through Amazon's Internet site.

This decision helped Amazon develop and continue to perfect what has become the industry's gold standard for Internet fulfillment. Amazon knew that outsourcing the operation of its fulfillment centers would not only prevent it from developing a core competitive advantage but also let others, namely, third-party providers, offer their services to Amazon's competitors.

By 2010, Amazon had established 11 fulfillment centers in North America, 8 centers in Europe, and 6 in Asia (see Table 11.1). It uses the North America centers to fulfill the orders it receives from the United States and Canada. These orders account for 53% of Amazon's revenue, and their volume has been growing at a 45% annual rate in recent years. The centers in Europe and Asia fulfill the orders that Amazon.com receives from customers in European Union countries, and Japan and China, respectively. These orders account for 47% of Amazon's revenue and have experienced a 47% annual growth rate in recent years.

Most of these fulfillment centers are located outside major urban centers, far away from prime real estate areas. They provide a low-cost alternative in terms of land value and real estate taxes to that associated with traditional brick-and-mortar stores operated by major retail chains.

Nevertheless, with these cost advantages comes the need for Amazon to transport the products ordered by customers to their destinations. These delivery costs account for a significant portion of all transportation costs in Amazon's supply chain. Table 11.2 presents a multiyear breakdown of these transportation costs in relation to the revenues Amazon received from customers paying for deliveries as well as overall fulfillment costs. These fulfillment costs include all delivery costs as well as those costs incurred in operating and staffing the fulfillment centers. They include costs attributable to buying, receiving, inspecting, and warehousing inventories, and picking, packaging, and preparing customer orders for shipment.

In direct contrast to its decision to keep its fulfillment centers' operations in-house, Amazon has chosen to contract third-party logistics (3PL) firms such as United Parcel Service (UPS) to execute the delivery of its orders. These firms offer multimodal transportation options that combine air- and motor-carrier modes to take Amazon's products from its fulfillment centers to its customers' destinations. The use of air transportation is more expensive than the use of motor carriers on a per-ton, per-mile basis. However, Amazon increased the use of air transport as it broadened its market to increasingly distant destinations from its fulfillment centers.

Generally, Amazon will send its products in full-truckload shipments from its fulfillment centers to third-party providers' airport hubs using motor-carrier transportation. This transportation mode will cost Amazon around $0.25 per

**Table 11.1   Cities with Amazon Fulfillment Centers**

| **North America** |
| --- |
| *Arizona*: Phoenix, Goodyear |
| *Delaware*: New Castle |
| *Indiana*: Whitestown and Plainfield |
| *Kansas*: Coffeyville |
| *Kentucky*: Campbellsville, Hebron (near CVG), Lexington, and Louisville |
| *Nevada*: Fernley and North Las Vegas |
| *New Hampshire*: Nashua |
| *Pennsylvania*: Carlisle, Chambersburg, Hazleton, Allentown, and Lewisberry |
| *Texas:* Dallas/Fort Worth |
| *Virginia*: Sterling |
| *Ontario (Canada)*: Mississauga (a Canada Post facility) |
| **Europe** |
| Glenrothes (Scotland): Amazon.co.uk warehouse |
| Bedfordshire (England): Marston Gate, near Brogborough |
| Inverclyde (Scotland): Gourock |
| Fife (Scotland): Glenrothes |
| Swansea (Wales): Crymlyn Burrows near Jersey Marine |
| Loiret (France): Orléans-Boigny (2000) |
| Loiret: Orléans-Saran (2007) |
| Hessen (Germany): Bad Hersfeld |
| Saxony (Germany): Leipzig |
| **Asia** |
| Ichikawa, Chiba (Japan) |
| Yachiyo, Chiba (Japan) |
| Sakai, Osaka (Japan) |

**Table 11.1   Cities with Amazon Fulfillment Centers (continued)**

| |
|---|
| Guangzhou (China) |
| Suzhou (China) |
| Beijing (China) |

*Source:* Adapted from Amazon.com.

pound since distances between fulfillment centers and air transport hubs are typically less than 100 miles. At the airport hubs, the third-party provider breaks the full-truckload shipments according to the orders' destinations and loads the orders onto cargo planes to transport them to hubs throughout the country. Air transportation for this leg typically costs Amazon around $1.05 per pound since air transportation distances between hubs are normally greater than 500 miles. Once the orders arrive at the hubs, they are sorted again according to their destinations' zip codes and sent in less-than-truckload shipments at an average cost of around $0.30 per pound based upon a usual distance of less than 100 miles between the air transport hubs and the final destination.

Amazon could lower its transportation costs by opening additional fulfillment centers closer to the markets it serves. This would reduce the lengths of haul

**Table 11.2   Shipping Revenues and Costs and Fulfillment Costs**

| | 2009 | 2008 | 2007 |
|---|---|---|---|
| **Revenues and Costs (in millions)** | | | |
| Outbound shipping revenue[a,b] | $ 924 | $ 835 | $ 740 |
| Outbound shipping costs | $1773 | $1465 | $1174 |
| Fulfillment costs | $2052 | $1658 | $1292 |
| **Percent of Net Sales** | | | |
| Outbound shipping revenue | 3.8% | 4.4% | 5.0% |
| Outbound shipping costs | 7.2% | 7.6% | 7.9% |
| Fulfillment costs | 8.4% | 8.6% | 8.7% |

*Source:*  Adapted from Amazon.com.

[a] Excludes amounts earned on shipping activities by third-party sellers where Amazon does not provide the fulfillment service.

[b] Includes amounts earned from Amazon Prime membership and Fulfillment by Amazon programs.

**Table 11.3   Fulfillment Center Information as of 2009**

| Square Footage | Value | Accumulated Depreciation |
|---|---|---|
| 11,848 (North America) 5739 (International) | $551,000,000 | $202,000,000 |

*Source:* Adapted from Amazon.com.

in the delivery of its orders and could even obviate the use of air transportation in much of its fulfillment operations. This strategy, however, could affect negatively the cost efficiency of its fulfillment center operations. Fulfillment centers carry fixed costs and overhead expenses that depend on real estate acquisition costs and taxes, and also on warehousing equipment depreciation and general and administrative expenses such as insurance and labor costs (See Table 11.3). As more fulfillment centers enter operation, Amazon loses economies of scale in light of the volume of orders processed at each facility.

Moreover, Amazon has deliberately designed its fulfillment centers to specialize in one of two product categories based on handling characteristics: sortable and bulk items. According to Amazon's own classification, sortable items include those products that are no bigger than a loaf of bread. These products include many of its fast-moving items, such as books and DVDs. Fulfillment centers specializing in the handling of these products are highly automated and use advanced sorting equipment and conveyors to move the products from storage to packaging to shipping. To justify its investment in this technology, Amazon must utilize the facility with a high volume of orders.

Bulk items include large items such as TV sets and other home appliances that typically carry high price tags as well. Because of their size and value, bulk products require direct handling by individual laborers in their storage and retrieval from inventory. Packaging and shipping is also labor intensive. The different product characteristics make it difficult for Amazon to combine fulfillment center operations involving bulk items with sortable goods and still maintain a high utilization of its human resources at its facilities.

# Amazon's Operational Decisions

Although the structure of Amazon's fulfillment centers' footprint has represented a critical set of decisions conducive to the realization of lower operating costs, Amazon has also focused its attention on the use of operational activities to build distinctive, strategically relevant capabilities that have attracted new customers and helped develop loyalty among existing ones.

Amazon made a strategic decision to run its own fulfillment centers. These investments have yielded important cost efficiencies that have propelled Amazon to an industry leadership position and enabled it to have a high level of control of its operations planning. For example, Amazon is able to quote customers the exact cutoff time for ordering to receive deliveries the next day. Virtually no other Internet retailer can offer this service for the breadth of products that Amazon sells.

Amazon continues to leverage its fulfillment centers to broaden the variety of inventory that it can offer customers. It has made the decision to store only its best-selling products in its fulfillment centers in order to ensure a fast inventory rotation. With a total of $2.1 billion in inventory and 12 inventory turns per year in 2009, Amazon is at the top of the industry in inventory effectiveness. However, it is still able to sell other less popular products through the use of drop-shipping arrangements with hundreds of suppliers. Through these arrangements, Amazon markets suppliers' inventory through its website, while suppliers are responsible for storing the products in their inventory and shipping out these goods from their inventory facilities once customer orders arrive at Amazon.com. Suppliers in these drop-shipping programs can keep most of the revenue from the sale of their products, while Amazon earns only a commission per product sold. In 2009, these arrangements accounted for 30% of Amazon's unit sales, and this share is expected to grow in the future.

In 2008, Amazon also introduced an innovative program through which it offers to handle the storage and shipping of its suppliers' inventory right out of its fulfillment centers. These kinds of arrangements are structured as part of a program called Fulfillment by Amazon. Vendors in this program send their products to Amazon's fulfillment centers for storage. Once customers order the products, Amazon fulfills the orders on the vendors' behalf. This includes picking and packing the products and combining them with other items ordered simultaneously by customers from Amazon or another vendor. Finally, Amazon will ship the suppliers' products from its fulfillment centers while providing tracking information and customer service support for the orders.

Globally, sellers using Fulfillment by Amazon stowed more than one million unique items in Amazon's fulfillment center network in 2009. Through this program, Amazon has been able to boost significantly the volume of orders processed through its fulfillment centers and increase facility utilization, particularly during off-peak seasons when overall demand is low. Moreover, through this program, Amazon earns additional revenue from storage and fulfillment service charges to its vendors. As detailed in Table 11.4, Amazon will charge storage fees for all units stored in every Amazon fulfillment center based on calendar month and vendors' daily average volume utilized (measured in cubic

**Table 11.4  Fulfillment by Amazon Fees**

| *Calculating Fulfillment Fees* |
| --- |
| Follow the steps below and the table below to determine the cost of fulfilling an item using Fulfillment by Amazon. |
| **Step 1—Inventory storage** |
| Use the table "Inventory Storage." Storage fees are charged for all units stored in an Amazon fulfillment center based on calendar month and daily average volume (measured in cubic feet). |
| **Step 2—Determine unit types** |
| **Media, nonmedia, and oversize**—Media units include books, music, software, video games, and videos (DVD, VHS). Nonmedia units include everything else. An "oversize unit" is any packaged unit, media, or nonmedia that does not fit within an area of 18 in. × 14 in. × 8 in. or weighing 20 lb or more. |
| **Step 3—Calculate fulfillment fee** |
| A. **Order handling**—Add $1.00 if your fulfillment order contains one or more nonmedia units. |
| B. **"Pick & Pack"**—A fee is applied to each unit in your fulfillment order. If a unit has a retail price less than $25, use the corresponding row for that unit in the table below. If the unit's retail price is $25 or greater, use the corresponding row for that unit. |
| C. **Weight handling**—For each unit, multiply the individual unit weight by $0.40. For an order with multiple units, add the fee for each individual unit to get the total fee. |
| **TOTAL**—The sum of A, B, and C is the fulfillment fee. |

| *Inventory Storage* | |
| --- | --- |
| This fee is assessed to every unit (un) for as long as it is in the fulfillment center | |
| *Monthly storage (per cubic foot)* | |
| January–September | $0.45/ft$^3$ per month |
| October–December | $0.60/ft$^3$ per month |

**Table 11.4 Fulfillment by Amazon Fees (continued)**

| Amazon Fulfillment | | | |
|---|---|---|---|
| The total fee to process a fulfillment order = order handling + Pick & Pack + weight handling | | | |
| *Fulfillment* | *Media* | *Nonmedia* | *Oversize* |
| **A. Order handling** | N/A | $1/order | N/A |
| **B. Pick & Pack** | | | |
| Price/un < $25 | $0.50/un | $0.75/un | $3.00/un |
| Price/un ≥ $25 | $1.00/un | $1.00/un | $3.00/un |
| **C. Weight handling** | $0.40/lb | $0.40/lb | $0.40/lb |

*Source:* Adapted from Amazon.com.

feet). Therefore, vendors pay only for the space they use. Amazon also charges fulfillment fees depending on the type of product shipped, the weight of the product, and the value of the orders.

In another innovative practice in its fulfillment centers, Amazon has implemented a shipment strategy through which it deliberately delays the release of its orders from inventory in accordance with the amount of time necessary to deliver the orders on time to their destinations. Orders are not released from inventory on a first-in-first-out basis. Instead, orders that require overnight delivery, for instance, will be released from inventory first, while orders for which customers have requested ground (seven-day) shipping will be released from inventory at a later date.

This practice has given Amazon a greater ability to plan the workflow at each of its fulfillment centers so that its labor and equipment at those facilities can operate at a constant, sustained rate throughout the week. The practice does carry some risks since delaying the release of the orders could result in unintended late deliveries. Furthermore, this practice will not be very effective when demand backlog is low. With fewer items in inventory, it can become very challenging to implement this strategy without running the risk of incurring excess stockouts.

Aware that delays in releasing orders from inventory can have a negative effect on customers who want instant gratification from their purchases, Amazon recently introduced a new "Local Express Delivery" option. In 2010 this option extended to customers in seven cities in the United States: New York, Philadelphia, Boston, Washington, Baltimore, Las Vegas, and Seattle. Through

**Table 11.5   Local Express Delivery Fees**

| Items | Per Shipment | Per Item |
|---|---|---|
| Automotive | $17.99 | $1.99/lb |
| Baby items | $17.99 | $1.99/lb |
| Books, VHS videotapes, software | $14.99 | $4.99 |
| CDs, music cassettes, vinyl, DVDs | $9.99 | $3.99 |
| Cell phones | $17.99 | $1.99/lb |
| Cell phone accessories | $17.99 | $1.99/lb |
| Computers | $17.99 | $1.99/lb |
| Electronics | $17.99 | $1.99/lb |
| Grocery | $17.99 | $1.99/lb |
| Jewelry, clothing items, shoes | $14.99 | $4.99 |
| Personal care, furniture, bed, bath, and home decor items | $17.99 | $1.99/lb |
| Luggage | $17.99 | $1.99/lb |
| Outdoor living and sports items | $17.99 | $1.99/lb |
| Tools and hardware | $17.99 | $1.99/lb |
| Toys | $18.99 | $1.99/lb |
| Video games | $9.99 | $1.99 |
| Any combination of the above items | Highest applicable per shipment charge | As above |

*Source:* Adapted from Amazon.com.

this option, customers can order eligible items any time prior to 10 a.m. or 1 p.m. (depending on the city), and Amazon will have the items delivered on the same day.

This service carries considerable costs, which sank dot.com-era businesses like Kozmo and Urbanfetch that offered same-day delivery services while charging little or no delivery fees. Many customers abused these companies mercilessly. Amazon, well aware of these cases (Amazon was an investor in Kozmo), has structured a set of delivery fees that clearly cover its costs. Table 11.5 provides a summary of the fees Amazon.com charges for "Local Express Delivery." The fees are quite steep, compared to charges for other delivery options such as next-day and two-day delivery. Some customers who are not price conscious may use same-day delivery regularly, but most will likely see same-day delivery as an option of last resort, used in case of emergency.

## Keeping the Virtuous Cycle Moving Forward

Amazon's virtuous cycle has been instrumental to the retailer's success. The company management team has made deliberate structural and operational decisions to ensure that the virtuous cycle keeps on churning in its favor. However, it is important to understand how these decisions have contributed to this objective. That is, how have these decisions, their implementation, and the results that Amazon has obtained contributed to maintaining its virtuous cycle?

Moreover, given the current state of Internet retailing and future trends on its horizon, which of these decisions are likely to remain relevant in supporting the virtuous cycle in the future? Are there opportunities for Amazon to improve upon these decisions in order to make its virtuous cycle run even better in the future?

# Chapter 12

# eShip-4U*

The ADM technology could potentially revolutionize the shipping industry, revitalize the business of online shopping, change the way people receive and ship packages, and eventually change their buying habits.

**—Amir Erlichman (HBS MBA '94), principal partner,
Yozma Group, venture capital funders of eShip**

eShip-4U (eShip) founder and CEO Dan Granot was both pleased and perplexed. eShip's partnership with Deutsche Post was working very well, and the automatic delivery machine (ADM) pilots in Mainz and Dortmund, now in their fourth month, were as successful as everyone at eShip had hoped. Yet, the key to entering the U.S. market was as elusive as ever. It was unclear what, if anything, from the partnership with Deutsche Post could be replicated in the United States.

In May 2002, Dan and other members of eShip's executive team had met with the firm's advisory board to discuss various U.S. entry strategies for eShip's revolutionary ADM. A network of ADMs was conceived to be analogous to the ubiquitous ATMs that were an everyday part of American life. The ADM technology would allow consumers to direct shipments to a nearby ADM for

---

* With permission, this chapter presents the case "eShip-4U" (Case number N1-603-076) written by Timothy M. Laseter and Roy D. Shapiro and published by Harvard Business School Publishing.

package pickup or return, 24 hours a day, 7 days a week (24/7). The ADM would also provide carriers such as Federal Express (FedEx), United Parcel Service (UPS), DHL, and the United States Postal Service (USPS), a centralized delivery point, thereby reducing the considerable costs of servicing suburban and rural residential homes. A central component of eShip's system was the web-based control and management software, dubbed the Last-Mile Information System (LAMIS). LAMIS provided an online, real-time, virtual hub between vendors (e.g., retailers, e-tailers), consumers, carriers, so-called landlords (those who owned the real estate on which the ADMs would physically be located), and the ADMs themselves. The system would notify consumers when their packages arrived at the designated ADM, generate an access code needed to retrieve the package, and enable vendors, carriers, and others to monitor capacity utilization, pickups, returns, technical problems, and a variety of other information.

Dan recalled that it had not been long ago when he had first introduced the ADM concept to Amir Erlichman, principal partner at the Yozma Group, an Israeli venture capital firm. Amir had been quite skeptical:

> While I immediately saw the potential in the technology and believed in the promise of the revolutionary ADM concept, I was doubtful about the investment. Can a small start-up like eShip with limited financial resources afford the cost of educating consumers and changing their buying habits? Plus, can eShip manage to position itself to squeeze enough value out of the package delivery food chain in an industry dominated by few big players like the private carriers and postal companies? Can we manage to build a lucrative international company here—one with a high-margin business, a significant annuity component, and a capacity to quickly grab market share worldwide? Will we be the ones to reap the fruits of our own invention in a large and growing online shopping market, or will someone else?
>
> At the same time, I did realize that the value of the ADMs was in its networking capability. Not only can you deliver packages via the ADMs, but also sell things just like vending machines. There was inherent flexibility built into the system and also the opportunity of cross-selling and personalized targeted selling to consumers. You can also sell advertising, rent out spaces like lockers, or collect and sell aggregate consumer data. Once you have the ADMs connected to the Internet, the possibilities are almost unlimited.

It had taken Dan a long time to convince Amir that eShip was capable of getting this revolutionary concept off the ground. While Amir had now become a strong advocate of the technology, Dan wondered how long it would take to convince consumers, business partners, and other investors about the benefit of ADMs.

Dan knew that his investors were eager for eShip to "go to the next level" by entering the United States. A trial run in two German cities, in partnership with the Deutsche Post, had been very successful. Another trial was also under way in Israel, with ADMs deployed at a chain of local gasoline stations/convenience stores. The question remained, however, of how best to approach the United States. Would simply copying one of these trials be either possible or effective, or was there another way to best enter this most lucrative and challenging of markets? Dan understood that eShip could not do this itself: Who would be the best partners for a successful entry into the United States?

## The Last Mile

Package delivery, dominated by giant players such as FedEx, UPS, and DHL, was a growing industry fueled by the ever-increasing volume of online purchases. In 2001, the U.S. residential package delivery market had been estimated at more than $7 billion (1.3 billion packages) per year. Driven by online retail, this market was expected to more than double by 2004 (eShip Business Plan, June 2001). The industry, however, had its own inherent operating problem: much like telecom operators' inability to reach, in a cost-effective way, the consumer's premise, the "last-mile" cost had long plagued carriers. It was estimated that local delivery represented as much as 64% of total U.S. distribution cost (Tim Laseter et al., 2000)

The reasons for the high last-mile cost to residential sites were twofold: First, unlike business-to-business (B2B) delivery for which shipment volume might be large, package deliveries to consumers were, in most cases, one package per delivery. The carrier had to construct an elaborate and expensive route for the delivery vehicle to drop off one package at a time. There were few economies of scale: "Physical delivery does not benefit from the network effect that supports other types of Information Economy businesses" (Tim Laseter et al., 2000).

Second, if the recipient was not at home, a second (or even third) delivery was required, which more than doubled the cost. More than two-thirds of American homes were not occupied during the business day. In the United States, 1.3 delivery attempts per package produced more than 600 million "Sorry we missed you" sticky notes every year (eShip Business Plan, June 2001).

The economics of last-mile cost were driven by three major factors:

■ The average travel per package per truck—a function of the population density of the delivery area

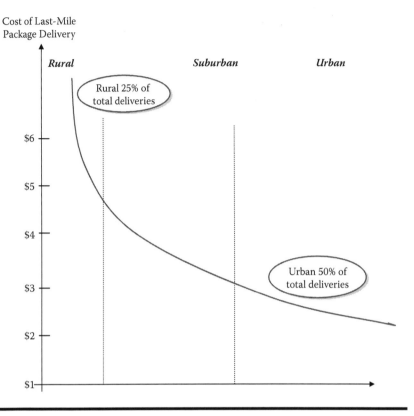

**Figure 12.1 Last-mile economics.** *Source:* **eShip company documents.** *Notes:* **(1) Business-to-business deliveries were estimated to incur less than $1 of last-mile cost. (2) The last-mile cost to serve a network of ADMs was estimated to be 16% of the last-mile cost incurred for residential deliveries.**

- The number of packages a truck can drop off per delivery—averaging close to one for residential deliveries
- The number of delivery attempts per package

Last-mile cost was greater in rural areas than suburban or urban areas. Indeed, in some rural areas, even first delivery was difficult to justify economically. (See Figure 12.1).

As carriers had become more aware of the cash drain they suffered in serving residential customers, they had started actively looking into potential solutions. FedEx, for example, had assigned a senior executive to develop new solutions or concepts. eShip's ADM technology offered one such solution.

# eShip*

eShip was established in September 2000 by a group of four professionals (see Box 12.1) committed to addressing the need for comprehensive last-mile solutions for package delivery. Incorporated in Delaware, eShip was located in Netanya, outside Tel Aviv, Israel. In 2002, the company had 24 employees, of whom 15 were involved in software development. eShip had received $3.8 million in first-round financing in September 2000 from two Israeli venture capital firms: the Yozma Group and Veritas Venture Partners. See Box 12.2 for short biographies of selected members of eShip's board of directors and advisory board.

eShip's ADM technology was developed not only to deal with last-mile economics but also to provide consumers with 24/7 convenience and the benefit of flexible, self-selected, shipping options (e.g., "Attempt delivery to my home twice, and if no one is at home, deliver to this nearby ADM"). Nir Kinory and his team of engineers and software developers had produced an ADM prototype, and a number of hardware and software patents had been filed, including those for specific technical achievements such as the algorithms that ensured maximum capacity utilization of the ADM carousel shelving system. With limited cash, eShip was eager to run a real-world trial to verify that the hardware, software, and network components would work together as expected and, as important, would provide value to the package delivery value chain.

However, Dan and his management team were not interested in having eShip become a hardware manufacturer beyond the prototype phase. Rather, they had made a decision early on to concentrate on software, technology, and network support. Storage/retrieval industry and ATM manufacturers had been approached to discuss outsourcing to allow eShip to concentrate on its core software development and the infrastructure skills that would best support operators of the ADM/LAMIS (Last-Mile Information System) network. Manufacturers in both Europe and the United States had expressed interest in producing the ADM hardware for eShip.

At this early stage of development, most of eShip's revenue came from the sales of the ADM machines. Longer term, the revenue sources would include

- ADM hardware
- ADM software plug fees
- ADM and LAMIS (network) software sales
- Network hosting
- Support fees
- Software upgrades

---

* eShip, "About Us/Management/Press Releases," eShip Website <http://www.eShip.com/html/about_us.html>, accessed May 2, 2002).

## BOX 12.1

## SHORT BIOGRAPHIES OF ESHIP MANAGEMENT TEAM

**Dan Granot (CEO)** has more than 20 years of experience in the shipping industry. Dan was the founder of Shigur Express and acted as its managing director. Since 1997, he has served as vice chairman of DHL Israel, where he holds 10% of company equity. In 1998, he managed the merger of Aviv Yael Daroma and the domestic section of Shigur Express. Dan holds a B.A. in economics from Tel-Aviv University and served as a lieutenant colonel in the Israel Defense Forces. He is 50 years old.

**Nir Kinory (Senior VP)** brings experience in the integration of various businesses and was a creator of the concept behind eShip-4u. Before establishing eShip-4u, Nir managed a privately held consulting firm. He formerly served as comptroller at Delta Galil Industries Ltd. (NYSE: DELT) and as a senior business consultant manager with the Israeli representative of ODI and E&Y. Nir holds a B.S. degree in information systems, cum laude, from the industrial engineering faculty of the Technion-Israel Institute of Technology, and an MBA from Bar-Ilan University. Nir served as a captain in the Intelligence Corps of the IDF. He is 39 years old.

**Yoav Koster (VP)** possesses deep experience in automation and mechanical development. He designs products for leading Israeli companies such as Iscar, IAI, Orbotech, Plasson, and more. The products that he develops combine motion control, automation, design, and value engineering. Yoav holds a B.S. and M.S. in mechanical engineering from the Technion-Israel Institute of Technology, and served as a captain in the IDF. He is 38 years old.

**Shalom Weiss (VP)** has 12 years of experience in creating systems that integrate software and hardware, including systems for the shipping industry. Before joining the team, Shalom served as development manager at Manna. His experience includes managing the software development department at Elmotech and participating in the development team of Amital Forwarding Software. Shalom served as vice president–R&D at Kepler. Shalom holds a B.S. in computer sciences from the Hebrew University of Jerusalem and is about to complete a master's degree in computer technology at Bar-Ilan University. Shalom served as a captain in the Intelligence Corps of the IDF. He is 40 years old.

## BOX 12.2

## SHORT BIOGRAPHIES OF SELECTED ESHIP
## BOARD, AND ADVISORY BOARD, MEMBERS

**Amir Erlichman**, since 1998, has been general partner, Yozma Venture Capital. Yozma is recognized worldwide as the creator of the Israeli venture capital industry and as a leading venture group since its establishment in 1993. Mr. Erlichman has played an active role in the selection and value creation of Yozma's portfolio companies, primarily in the fields of software and the Internet. Having lived in the United States between 1988 and 1998, Mr. Erlichman has a wealth of experience in the U.S. capital markets. Prior to joining Yozma, he was an investment banker with Lehman Brothers in New York, specializing in mergers, acquisitions, public offerings, and private placements of high-technology companies. Mr. Erlichman also gained significant exposure to the U.S. financial markets with Credit Suisse First Boston. He holds a B.S. with highest distinction in computer engineering from Polytechnic University in New York and an M.B.A. from Harvard Business School.

**Robert Kuijpers**, former chief executive officer of DHL Worldwide Express, has held various executive positions at the company and is recognized worldwide as a pioneer and market leader of the global air express industry. Rob is a member of the board of directors at MyCustoms and a regional advisory board member of the London Business School.

**Tim Laseter** is a member of the Darden school faculty at the University of Virginia. Prior to joining in 2002, Laseter was a partner in Booz Allen Hamilton's operations practice with concentrations on operations strategy, supply chain management, and sourcing for a wide variety of global businesses. Prior to joining Booz Allen, Laseter worked in manufacturing operations at a joint venture between Siemens and Corning. Laseter is the author of *Balanced Sourcing: Cooperation and Competition in Supply Relationships* and a number of papers. A frequent speaker at business conferences, Laseter has presented to executive audiences in Europe, South America, and Asia as well as throughout the United States.

**William Henderson**, Former USPS postmaster general, has more than 30 years of experience with package shippers, post equipment manufacturers, and logistics service providers. Henderson has led the United States Postal Service through 7 years, encompassing a period of fantastic progress. In

1994, Henderson began serving as chief operating officer of the USPS, and in 1998 he was appointed postmaster general and CEO, with responsibility for nationwide postal operations: the daily processing, transportation, and delivery of more than 650 million pieces of mail to more than 130 million addresses. Throughout his tenure, Henderson focused the organization on maintaining affordability and achieving industry growth.

# The Deutsche Post Pilot

On January 21, 2002, Germany's Deutsche Post World Net commenced ADM trial service for the general public in the cities of Dortmund and Mainz. The free, subscription-based service was the first opportunity for eShip to see the ADM system working in an existing residential delivery context.

## *Deutsche Post: A Company in Transition*

In January 1995, the German Bundespost's 500-year-old postal division became a government-owned corporation, Deutsche Post AG. Dr. Klaus Zumwinkel, chairman of the board, envisioned the new corporation expanding beyond domestic mail and express services—into logistics, financial and information services, mail, and express services on a global basis. The impending loss of the domestic letter-delivery monopoly (forecast to be, perhaps, as soon as 2003) was a major factor driving this business model change (Ewing 2000).

Beginning in 1997, Dr. Klaus Zumwinkel made a series of strategic acquisitions, including Danzas (logistics, global air freight forwarding), AI (air freight forwarding), Postbank (financial services), and a controlling interest in DHL International (worldwide express) (Zumwinkel 2001).

On November 20, 2000, Deutsche Post went public and was listed on the Frankfurt Stock Exchange. The IPO raised 6.6 billion euros—the second largest German IPO (after Deutsche Telekom). This ended a dramatic 10 years under Dr. Zumwinkel, during which employees had been reduced from 380,000 in 1990 to 240,000 in 2001. FY2001 revenues were 35 billion euros: mail delivery (33% of sales), express (18%), logistics (26%), and financial services (22%) (Deutsche Post World Net 2001).

In early 2001, seeking an e-commerce innovation that would demonstrate Deutsche Post's leadership in e-commerce logistics, and as a preemptive strike against other European competitors, Deutsche Post sponsored a competition for "last-mile" delivery and logistics solutions. eShip, along with 40 other com-

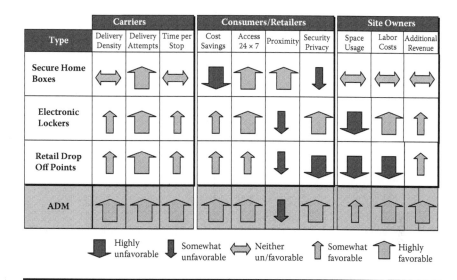

Figure 12.2 eShips's evaluation of the strengths/weaknesses of alternative last-mile solutions. *Secure home boxes* are lock boxes the size of a large cooler that are installed and attached to an entrance to the home. [a]*Electronic luggage lockers* are centrally controlled lockers in commercial/multiunit sites. [b]*Retail package drop-off points* are networks of retail outlets, such as gas stations or convenience stores, that hold packages for pickup by the public. Generally, they become part of a delivery network for an expected increase in foot traffic. [c]*Source*: eShip Business Plan, June 2001. [a]Start-ups include Z-Box (US), Brivo (US), Bearbox (UK), and Condelsys (Germany). [b]Start-ups include Delivery Station (US), ByBox (merged with Dynamid, US), ShopperBox (US), and Fraserbox/Dropzone1 (UK). [c]Start-ups include Paxzone (US), Collect Point (Europe), and e-Stop (UK).

panies, entered its ideas and products into the competition. See Figure 12.2 for examples of alternative last-mile solutions, and eShip's assessment of them.

Deutsche Post evaluated the proposals and, in June 2001, chose five to participate in a 1-month indoor test. eShip made the cut. Finally, two companies were chosen for the full "outdoor" test: the "high-tech" solution offered by eShip, and a "low-tech" solution offered by KEBA AG of Austria. During an interview held on January 22, 2002, with Dan Granot and Amir Erlichman, they mentioned that the Deutsche Post commenced its test on November 15, 2001, initially limiting trial use to parcel deliveries to business customers. Initial clients included Siemens, Deutsche Telekom, Bosch, and HP, who shipped repair and replacement parts for pickup and return by engineers and field technicians.

# The Packstation 24 Trial Run

For the initial ADM trial with the German public, Deutsche Post selected the cities of Dortmund (population 600,000) and Mainz (population 188,000). To promote the new service, some 1.4 million brochures were prepared and distributed, and Deutsche Post sponsored various festival-like events in both cities. The service was marketed as a new concept that allowed recipients of parcels to select the package delivery location of their choosing: their homes, postal retail outlets, or self-selected ADM locations. Once a parcel was delivered to an ADM, the customer would be informed via email or voice mail, and the parcel could be retrieved 24/7.

The service, which Deutsche Post had named "Packstation 24," was free, but customers were required to register. Any interested resident could apply in one of three ways: (1) by filling in the reply postcard attached to the brochure, (2) by phoning a service hotline, or (3) by logging onto a dedicated website. A welcome pack containing a customer card, PIN number (used to retrieve parcels inside the ADM), and letterbox sticker would then be sent to the customer.

On January 21, 2002, Packstation service began, and within 90 days, more than 25,000 customers had applied, according to information provided by Dan Granot during an interview on April 11, 2002. There were seven ADMs deployed in Dortmund, with four in post offices or busy street corners, two on gas station tarmacs, and one at the central train station. In Mainz, five ADMs had been deployed, with two at gas stations, one at the central train station, one in a post office, and one on a downtown street. Twelve KEBA boxes were also deployed in Dortmund and Mainz. The server running the LAMIS software was housed in a Deutsche Post facility in Frankfurt, with eShip technicians providing full-time support of the daily operation of the network.

Boris Mayer, project manager at Deutsche Post, seemed confident of success.

> Acceptance of the machines has been very high, particularly among our business customers. We are convinced that our private customers will also use the new service, especially as well-known mail-order firms and online retailers such as Quelle, Amazon, Yves Rocher, Klingel, and Conley's Modekontor want to use Packstation. If the pilot test for private customers runs as successfully as with our business customers, we will not only expand the service through additional locations, but will also integrate further self-service options (Deutsche Post 2002).

During an interview on April 11, 2002, Dan Granot mentioned that Deutsche Post was planning a staged rollout of ADM service with a potential increase to 66 ADMs in and around Frankfurt beginning in September 2002.

## The ADM

### ADM Hardware

Consumers could have packages delivered to any ADM in the network and retrieve them anytime. In addition, consumers could drop off, or return, packages to ADMs at their convenience. When a package was delivered to an ADM, the consumer would receive a PIN number via email, or potentially via cell phone, pager, or Instant Messenger Services. When the consumer entered the correct PIN number, the ADM's internal carousel would rotate, and the cell that held the consumer's package would open. The consumer could then retrieve the package. See Figures 12.3 and 12.4.

Each ADM could hold up to 180 parcels of different sizes. In the standard configuration, the parcel could be up to 21 inches × 18 inches × 24 inches in size. The external dimensions of the ADM were 2.24 meters (7.3 feet) tall, 1.36 meters (4.5 feet) deep, and 2.47 meters (8.1 feet) wide, a footprint comparable to

**Figure 12.3   ADMs in action: (a) ADM design.** *Source:* **eShip company documents. (continued)**

**Figure 12.3** (continued) ADMs in action: (b) ADM deployed in Europe by Deutsche Post. *Source:* eShip company documents.

**Figure 12.3** (continued) ADMs in action: (c) A Deutsche Post employee loading parcels. *Source:* eShip company documents.

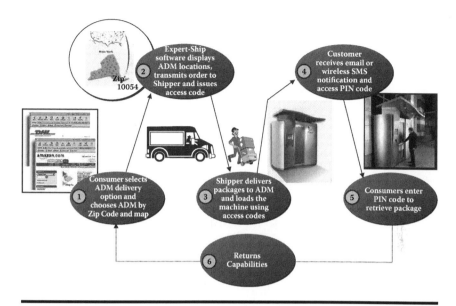

**Figure 12.4    The ADM network.** *Source:* **eShip Business Plan, June 2001.**

two to three soda vending machines. A smaller version, the "Mini-ADM," could hold up to 50 parcels of assorted sizes.

Initially, the ADM "package" (to include ADM hardware, ADM software plug with LAMIS access, and a 5-year maintenance contract) was to be priced at $45,000. As the volume of production increased, it was anticipated that this price would decrease considerably. Estimated operating costs were $200–300 per month. This included $75–125 in land costs; $50–60 in connection fees (electricity/Internet) and supplies (paper); $50 for insurance; and $20–50 in other expenses (including marketing). The Mini-ADM was priced at about half the price of the standard configuration ADM.

## The Network

More than a stand-alone machine, each ADM linked to a complex network of hardware and software, potentially connecting thousands of businesses. In addition to the ADM hardware, the network consisted of the central server software—monitoring and controlling all ADM machines via the Internet—as well as the client software that resided on local ADM machines. The network was able to track and allocate available space inside ADMs on a real-time basis and to ensure that packages were delivered to, and picked up by, the right person.

At the center of the network was the central server software called LAMIS. The software was fully web enabled and was capable of controlling a network of ADMs on a real-time basis. LAMIS would be either connected to a network operator system or to eShip's Data Application Server (DAS), which functioned as a virtual hub between consumers, nonstore merchants (e-tailers, catalog merchants, telemarketers, etc.), carriers, and the ADMs. LAMIS would also allow users to identify the most conveniently located ADM, notify users when their packages arrived at the ADM, provide users with an access code to pick up their packages, and notify merchants and/or carriers when the packages were picked up. Moreover, the system captured a variety of other information including barcode information for each package, the available free capacity of each machine, and what maintenance was needed.

The web-enabled client-end software, deployed in the individual ADM, handled the communication between ADMs and LAMIS through telephone, cellular, or satellite networks. In addition, the local ADM software also controlled specific machine actions, for example, matching PIN numbers or the opening of the appropriate cell to dispense the right package to a customer. eShip had filed for patents on both the ADM design and the associated software.

## Entering the U.S. Market

Although the Deutsche Post pilot provided one potential model of successful deployment of ADMs, replicating it in the United States remained a challenge. First, no single company in the United States provided the same mix of services as did the recently privatized Deutsche Post. The USPS retained a monopoly on residential delivery similar to Deutsche Post but did not have extensive third-party logistics (3PL) business like Deutsche Post's Danzas.

The USPS had been facing challenges from a number of directions. Competition from private firms—in particular UPS and FedEx, equipped with state-of-the-art technology—had been fierce. In the overnight shipping business, the USPS was a distant third. Though generating $60 billion in revenues per year, the USPS had run at a deficit for several years, triggering the U.S. Congress to push for increased efficiency and lower expenses. In 2002, Idealliance.org reported that Congress had decreed that the USPS would undergo $5 billion worth of cost-cutting initiatives through 2006, including a potential reduction in the number of post offices and, perhaps, even in the number of days of delivery in some areas (Idealliance.org, 2002). By law, the USPS was required to serve many remote areas at great expense that competing carriers could avoid. Most of Alaska, for example, had no UPS or FedEx presence due to its high cost to serve. See Table 12.1 for market share and other data on the USPS, UPS, and FedEx.

**Table 12.1   The U.S. Package Delivery Competitive Landscape**

| Profile, 1998 | USPS | UPS | FedEx |
|---|---|---|---|
| Year founded | 1775 | 1907 | 1973 |
| Employees | 792,000 | 327,000 | 192,000 |
| Revenues | $60 billion | $25 billion | $17 billion |
| Annual package volume | 1.9 billion parcels | 3.14 billion parcels | 1.7 billion parcels |
| Daily delivery points | 130 million | 12.4 million | 4.6 million |
| Facilities | 38,159 | 1,713 | 3,200 |
| Ground vehicles | 203,000 | 157,000 | 45,000 |
| Aircraft (owned) | 63 | 224 | 650 |
| *Market Shares* | | | |
| Market Segment | Share Percentage | | |
| Ground parcels | 9% | 75% | 11% |
| Overnight air | 6% | 31% | 44% |
| 2nd-day air | 45% | 16% | 26% |
| E-commerce | 33% | 55% | 10% |

*Source:* National Association of Letter Carriers, "Market Wars. How Postal Service Rivals are Clambering for Position in the US," http://www.union network.org/unipostal.nsf, May 3, 2000.

The argument had been made that the USPS could, nationwide, deploy ADMs and ensure consumer adoption by leveraging its current distribution and retail infrastructure—including 38,000 U.S. post offices. However, since 9/11 and the subsequent anthrax scare, the USPS had been focused more on security than on new cost-saving technologies. According to eShip management, "Discussions with USPS executives were hard to even schedule [in such an environment]. Dealing with the bureaucracy of the USPS would be a challenge. It would take time to bring the ADM to market this way."

FedEx, though historically B2B focused, had recently expanded into additional channels, including home delivery. When eShip approached FedEx in May 2001, it discovered that the company was experimenting with a similar prototype machine of its own design. Though eShip had had several subsequent discussions and had demonstrated the ADM to FedEx executives in November 2001 at the National Postal Forum in Denver, talks about collaboration continued to move slowly while FedEx worked toward its own pilot, at its own pace.

Neither had eShip's meetings with UPS generated any more optimism. Though interested in ways to better serve the consumer, it seemed to eShip management that the UPS retail strategy emanated from its recent acquisition of "Mail Boxes, Etc." The 3000+ Mail Boxes, Etc. operations could potentially be excellent locations for ADMs, but moving forward would be onerous since the locations were independent franchises and, thus, not under UPS control.

At the recent advisory board meeting, CEO Dan Granot expressed additional concerns,

> It's not just the timetable of dealing with the US Postal Service, FedEx, or UPS. I'm also concerned that our small company can get squeezed by any one of the three. The advantage of replicating the Deutsche Post business model is that carriers see the immediate financial benefit of last-mile savings in their current operations, much like the banks saw the benefits of ATMs in reducing teller costs. But, because they control deliveries, it is hard for us to extract a significant share of the enormous value we create.

Another possibility under discussion was what Amir Erlichman, an active member of the eShip advisory board, had dubbed the "independent operator" model.

## The ATM/ADM Analog and "Independent Operator" Model

The penetration of ATMs into nonbank locations offered an interesting analogy. The ATM was originally conceived as a proprietary cost savings measure by banks, meant to lower customer reliance on tellers for cash withdrawal transactions. All of the first ATMs, which appeared in the late 1960s and early 1970s, were located at banks (Jane Blake 2002). In the 1980s, national credit card networks such as Cirrus and Plus, owned, respectively, by MasterCard and Visa, connected ATMs and allowed for cross-bank access to funds—with no surcharges. Also, as competition for bank accounts increased, more ATMs were deployed with more features, for example, check deposits and transfers. In April 1996, the national networks lifted the ban on surcharges, and ATMs became revenue generators. The number of nonbank-located ("off premise") ATMs grew dramatically beginning in the mid-1990s, and by the end of 2001, more than half of the 273,000 ATMs in the United States were "off premise." According to a report issued by International Merchant Services (2002), for those companies hosting these "off-premise" ATMs, revenues generated included:

- Surcharges (merchants typically kept 80% of fees of $1.00–$4.00).
- Incremental sales (25% of the $60 average cash withdrawal was spent on-site).
- Savings from customers using cash rather than credit cards (eliminating a fee for the merchants of 2% or more).

An important driver of ATM penetration into nonbank locations was the rise of independent sales/service organizations (ISOs), of which there were some 250 in the United States in 2002. ISOs acted as the intermediaries between ATM manufacturers and merchants/landlords (convenience stores, shopping malls, casinos, etc.), providing a range of services, including analyzing alternative ATM locations, contract negotiation, installation, cash management, maintenance, and support (Jane Blake 2002).

Servicing an ATM fell into two categories: "first line" (e.g., cleaning, cash replenishment, paper refill, and other regularly required tasks) and "second line" (e.g., technical maintenance, repairs, and general troubleshooting). ISOs often subcontracted some of these tasks to third parties.

Building upon the ATM analogy, Amir believed, ADMs might generate revenues for their "independent operators" (IOs) in several ways. One was through the charging of rent or transaction fees to carriers who would be the direct beneficiaries of last-mile cost savings. Another potential source of revenue could be using the ADM as an additional product distribution and/or marketing channel. For example, one of the early eShip pilots had been conducted in Israel with the PAZ chain of gas stations and colocated Yellow brand convenience stores. Local partnerships had been developed with Kodak for photo developing (film drop-off and pickup), a cellular phone operator (to drop off handsets for repair and to retrieve new handsets), banks, and other businesses that believed they could benefit by interacting with consumers through ADMs. There was also the potential benefit to the landlord of increased foot traffic from customers visiting the site to pick up or drop off an item at the on-site ADM.

While the IO model offered many apparent advantages, there were still many issues to be resolved. The president of an ISO—an ATM independent sales/service organization—was less sanguine than eShip executives:

> I see the logic behind the ADM, but given the complexity of the system, providing strong service and support to merchants is going to be crucial. What are you going to do about educating shop owners on this thing? How about parts distribution, inventory management, training third parties in repairing it? You're going to need a 24-hour 1-800 number for emergencies. After all, we're not talking about withdrawing cash. If an ATM breaks down, there's going to

be another ATM around. Here, you're talking about a package from grandma.

Where's the incentive for the merchant to install an ADM? Where is the revenue generation? This isn't an ATM, with cash being withdrawn and spent on-site.

Ultimately, I think that the carriers are going to have to take a lead deploying these things. I can't see there being enough of a benefit to merchants to take the financial risk of buying ADMs.

He concluded, "But, we'd be more than happy to enter into a service contract with eShip."

## Partnering with E-Tailers

Another possibility was partnering directly with a large e-tailer or mail-order firm. In 2000, FedEx cited a CARAVAN Research study reporting that 70% of those customers polled linked their satisfaction with an online or catalog retailer directly to their satisfaction with the delivery experience. That same study reported that more than 44% said that premium service options such as appointment and evening delivery would increase their propensity to purchase online. Another study by eShip estimated that 44% of online purchases were abandoned at the last step when consumers saw the shipping cost. Providing consumers a reliable, lower-cost, 24/7 shipping choice through an ADM might allow an e-tailer to recover some of those lost sales and, perhaps, generate additional sales. Also, the physical presence of ADMs in high-visibility areas might offer increased brand awareness for online business-to-customer (B2C) businesses.

### *A Boston Pilot?*

During the May 2002 Advisory Board meeting, the notion of pilot in the city of Boston had arisen. Amir Erlichman had commented, "I think the real key is to just get a demonstration going in the United States. Everyone who sees the ADM in operation immediately sees the real potential, but few grasp it based upon our 2-D drawings or even the promotional video. If we could get an ADM installed on the HBS campus, it'd be a great sales tool."

Rob Kuijpers added his perspective: "I'm absolutely in favor of a pilot, but one machine on the HBS campus isn't likely to have enough impact. We'd need a network of machines to really make a mark. Can we afford to do this on our own?"

Dan Granot replied: We'd need to find a partner. As my venture capital financiers continue to remind me, our cash on hand won't hold us much beyond the end of the year at our current burn rate estimates, and those estimates don't include building ADMs without paying customers. At the same time, a reasonably sized pilot, say, 20 machines, could be run in Boston for an investment of not much more than $1 million—$900 thousand for the ADMs, and some additional investment for start-up costs and other overhead to get the business launched. That's not out of the reach of an individual entrepreneur—preferably one who already has property holdings like fast food or convenience stores where the machines could be placed. Or, we might be able to get one of the large e-tailers like Amazon to back us.

Tim Laseter, looking up from his computer, commented: I've got some data. Looking at my files, Boston has many positive characteristics—beyond being the home of the Harvard Business School. First, according to a *Washington Post* article in October 1999, 46% of the adult population had Internet access. According to the 2000 census, Boston's population was 590,000 in the city and three million in the greater metropolitan area.

Rob interjected: OK, maybe Boston's a good target city, and I agree that $1 million in funding shouldn't be impossible to get, but how does this solve our problem? Don't we still need the carriers to participate?" "Not necessarily," replied Tim. "If major e-tailers delivered in bulk to Boston, a local courier could fill the 20 machines with a few minimum-wage employees and a small delivery van.

Nir Kinory pitched in: I think Tim's right. By our estimates, it takes less than 10 seconds per package to load a machine. Filling a completely empty machine with 180 packages would take 30 minutes or less. Of course, we expect the average package to stay in the machine a day or two, and we certainly don't expect 100% utilization, so the loading time for a typical day would probably be no more than quarter of an hour. Of course, you'd have to factor in some driving time as well, but I'd bet that a few couriers could easily cover all 20 machines.

Bill Henderson joined in: OK, so the machines could be loaded pretty cheaply—if the packages are in Boston. Who's going to ship them there, and why would they prefer an ADM?

Tim responded: An online retailer like Amazon.com or a cataloger like Land's End might be interested in the ADM for the same reason that FedEx or UPS would be—to save money and potentially improve customer service.

Yoav Koster asked: How would Amazon or Land's End save money? Isn't the shipping charge simply passed on to the consumer?

Tim looked up again from his computer: Actually, most retailers treat shipping as a profit center. Look at Amazon's website and you'll see that they have a detailed table of shipping rates depending on the type and quantity of items. For standard service, 3–7 days, an order of a book and two CDs would incur a shipping charge of $5.97. If the customer wants it faster, the charge jumps to $10.96 for the two-business-days service or $17.96 for next-day service! I'm certain that they negotiate rates that allow them to make money at those prices.

Bill Henderson: Tim's right about that. I can't provide you any specifics due to nondisclosure restrictions, but it's not hard to figure out that there is a profit. Just go to the USPS.com site and test it yourself. If I remember correctly, Amazon serves Boston out of their distribution center in New Castle, Delaware, which is less than 350 miles from Boston.

Amir looked up from his computer: Bill's right. I tested a 12 inches x 12 inches x 4 inches package weighing five pounds going from New Castle to Boston. Even a small business requesting the pickup of a single package can ship for only $5.71. With Amazon's volumes and the savings from bulk pickup at their site, I'm sure they get a much better price.

"Check out the UPS.com site for expedited delivery rates. I bet you will find an even bigger difference, at least between New Castle and Boston," noted Bill. After the briefest pause, Amir replied, "Right again. The same package with second-day delivery from UPS is $9.19; $15.40 for next day."

Undaunted by the enthusiasm in the room, Yoav returned to his main argument, "OK, OK, so they make a profit on packages. That still doesn't explain why or how they could make more money through us, unless the shippers give them the savings. In fact, we've added additional costs by having people load the ADMs; haven't we?"

"You're right. If Amazon continued to ship individual packages through UPS and USPS. But, imagine that Amazon could contract with a third-party logistics company to run a dedicated truck from New Castle to Boston each night after customer orders are picked and packaged. The 3PL would typically charge no more than $1.50 per mile for an 18-wheeler that can hold up to 40,000 pounds. That would be a lot cheaper than sending 8000 five-pound packages via UPS or even USPS! Furthermore, the packages would arrive at the ADM the next day rather than at the consumer's doorstep five business days later. Customers might even pay a premium over the base service for the faster delivery."

"Wait a second," exclaimed Rob. "Did you say 8000 packages per night? I can't believe that Amazon, or any other retailer, ships that many packages to Boston each night!"

"I'm sure you're right that it's not 8000. I just used that number because it was the maximum capacity of the truck. I don't think any of us know what the real number would be, but my guess is that the economics of this model could break-even for a retailer at a reasonably low number of packages. At least I hope so," replied Tim.

After having pulled up some numbers from the web, Amir came to Tim's defense, "Land's End sold $1.6 billion last year; Amazon sold $2.2 billion, just in the United States. Even if the average order size is $100, that's a lot of shipments. And if the typical Amazon order is $50, which sounds right for the one book and two CDs that we were assuming earlier, the number of orders doubles.

"But, would that be enough to justify an investment of $1 million—just to serve Boston? It still isn't obvious to me that it is," Rob retorted.

Amir jumped up from his computer and exclaimed: It doesn't have to be enough. In fact, it's just a start. We can sell a whole host of products from the ADM like prepaid cell phones or stamps. ATM operators sell ads on their touch screens, so I don't see why we can't do the same. If our independent operator gets the right retailers on board—like a drug store chain—we could use the ADM to issue prescriptions or exchange film for developed pictures. No more waiting in line! The customers will love it. The increased foot traffic alone would probably justify the machine, particularly since ours can sit on a sidewalk or in the parking lot and not take up valuable retail floor space.

Nir Kinory weighed in: Amir has some good ideas, but I think we're missing some of the biggest lessons from our pilot in Germany. We now know that B2B deliveries offer even bigger profit margins than B2C. Surely, we can find some comparable opportunities in the United States. Maybe the 3PL we use for bulk delivery has some B2B service part deliveries that would benefit from ADMs.

Dan stepped in to regain control of the meeting: I'm glad that my advisory board and management team share such passion for our invention. Though there are questions, I think our discussion demonstrates that there may be merit in a one-city pilot. And, it sounds like we have a pretty good grasp of most of the drivers of the economics from what we've just talked about. Your intuition, Tim, that the savings potential for the delivery model alone is large enough to justify the investment may be right, but I think we need to run some numbers to prove our case. I'm particularly interested in determining which assumptions have the greatest impact on the economics of that model.

# References

Deutsche Post World Net, Annual Report 2001, Deutsche Post World Net Web site <http://investorrelations.dpwn.de/index_en.html>, accessed May 4, 2002.

Deutsche Post, Packstation Also Now for Private Customers, Deutsche Post Press Archive, January 4, 2002, <http://www.deutschepost.de/postagen/index.html?inhalt=/postagen/news/index_archiv.html>, accessed May 4, 2002.

Dr. Klaus Zumwinkel, Deutsche Post World Net in Transition, Pitney Bowes PostInsight Web site, March 26, 2001 <http://www.postinsight.pb.com/files/ZumwinkelText.pdf>, accessed May 4, 2002.

eShip, About Us/Management/Press Releases, eShip Web site, <http://www.eShip.com/html/about_us.html>, accessed May 2, 2002.

FedEx Launches New Home Delivery Service, FedEx Corporation Press Releases, <http://www.fedex.com/us/about>, accessed March 14, 2000.

Idealliance.org, Postal Service Presents "Transformation Plan" to Congress, <http://www
.idealliance.org/news/2002/ci0409.asp>, accessed April 9, 2002.

International Merchant Services, ATM Profitability Calculator, International Merchant
Services Web site, <http://www.atm24.com/anatomy/profitabilityCalculator.asp>
accessed May 1, 2002.

Jack Ewing, Pushing the envelope at Germany's post office, *BusinessWeek*, September 11,
2000. <http://www.businessweek.com/2000/00_37/b3698220.htm>, accessed May
4, 2002.

Jane Blake, Off-Premise ATMs: New Opportunities for Savvy Entrepreneurs,
ATMmarketplace.com News and Research section, <http://www.atmmarketplace
.com/research_story.htm?article_id=4960&pavilion=3>, accessed May 4, 2002.

Tim Laseter et al., The last mile to nowhere: Flaws & fallacies in Internet home-delivery
schemes. *strategy+business*, © 2000, Booz-Allen & Hamilton, p. 5.

## Chapter 13

# FreshDirect: Expansion Strategy*

Jason Ackerman, president and CEO of FreshDirect, tossed the copy of the *New York Times* article on the table and complained:

> I appreciate the free publicity, but yet another reporter just doesn't get it. There is no reason to compare us to Webvan or other dot-com grocers that closed down in 2001. We're not a "last mile" delivery business; we are a specialty producer selling directly to consumers. It's all about higher quality food at lower prices.

In 2003, FreshDirect had a customer base of 120,000, with 2500 more signing up each week, a retention rate of more than 64% and an average order size of $100. The company, with its 300,000-square-foot state-of-the-art processing facility, was located just outside Manhattan and had generated an operating profit a year ahead of schedule. FreshDirect had 30% to 40% gross margins that were higher than the industry average and was targeting revenues of $2 billion by 2007. Ackerman was confronting the key issue of capacity utilization when he started exploring new channels such as mail-order and institutional markets.

---

* With permission, this chapter presents the case "FreshDirect: Expansion Strategy" (Case number UVA-OM-1115) written by Debashish Chatterjee under the supervision of Timothy M. Laseter and published by the University of Virginia Darden Graduate School of Business.

# FreshDirect: Home Grocery Delivery

A la carte convenience may sound like an oxymoron to New York residents, but that is what FreshDirect aspired to provide. The company had been on track, hitting $90 million in revenues in its first year. With labor costs 60% lower than other gourmet grocery stores, and with a growing customer base, it had become profitable earlier than expected. FreshDirect was not another dot-com trying to make a business out of the Internet (see "What FreshDirect Learned from Dell," by Tim Laseter et al., *strategy+business*, issue 30). Like Webvan, FreshDirect accepted orders through the Internet for direct home delivery. But that is where the similarity ended. FreshDirect concentrated on offering fresh made-to-order food and treated home delivery as a necessary evil rather a key component of the value proposition. Customers could specify the thickness and size of a T-bone steak, choose the type of marinated sauce to go with it, instruct whether the whole fish was to be split or not, and even select the state of ripeness of tomatoes and other fruit. By ordering directly from farmers, dairies, beef processors, and dockside fish markets and completing the final processing on a made-to-order basis in its own facility, FreshDirect offered a fresher product with minimal spoilage. As such, FreshDirect took more inspiration from Dell than from Webvan.

About 74% of FreshDirect's sales came from perishables. It delivered fresher food than that offered by the local grocery stores and at a price about 25% to 30% lower. The elimination of middlemen suppliers helped reduce costs. FreshDirect also figured out how to largely eliminate the 8% to 30% spoilage of meat, fish, and produce experienced by traditional grocers due to shelf-life limits. By cutting, packaging, and baking according to individual orders, FreshDirect eliminated the waste of precut or prepackaged items that must be discounted before shelf-life limits expired and ultimately trashed after that limit was reached.

The Direct Business Model (Figure 13.1) gave FreshDirect significant advantages. By cutting out the middlemen, it ensured fresher food at lower prices. Ackerman did not think that the Internet provided any real competitive advantage. He used it only because it provided lower cost of access to consumers, unlike Webvan's founders who thought that they had a competitive advantage simply by being Internet based. In the fall of 2003, FreshDirect had 120,000 customers, and was adding 2500 new ones each week. The average order was about $100, and 78% of its customers had reordered. FreshDirect did not plan to offer continuous free delivery or delivery precision (same-day delivery within a half-hour time window) like Webvan. Delivery crews on its fleet of 23 trucks averaged 9 to 10 deliveries per hour (three times more than Webvan), based on two-hour appointment slots during evening and weekends hours to avoid the

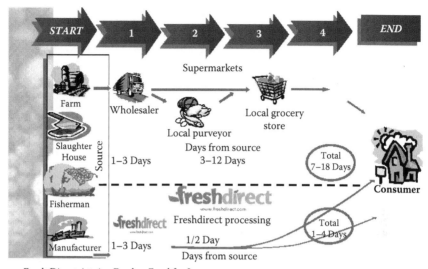

Fresh Direct Attains Fresher Food for Less
Source: Fresh Direct Corporate Presentation

**Figure 13.1   FreshDirect's supply chain.**

worst of New York City's traffic. The suburban model of delivery was different. Refrigerated trailers waited at aggregation points such as train stations and office parks, where customers could pull up on their way home from work and collect the groceries they had ordered.

Co-CEO Joseph Fedele, a 27-year veteran of the food business, claimed that FreshDirect had the "most automated plant in food processing." It resembled a gigantic restaurant kitchen occupied by more than 1000 people working in sweaters and coats from 1:00 a.m. to 7:00 a.m. who fulfilled 3500 orders each day by pulling orders off computers, cutting and packing the meat, bagging the produce, and then putting the orders in boxes. The plant was capable of processing 10,000 orders in a 10-hour shift, so there was room for growth.

FreshDirect's processing plant looked less like a distribution center and more like a manufacturing facility as it butchered meat from whole carcasses; made its own sausage; cut up entire salmon; roasted and ground coffee; baked bread, pastries, and desserts from scratch; ripened fruits and vegetables; and cooked meals. On average, FreshDirect's seafood department had about one day's worth of inventory, compared with the seven to nine days at the seafood counter of a well-run grocery store. The plant had 12 different temperature zones to cater to different requirements for each type of food. For instance, meat was cut in rooms cooled to 38 degrees to prevent bacterial contamination. Sanitary conditions were a top priority. Sophisticated software managed food deliveries and could pinpoint an order location to within 20 feet.

Unlike Webvan, which expanded rapidly in many cities, FreshDirect was following a methodical approach of expanding neighborhood-by-neighborhood in its sole market of New York City. The management team viewed flawless execution as critical to building a long-term, repeat-customer base with delivery proving to be the biggest challenge. Despite the desire for controlled growth, the excess capacity in critical processing areas such as the meat department troubled Ackerman:

> We are only using the equipment on one shift currently to meet our local delivery schedule.
>
> Furthermore, if we had more volume, we could invest in more automated equipment, which could further lower our processing cost. Although I am not sure about the other channel possibilities, it feels like a lost opportunity to me not to use our meat-processing capacity more fully. Maybe we could sell to local restaurants or ship steaks by mail like Omaha Steaks.

## Beef Industry Background

As the largest segment of U.S. agriculture, the beef industry provides more than 1 million jobs, including the farmers and ranchers who produce cattle; stocker operators; cattle feeders who bring the cattle to market weight; as well as hundreds of various allied industry partners like packers, transporters, and retailers. Cattle sales of $1 generates $5 in additional business activity. With around 100 million head, the United States has less than 10% of the world's cattle inventory, but it produces nearly 25% of the world's beef supply. Although the inventory of cattle has dropped steadily over the past decade, beef production continued to grow through 2002 thanks to the use of new breeds, computerization, and increased mechanization. The current trend shows a drop in beef production but a continued increase in retail sales due to rising prices (Table 13.1).

Consumers spent $65 billion on beef in 2002, and beef's share of total meat expenditures was 46.1% (pork, chicken, and turkey came next in that order). Per capita spending on beef was $213, which corresponded to 69.5 pounds on a retail weight basis. Steak is the single most popular beef dish, accounting for 14% of all in-home beef-eating occasions, while hamburger is second at 9%. According to ACNielsen, sales of prepared-beef items at supermarkets grew more than 67% in 2000, versus 1998 due to the growing number of new convenient beef items available on store shelves.

**Table 13.1  Cattle Numbers and Beef Production**

| Year | Total Cattle Inventory (thousands) | Cows (thousands) | Beef Production[a] (lb in millions) | Total Retail Value of Beef Consumed ($ in billions) |
|------|------|------|------|------|
| 1996 | 103,548 | 44,739 | 25,421 | 50.7 |
| 1997 | 101,656 | 43,776 | 25,420 | 50.1 |
| 1998 | 99,744 | 43,084 | 25,634 | 51 |
| 1999 | 99,115 | 42,878 | 26,400 | 54.6 |
| 2000 | 98,198 | 42,759 | 26,777 | 58.5 |
| 2001 | 97,277 | 42,590 | 26,108 | 63.9 |
| 2002 | 96,704 | 42,229 | 27,090 | 65.2 |
| 2003 | 96,100 | | 26,502 | |
| 2004 | 94,900 | | 25,780 | |

*Source:* USDA (past reports and forecasts).

[a] Carcass weight.

Several breed associations have attempted to market a branded product with their breed name on the package. In many cases, they have backed up the labels with extensive advertising programs. Many exotic breeds attempted to market "lite" beef with fewer calories and less fat. Other companies have introduced organic and "natural" beef products. Of the more than 200 companies that have tried to discover and exploit such niche markets, less than a dozen remained in business in the 1990s. The industry continues to search for ways to successfully brand beef, seeing it as a way to increase sales. The most successful branded product has been certified Angus beef. This brand features highly marbled Angus beef. Traditionally, beef prices increase in the spring and early summer months as retailers prepare to stock up for the "grilling-out" season.

Participants in the traditional beef supply chain include the producer, feedlot and slaughterhouse, packer, and the retailer (Figure 13.2). Although the relative mix of share of value varied dramatically from month to month due to the commodity pricing response of supply and demand imbalances, the industry appeared to have gone through a significant structural change over the past decade. The retailer's share reached a historically unprecedented level in excess

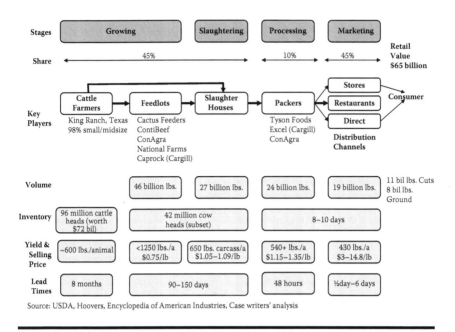

Figure 13.2 Beef Industry Supply chain.

of 45% in 2001 and seemed poised to remain well above the rates experienced at the beginning of the decade. During the 1990s, the packer's share had nearly doubled from a mere 5% to around 10% at the end of the decade. As a result, the producers' share had dropped precipitously from around 60% to less than 50% of beef's retail value as fed-cattle prices declined with the increasing supplies of market-ready cattle.

## Cattle Farmers

Producers—which include individual farmers and ranchers, farmers' cooperatives, and public and private corporations—breed and raise cattle. Tyson Foods, Inc., became the largest supplier of beef, poultry, and pork in 2001 when it acquired IBP, Inc. The combined company is expected to generate sales of $24.7 billion in 2004 (Standard & Poor's projections). Its competitors include ConAgra Foods, Inc., Pilgrim's Pride Corp., Cargill, Inc., Sanderson Farms, Inc., Smithfield Foods, Inc., and Hormel Foods Corp.

Most cattle farms are small, privately owned operations. The largest cattle ranch with a herd of 60,000 is the family-owned King Ranch in Texas, but around 85% of beef production comes from the one million independent U.S.

farms, each with fewer than 500 head of cattle. (In fact, 800,000 of the one million cattle farms have 50 or fewer head of cattle.) The sale of cattle and calves remains the largest segment of the American agricultural economy, and cattle-men own or manage more land than any other single industry. In the meadows of Montana or the irrigated pastures of California, one acre of land supports a cow and her calf for an entire year, while it may take hundreds of acres to pro-vide the same support in the deserts of the Southwest.

It is difficult to find a ranch in America today that will be profitable. Ranches are often priced according to cow/calf unit, which is the amount of land necessary to run a cow and her calf for one year. This calculation is used to figure the car-rying capacity of the land. Typically, a ranch today sells anywhere from $1500 to $3000 per cow/calf unit. Not surprisingly, farms often remain in the same family for multiple generations. Cattle farmers try to maintain an appropriate mix of breeding and commercial stock. The breeders typically give birth each spring to a single calf after a 9-month gestation period, and can be productive for breeding and nursing for 8 to 10 years. The average calf weighs between 80 and 85 pounds at birth and lives on a diet of grass and its mother's milk. The calves run beside their mothers until they are weaned at 6 to 8 months. At this age, the calves usually weigh between 500 and 550 pounds, although there are significant variations due to management and feed conditions. Weaned calves may continue to live in pastures or go straight into the feedlot for the final fin-ishing stage.

## Feedlots and Slaughterhouses

The early 2000s showed a continued trend toward larger feedlot operations despite a cloud of environmental suspicion regarding the damage caused by waste runoff, as well as the effect of growth hormones injected into cattle to promote quick weight gain. According to the United States Department of Agriculture (USDA), nearly 11 million cattle and calves were in large feedlots (10,000 head or more), being fattened for eventual slaughter at the beginning of April 2003. The mix was roughly two-thirds steer and one-third heifer, 70% of which could be found in three states: Texas (2.7 million), Kansas (2.3 million), and Nebraska (2.2 million). In these and other large cattle-feeding states, it is not uncommon to see feedlots capable of holding more than 100,000 head of cattle at any one time. In the mid-1960s, there were 200,000 feedlots scattered around the country, but today that figure has dropped by half.

Cactus Feeders of Amarillo, Texas, is ranked first among U.S. cattle feed-ers and owns feedlots with a capacity for 480,000 head of cattle. It reported revenues of $625 million in 2001. Capable of feeding 405,000 cattle at one time and marketing nearly one million fed cattle during the course of a year, ContiGroup's division, ContiBeef, runs the second-largest cattle feedlot operation in the nation. ConAgra Cattle Feeding of Greeley, Colorado, ranked third, owning four lots with a capacity for feeding 320,000 head. National Farms, Inc., of Kansas City, Missouri, ranked fourth, owning seven lots with a capacity for 274,000 head. Caprock Industries (a division of Cargill) of Amarillo, Texas, ranked fifth nationally among cattle-feeding businesses, owning four lots with a capacity for feeding 263,000 head of cattle. Today, the largest 2% (around 2000 feedlots) process 95% of the nation's total head of cattle.

Feedlots typically process young beef cattle for 110 to 150 days on a feed ration containing grain, by-products, and hay that gives American beef its unique taste known throughout the world. During this finishing period, a typical cow will go from a starting weight of 600 pounds up to a finished weight of 800 to 1250 pounds and yield a price from $600 to $900 per head.

## Packers

The colonial farmers of New England, who were the first meatpackers in the United States, used salt to preserve meat. As the nation expanded westward, slaughterhouses were built near population centers so meat could reach the table before it spoiled. For sanitary reasons, meatpacking operations could only be carried out during the cold winter months, with ice used for refrigeration. The development of mechanical refrigeration and refrigerated railroad cars in the second half of the nineteenth century changed all that. The twentieth century drove consolidation into large facilities with mechanized disassembly, conveyor procedures, sanitation systems, and packing methods that provided an advantage over the traditional small plants. Over the past two decades, the industry has simultaneously consolidated and relocated to the heartland. Slaughterhouses moved closer to the feedlots where the animals were raised to reduce the stress, weight loss, and injury during the long journeys in crowded cattle cars and trucks. Moving away from the urban areas with their highly skilled and generally unionized workers into the rural communities also offered the advantage of lower costs.

Since the mid-1980s, more than 405 packing plants have shut their doors, and three large corporations, Tyson, ConAgra, and Cargill, have controlled nearly 80% of the U.S. boxed-beef production. To be competitive, a packing house aims to process more than 500,000 head per year. Consider, for example, IBP, now part of Tyson. At the company's plant in Dakota City, Nebraska, animal carcasses are carried more than 20 miles of conveyor systems. Within 48 hours, a 650-pound carcass can be broken, cut, and packed into 65- to 80-pound boxes for shipment to supermarkets. The company continues to shift plants and production to areas that offer the most strategic advantage to the meat markets.

From the slaughter- and packinghouses, beef flows into one of three primary distribution channels. Nearly 70% of beef is sold through grocery stores, while about 29% reaches consumers through restaurant and institutional sales. A small percentage of less than 1% of beef is sold direct via mail order or over the Internet.

## Grocery Stores

Beef is still largely sold as a generic product in retail grocery stores, whereas chicken and pork are often sold as "branded" products with special packaging and attractive labels. Smaller players in the beef industry have launched many private-label brands with little success as the industry struggles to find an effective marketing approach. The meatpacking industry is concentrated in the hands of three major packers that have shown a reluctance to enter the branded-meat business, which will likely continue to hamper opportunities to expand the branding of beef. The decrease in the per capita consumption of beef over the past decade may have been, at least in part, driven by poor brand-marketing relative to the growth of the meat categories of pork and chicken.

According to the U.S. Census Bureau's Statistical Abstract, there were 163,000 grocery stores, including 24,600 supermarkets (defined as having at least $2.5 million in annual sales). In 2000, these supermarkets reported total annual sales of $453.8 billion. According to the 1999 *Food Marketing Industry Speaks*, the median number of supermarket items was 40,333.

Based on research conducted by ACNielsen, annual trips to the grocery store declined from an estimated 86 in 1998 to 75 in 2001, whereas annual trips to super centers, which merged the traditional grocery and discount store into one, increased from 14 to 18 during the same time interval. In the early 2000s, Wal-Mart passed traditional grocery chains to become the nation's leading grocer, with a 12% market share in 2002. The remainder of the grocery business was dominated by the multiunit and regional supermarket chains: Kroger, Albertsons, Safeway, A&P, Winn-Dixie, Supervalu, Publix, and Food Lion.

The meat department usually ranks second in volume of sales, amount of space occupied, number of items stocked, and total profit—the grocery department ranking first in all these areas. Compared to the grocery department, however, the meat department has a higher gross profit along with higher expenses. This department is important because store loyalty can be built and retained by an outstanding meat department. Family meals are often built around a meat dish, the success of which is judged by the meat's flavor and tenderness.

Although meat is usually broken down into progressively smaller cuts as it moves from the producer to the consumer, there has been a move away from processing meat inside the supermarket toward a model of central processing plants. Central processing can ensure uniformity of quality, improve bacteria control, and reduce shrinkage while simultaneously reducing space and training needs at the store. Meat department employees can now have more time for personal contact with customers to help them with tips on meat preparation, cooking, and serving. There are objections to this move, however, as jobs get eliminated at the store. Another effect is that the industrywide breaking and trimming of meat standardizes cuts, thereby reducing the store's ability to customize.

Beef is the largest single-product category in the meat department; its sales volume is more than that of any other single-product category in the entire supermarket. It accounts for about one-third of the dollar sales in its own department and close to 8% of the supermarket's total dollar sales. This volume has resulted in beef being the basis for many of the day-to-day promotions at the supermarket.

## Restaurants

The biggest companies operating eating places include those operating single-concept chains, like McDonald's, which recorded total sales of $15.4 billion in 2002. According to analysts, at least 96% of Americans between the ages of 16 and 65 have eaten at one of the 30,000 McDonald's restaurants worldwide. Burger King is the second-largest restaurant chain with sales of $1.7 billion in 2002. In 1999, Burger King served nearly 1.6 billion Whoppers and received more than 14 million customers daily. Other major chain operations such as Applebee's, T.G.I. Friday's, Ruby Tuesdays, and The Outback forgo the self-service model of fast food in favor of a "casual dining" format with waitstaff, alcoholic beverage service, and higher-than-average pricing.

While the megachains have national-brand recognition, the industry is actually quite fragmented. According to the National Restaurant Association, in 2003, there were more than 870,000 restaurants in the United States with sales totaling $426 billion. More than 70% were independent, single-unit businesses with fewer than 20 employees. According to the National Restaurant Association in 2000, a full-service food-and-drink establishment had average annual revenues of $650,000, and a fast-food restaurant took in an annual average of $585,000, roughly 28% of which was cost of goods sold.

# Direct Retail: Omaha Steaks

Omaha Steaks ranks as the nation's largest direct marketer of steaks and other frozen gourmet foods with sales of $325 million and more than 1.5 million customers worldwide. The company manufactures, markets, and distributes a wide variety of premium steaks, red meats, and other gourmet foods. These products are custom cut and packaged to serve the needs of various markets. A family business since its founding in 1917, Omaha Steaks has grown into a major entity employing more than 1800 employees (Figure 13.3). Headquartered in Omaha, Nebraska, its facilities include two manufacturing plants, a distribution center, and a freezer warehouse. In 1999, Omaha Steaks opened new corporate and marketing offices adjacent to its expanded telemarketing facility.

Markets nationwide and overseas include food service, mail-order, incentive, telesales, retail stores, licensed-restaurants sales to specialty and food stores, and interactive sales. Omahasteaks.com was founded as a separate company to provide more comprehensive service and an incredible shopping experience for their customers. The brand, Omaha Steaks, has been promoted and advertised for 35 years and is positioned as the ultimate in superb service and quality.

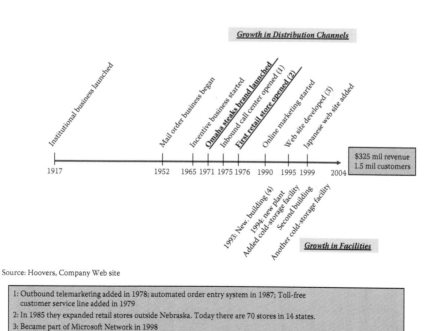

Source: Hoovers, Company Web site

1: Outbound telemarketing added in 1978; automated order entry system in 1987; Toll-free customer service line added in 1979
2: In 1985 they expanded retail stores outside Nebraska. Today there are 70 stores in 14 states.
3: Became part of Microsoft Network in 1998
4: 60,000 sq ft Building to house Marketing, HR, IT and Call Center (Same size new building in 1999)

**Figure 13.3  Omaha Steaks history.**

## *Production*

By 1990, it became clear there was no more room at the Omaha Steaks plant. A building was purchased in South Omaha and transformed into a distribution center. Huge consumer demand for Omaha Steaks persuaded the company to open a new plant in Snyder, Nebraska, in 1994. To support sales growth, the company purchased one cold-storage facility in 1998 and another in 2000.

Concern for food safety and plant sanitation pervades the manufacturing processes. Testing frequency and standards are maintained that exceed the levels demanded by the USDA. During the explosive growth of the 1980s and 1990s, the company expanded all its facilities, including production, administration, and marketing. In 1993, it completed a 60,000-square-foot building in Omaha to house the call center, marketing, human resources, and information technology departments. In 1999, it completed another building of the same size.

## *Shipping*

Omaha Steak's standard shipping method delivers packages within seven business days or less from the day the order is received. The company currently uses UPS and FedEx for delivery. These delivery companies can leave a package at the front door so one does not have to be home to receive a package. Express and overnight delivery options are also offered. Products are shipped in a polystyrene cooler packed with dry ice to ensure that the meat arrives frozen and in perfect condition.

## Direct Retail: Online Grocer

In early 2003, there were only a few names remaining in the online grocery sector, but regional bricks-and-mortar grocery stores were preparing to try their luck with the Internet. Surprisingly, Peapod weathered the storm of dot-com failures and remained open for business, thanks to investment by the Netherlands retailer Royal Ahold. Albertson's opened online outlets in the Seattle and San Diego areas. Using existing stores and employees to fill orders, the company slowly created a profitable niche for itself. Publix Supermarkets also launched an online shopping option based in the southeastern states. In August 2002, Vons began offering online shopping in Southern California. The chain's parent company, Safeway, already offered the service in Northern California and Oregon. All of these enterprises worked in conjunction with bricks-and-mortar partners, thus eliminating the need for costly warehouse construction.

Tesco, a British grocer, also met with good fortune online. A top supermarket chain in the United Kingdom, Tesco used the hybrid model of online ordering and order fulfillment through its traditional grocery stores. Some analysts attributed Tesco's success to the thickly populated London landscape. Delivery people were able to complete seven or eight drop-offs an hour due to the close proximity of London homes. This situation contrasted with the typical U.S. market where drivers face extensive suburbs and commuter traffic, limiting their deliveries to three or four an hour. In the early 2000s, Tesco did not believe the United States was a lost cause in the online grocery industry, and so, in June 2001, formed a partnership with Safeway and its online arm, Groceryworks.com.

## Farm to Fork: Supply Chain Coordination

Most companies involved in the beef industry tended to agree that one "stage" of the beef industry value chain always seemed to temporarily benefit at the expense of another. With the current system, when beef prices increased, feedlot owners benefited because they marketed more "finished" animals. When there were too many cattle on the market, the beef producer was pressured to lower prices while the slaughter plants realized high profit margins due to an inelastic supply curve for beef at the farm level. The industry was trying to find a better way to organize beef production and sales from "conception to consumption" so that everyone involved benefited from taking the risks of production in the increasingly volatile global beef market. Increased vertical integration and quality-based pricing structure appeared the most likely paths forward. The beef industry was under increased competitive pressure from the pork and poultry industries. Both the pork and poultry industries—which had significantly increased their shares of the meat market in recent years—were heavily vertically integrated.

## A Question of Priorities

Jason Ackerman thought about the potential channels of expansion that competitor Omaha Steaks had used and pondered the options for FreshDirect. He looked at the history of leading mail-order houses of the 1980s, which showed that Omaha Steaks had grown from a worth of $25 million to $325 million in 20 years. Mail order had low barriers to entry and required limited capital investment. Customers had been buying various foods in the past by mail for a variety of reasons, including convenience, lower prices, or simply the novelty.

On the other hand, the institutional segment was worth $11 billion in New York City alone, including corporate meeting planners, caterers, and hotels. In such a large market, FreshDirect's goal of $500 million with the current capacity seemed plausible, but it required building relationships and setting up a sales organization. Which path would best leverage the operations strategy of FreshDirect?

# Chapter 14

# Musictoday, LLC: Managing Inventory for Night Train*

On a frosty morning in January 2004, Jack Murphy sat at his desk and thought about how he could get his client Night Train back on track. Murphy was vice president of operations for Musictoday, a provider of e-commerce, ticketing, and merchandising services to the music industry. For a wide variety of artists, Musictoday sold tickets to live events, built custom Internet stores, and fulfilled orders for merchandise, including CDs, T-shirts, hats, posters, and stickers (see Figure 14.1 for representative items). Musictoday also packed and shipped those orders from an inventory that the company stocked in its warehouse located in Charlottesville, Virginia.

Although the band Night Train was a relatively small client for Musictoday, the company liked to provide a high level of service to all of its clients. Over the previous few months, during the peak of the holiday season, Musictoday had stocked out of Night Train inventory during critical sales periods and had thus lost important revenue opportunities. At the same time, Murphy found

---

* With permission, this chapter presents the case "MusicToday LLC: Managing Inventory for Night Train" (Case Number UVA-OM-1204), written by Jay Ashton and Vincent Gu, under the supervision of Timothy Laseter, and published by the University of Virginia Darden Graduate School of Business. A multimedia version of the case is available from Darden Business Publishing.

Hat from the Rolling Stones

CD from the artist Mike Doughty

T-shirt from the artist Moby

Guitar tablature book from the band Evanescence

Key chain from the Blue Man Group

**Figure 14.1   Sample artist merchandise sold by Musictoday, LLC.**

that the replenishment-order quantities had varied dramatically, oftentimes with small expedited receipts from certain suppliers that probably cost Musictoday a premium to process. These wide swings in ordering may have been due to the informal way that Musictoday buyers operated, but it might also have been due to the involvement of the artists. Although Musictoday placed some orders directly to the CD distributors and promotional-products companies, at other times, the buyers simply forwarded a recommended order quantity to the artists who then placed the order with the supplier for shipment to Musictoday's fulfillment center.

Although stock-outs were terribly disappointing to clients, lost sales were even more painful to Musictoday's own operation. While artists captured the majority of their value through CD sales and touring, Musictoday's main source of revenue was merchandise sales. Worse still, any extra costs of receiving expedited orders directly hit Musictoday's bottom line because the company received a fixed percentage of merchandise sales revenue as its fee. Murphy realized that improving his inventory-planning process was critical to Musictoday's long-term success, and that it was now time to tackle this problem.

## From One Band to Many

The roots of Musictoday trace back to the early days of the Dave Matthews Band, when the band's manager began selling T-shirts at small venues in and around Charlottesville. As the band grew into a successful national act, the merchandising operation grew into a multimillion-dollar business. Musictoday was formed in 1998 when the manager of the Dave Matthews Band merged his web services company, Red Light Communications, with his merchandise-fulfillment operation, MMF.

Once formed, Musictoday quickly began attracting the business of some of the best-known and most successful artists in the industry. As the company scaled up its operation, it began to offer a comprehensive merchandising solution to its clients. Not only did the company stock, handle, and manage inventory for clients, it also built custom commerce-enabled Internet sites for the artists. Thus, from inventory management to the point-of-sale and finally to the pick-pack-ship operation, Musictoday offered a compelling solution to any artist who wanted to sell merchandise without the hassle of managing an online merchandising operation.

This value proposition helped Musictoday grow into a leading merchandise service and sales operation for the music industry. Clients included a wide range of artists such as the Rolling Stones, Eminem, Dave Matthews Band, Metallica, Dixie Chicks, the Grateful Dead, O.A.R., Particle, and Jason Mraz, along with many smaller but promising artists like David Gray, DJ Logic, and Soundtribe Sector 9.

Musictoday stocked artist merchandise at their 50,000-square-foot warehouse in Charlottesville. Most of the merchandise was sold on consignment for their clients, which meant that the artists maintained ownership of the merchandise until it reached the consumer. When orders were received from Musictoday's e-commerce operation, Murphy's fulfillment division was responsible for the pick-pack-ship operation, picking the order items from inventory, packing the order for delivery, and shipping the order via the selected carrier. Orders for items that were in stock were normally shipped within 24 hours via the U.S. Postal Service (USPS). Express orders received by 3:00 p.m. were shipped out the same day via expedited shipping. Each evening, large USPS and United Parcel Service trucks would pull up to Musictoday's docks to receive the processed orders and send them on their way.

## The Problems of Success

Musictoday's rapid growth into a full-service merchandise operation was spectacular by any standard. Between 1998 and 2003, the number of clients for which Musictoday stocked and sold merchandise grew by a compounded annual rate of 66%* (see Figure 14.2 for data showing Musictoday's growth).

In addition to lining up an ever-expanding list of big-name clients, Musictoday also experienced significant increases in both the number of merchandise items offered for sale and, accordingly, sales revenues. Over the 5-year period leading up to 2003, revenue from Musictoday's merchandising operation grew at a compounded annual rate of 52%. Moreover, between 2001 and 2003, the number of merchandise orders that Murphy's operation was handling grew at a compounded annual rate of 43%.

By 2003, Musictoday was processing approximately 1500 orders on an average day, and the system it had built was beginning to experience some growing pains. While an average day saw significant volume, it was the cycle peaks that truly strained the operation. Merchandise sales experienced two major cycles. The first cycle occurred during the holiday sales season, when orders during the fourth quarter jumped fairly dramatically. While this holiday sales cycle was not exclusive to the music industry, Musictoday's other sales cycle was not experienced by other retailers. It was during the summer months, when college students were on vacation and many bands touring, that merchandise sales experienced another significant lift.

## Getting the Train Back on Track

Murphy wasn't quite sure how to begin tackling the stock-out problem that had plagued Night Train over the previous holiday season. He decided early on that his first goal should be to determine a reorder point for every Night Train SKU[†] stocked by Musictoday to avoid missing sales revenue due to stock-outs without

---

\* All primary growth data were gathered by telephone interview from a Musictoday executive on April 20, 2004. Certain data has been disguised.

† Stockkeeping unit: Term used by retailers to identify an individual item at the lowest level of product detail.

**Number of Merchandise Clients: 1998–2003**

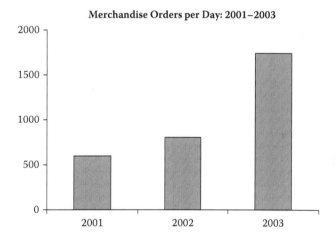

**Merchandise Orders per Day: 2001–2003**

**Figure 14.2    Growth at Musictoday, LLC.**

incurring needless costs. Murphy wasn't quite sure what would be an appropriate service level. He also wasn't convinced that the service level should be the same across all product categories. As an initial target, however, Murphy felt that Musictoday should have all Night Train merchandise in stock and available for sale at least 90% of the time. After running his initial analysis, he decided that he could look at how adjustments to the service level would affect his safety stock levels and ultimately his costs.

Murphy next thought about the most important factors that would influence his safety stock inventory levels. To get started, he gathered data on Night Train SKUs from the past 52 weeks (see Figure 14.3). The historical

**Demand for Night Train Products in 2003**

| Item Number | Item Description | Week Ending Date | | | | | | | | | | | | | Q1 2003 Sales |
|---|---|---|---|---|---|---|---|---|---|---|---|---|---|---|---|
| | | 5-Jan | 12-Jan | 19-Jan | 26-Jan | 2-Feb | 9-Feb | 16-Feb | 23-Feb | 2-Mar | 9-Mar | 16-Mar | 23-Mar | 30-Mar | |
| NTCD06 | NT Yankee Hotel Foxtrot CD | 577 | 644 | 514 | 480 | 351 | 534 | 508 | 380 | 666 | 230 | 260 | 608 | 387 | 6,139 |
| NTCH01TBBK | NT Black Toboggan Hat | 56 | 37 | 46 | 94 | 71 | 57 | 69 | 62 | 74 | 43 | 65 | 57 | 83 | 814 |
| NTCT08SXWH | NT Moon Buggy T-shirt SS White | 184 | 130 | 180 | 102 | 119 | 188 | 74 | 98 | 89 | 163 | 84 | 147 | 101 | 1,659 |
| NTCT10SXWH | NT Farm Wheel Ringer T-shirt SS White | 37 | 78 | 79 | 53 | 44 | 69 | 43 | 66 | 76 | 35 | 87 | 55 | 78 | 800 |
| NTCD12 | NT Farm Wheel Rolls CD | 360 | 351 | 289 | 236 | 184 | 137 | 199 | 187 | 255 | 305 | 187 | 329 | 162 | 3,181 |
| NTCT26SXGT | NT Old School Logo T-shirt SS Granite | 138 | 93 | 151 | 103 | 115 | 93 | 122 | 125 | 68 | 58 | 109 | 72 | 146 | 1,393 |

**Receipts of Night Train Products in 2003**

| Item Number | Item Description | 5-Jan | 12-Jan | 19-Jan | 26-Jan | 2-Feb | 9-Feb | 16-Feb | 23-Feb | 2-Mar | 9-Mar | 16-Mar | 23-Mar | 30-Mar | Q1 2003 Sales |
|---|---|---|---|---|---|---|---|---|---|---|---|---|---|---|---|
| NTCD06 | NT Yankee Hotel Foxtrot CD | 1,000 | | | 5,000 | | | | | | | | | 2,000 | 8,000 |
| NTCH01TBBK | NT Black Toboggan Hat | | 500 | | | | | | | | 250 | | | | 750 |
| NTCT08SXWH | NT Moon Buggy T-shirt SS White | | | | | | 500 | | | 2,000 | | | | | 2,500 |
| NTCT10SXWH | NT Farm Wheel Ringer T-shirt SS White | | | | 500 | | | | | | | | | | 500 |
| NTCD12 | NT Farm Wheel Rolls CD | | | | | | 1,000 | | | | | | | | 1,000 |

| NTCT26SXGT | NT Old School Logo T-shirt SS Granite | | | | | | | 500 | | | | | | | 500 |
|---|---|---|---|---|---|---|---|---|---|---|---|---|---|---|---|

*Week Ending Inventory of Night Train Products in 2003*

| Item Number | Item Description | 5-Jan | 12-Jan | 19-Jan | 26-Jan | 2-Feb | 9-Feb | 16-Feb | 23-Feb | 2-Mar | 9-Mar | 16-Mar | 23-Mar | 30-Mar | Q1 2003 Sales |
|---|---|---|---|---|---|---|---|---|---|---|---|---|---|---|---|
| NTCD06 | NT Yankee Hotel Foxtrot CD | 988 | 344 | (170) | 4,350 | 3,999 | 3,465 | 2,957 | 2,577 | 1,911 | 1,681 | 1,421 | 813 | 2,426 | 1,438 |
| NTCH01TBBK | NT Black Toboggan Hat | 297 | 760 | 714 | 620 | 549 | 492 | 423 | 361 | 287 | 494 | 429 | 372 | 289 | (8) |
| NTCT08SXWH | NT Moon Buggy T-shirt SS White | 360 | 230 | 50 | (52) | (171) | 141 | 67 | (31) | 1,880 | 1,717 | 1,633 | 1,486 | 1,385 | 1,025 |
| NTCT10SXWH | NT Farm Wheel Ringer T-shirt SS White | 2,451 | 2,373 | 2,294 | 2,741 | 2,697 | 2,628 | 2,585 | 2,519 | 2,443 | 2,408 | 2,321 | 2,266 | 2,188 | (263) |
| NTCD12 | NT Farm Wheel Rolls CD | 4,309 | 3,958 | 3,669 | 3,433 | 3,429 | 4,112 | 3,913 | 3,726 | 3,471 | 3,166 | 2,979 | 2,650 | 2,488 | (1,821) |
| NTCT26SXGT | NT Old School Logo T-shirt SS Granite | 1,584 | 1,491 | 1,340 | 1,237 | 1,122 | 1,029 | 1,407 | 1,282 | 1,214 | 1,156 | 1,047 | 975 | 829 | (755) |

**Figure 14.3   First quarter 2003 sales, receipts, and inventory data for Night Train merchandise. (continued)**

*Demand for Night Train Products in 2003*

| Item Number | Item Description | 6-Apr | 13-Apr | 20-Apr | 27-Apr | 4-May | 11-May | 18-May | 25-May | 1-Jun | 8-Jun | 15-Jun | 22-Jun | 29-Jun | Q2 2003 Sales |
|---|---|---|---|---|---|---|---|---|---|---|---|---|---|---|---|
| NTCD06 | NT Yankee Hotel Foxtrot CD | 234 | 377 | 423 | 245 | 543 | 457 | 436 | 329 | 942 | 1,410 | 1,278 | 1,568 | 1,281 | 9,523 |
| NTCH01TBBK | NT Black Toboggan Hat | 38 | 49 | 93 | 80 | 38 | 81 | 36 | 49 | 155 | 173 | 168 | 171 | 196 | 1,327 |
| NTCT08SXWH | NT Moon Buggy T-shirt SS White | 82 | 139 | 105 | 128 | 76 | 107 | 149 | 138 | 198 | 350 | 450 | 393 | 416 | 2,731 |
| NTCT10SXWH | NT Farm Wheel Ringer T-shirt SS White | 74 | 51 | 88 | 48 | 68 | 43 | 88 | 66 | 127 | 168 | 178 | 190 | 196 | 1,385 |
| NTCD12 | NT Farm Wheel Rolls CD | 333 | 144 | 330 | 327 | 332 | 204 | 358 | 237 | 371 | 734 | 721 | 707 | 727 | 5,525 |
| NTCT26SXGT | NT Old School Logo T-shirt SS Granite | 72 | 102 | 115 | 74 | 144 | 73 | 87 | 104 | 271 | 291 | 385 | 390 | 300 | 2,408 |

*Receipts of Night Train Products in 2003*

| Item Number | Item Description | 6-Apr | 13-Apr | 20-Apr | 27-Apr | 4-May | 11-May | 18-May | 25-May | 1-Jun | 8-Jun | 15-Jun | 22-Jun | 29-Jun | Q2 2003 Receipts |
|---|---|---|---|---|---|---|---|---|---|---|---|---|---|---|---|
| NTCD06 | NT Yankee Hotel Foxtrot CD | | | | | | | | 5,000 | | | | | 2,000 | 7,000 |
| NTCH01TBBK | NT Black Toboggan Hat | | | | | 1,000 | | | | | 500 | | | | 1,500 |
| NTCT08SXWH | NT Moon Buggy T-shirt SS White | | | | | | | | | 2,000 | | | | | 2,000 |
| NTCT10SXWH | NT Farm Wheel Ringer T-shirt SS White | | | | | | | | | | | | | | — |
| NTCD12 | NT Farm Wheel Rolls CD | | | 1,000 | | | | | | | 1,000 | | 1,000 | | 3,000 |

| Item Number | Item Description | 6-Apr | 13-Apr | 20-Apr | 27-Apr | 4-May | 11-May | 18-May | 25-May | 1-Jun | 8-Jun | 15-Jun | 22-Jun | 29-Jun | Q2 Inventory Change |
|---|---|---|---|---|---|---|---|---|---|---|---|---|---|---|---|
| NTCT26SXGT | NT Old School Logo T-shirt SS Granite | | | | | | | 500 | | | | 500 | 500 | 500 | 2,000 |
| *Week Ending Inventory of Night Train Products in 2003* | | | | | | | | | | | | | | | |
| NTCD06 | NT Yankee Hotel Foxtrot CD | 2,192 | 1,815 | 1,392 | 1,147 | 604 | 147 | (289) | 4,382 | 3,440 | 2,030 | 752 | (816) | (97) | (2,289) |
| NTCH01TBBK | NT Black Toboggan Hat | 251 | 202 | 109 | 29 | 991 | 910 | 874 | 825 | 670 | 997 | 829 | 658 | 462 | 211 |
| NTCT08SXWH | NT Moon Buggy T-shirt SS White | 1,303 | 1,164 | 1,059 | 931 | 855 | 748 | 599 | 461 | 2,263 | 1,913 | 1,463 | 1,070 | 654 | (649) |
| NTCT10SXWH | NT Farm Wheel Ringer T-shirt SS White | 2,114 | 2,063 | 1,975 | 1,927 | 1,859 | 1,816 | 1,728 | 1,662 | 1,535 | 1,367 | 1,189 | 999 | 803 | (1,311) |
| NTCD12 | NT Farm Wheel Rolls CD | 2,155 | 2,011 | 2,681 | 2,354 | 2,022 | 1,818 | 1,460 | 1,223 | 852 | 1,118 | 397 | 690 | (37) | (2,192) |
| NTCT26SXGT | NT Old School Logo T-shirt SS Granite | 757 | 655 | 540 | 466 | 322 | 249 | 662 | 558 | 287 | (4) | 111 | 221 | 421 | (336) |

**Figure 14.3    (continued) Second quarter 2003 sales, receipts, and inventory data for Night Train merchandise.**

**Demand for Night Train Products in 2003**

| Item Number | Item Description | 6-Jul | 13-Jul | 20-Jul | 27-Jul | 3-Aug | 10-Aug | 17-Aug | 24-Aug | 31-Aug | 7-Sep | 14-Sep | 21-Sep | 28-Sep | Q3 2003 Sales |
|---|---|---|---|---|---|---|---|---|---|---|---|---|---|---|---|
| NTCD06 | NT Yankee Hotel Foxtrot CD | 1,159 | 1,165 | 1,562 | 1,327 | 1,532 | 1,434 | 1,408 | 1,265 | 819 | 288 | 394 | 552 | 427 | 13,332 |
| NTCH01TBBK | NT Black Toboggan Hat | 220 | 172 | 214 | 215 | 184 | 216 | 214 | 162 | 105 | 42 | 36 | 37 | 40 | 1,857 |
| NTCT08SXWH | NT Moon Buggy T-shirt SS White | 328 | 404 | 327 | 448 | 387 | 355 | 403 | 338 | 288 | 130 | 111 | 132 | 191 | 3,842 |
| NTCT10SXWH | NT Farm Wheel Ringer T-shirt SS White | 163 | 190 | 176 | 160 | 203 | 191 | 169 | 174 | 95 | 56 | 83 | 47 | 75 | 1,782 |
| NTCD12 | NT Farm Wheel Rolls CD | 662 | 725 | 729 | 852 | 777 | 613 | 661 | 710 | 453 | 265 | 347 | 159 | 297 | 7,250 |
| NTCT26SXGT | NT Old School Logo T-shirt SS Granite | 389 | 330 | 393 | 380 | 346 | 360 | 339 | 296 | 255 | 114 | 107 | 118 | 141 | 3,568 |

**Receipts of Night Train Products in 2003**

| Item Number | Item Description | 6-Jul | 13-Jul | 20-Jul | 27-Jul | 3-Aug | 10-Aug | 17-Aug | 24-Aug | 31-Aug | 7-Sep | 14-Sep | 21-Sep | 28-Sep | Q3 2003 Receipts |
|---|---|---|---|---|---|---|---|---|---|---|---|---|---|---|---|
| NTCD06 | NT Yankee Hotel Foxtrot CD | 2,000 | 2,000 | 3,000 | 3,000 | 1,000 | 1,000 | 1,000 | 5,000 | 3,000 | | | | 2,000 | 16,000 |
| NTCH01TBBK | NT Black Toboggan Hat | | | | 1,000 | | | 500 | | | 500 | | | | 2,000 |
| NTCT08SXWH | NT Moon Buggy T-shirt SS White | | | 2,000 | | | | | 2,000 | | | | | | 4,000 |
| NTCT10SXWH | NT Farm Wheel Ringer T-shirt SS White | 250 | | | | | | 500 | | | | 500 | | | 1,250 |
| NTCD12 | NT Farm Wheel Rolls CD | 2,000 | | 1,000 | | 1,000 | 1,000 | | 5,000 | | | | | | 10,000 |

| Item Number | Item Description | 6-Jul | 13-Jul | 20-Jul | 27-Jul | 3-Aug | 10-Aug | 17-Aug | 24-Aug | 31-Aug | 7-Sep | 14-Sep | 21-Sep | 28-Sep | Q3 Inventory Change |
|---|---|---|---|---|---|---|---|---|---|---|---|---|---|---|---|
| NTCT26SXGT | NT Old School Logo T-shirt SS Granite | 500 | 500 | 500 | 500 | | | 500 | | 500 | | | | 500 | 3,500 |

Week Ending Inventory of Night Train Products in 2003

| Item Number | Item Description | 6-Jul | 13-Jul | 20-Jul | 27-Jul | 3-Aug | 10-Aug | 17-Aug | 24-Aug | 31-Aug | 7-Sep | 14-Sep | 21-Sep | 28-Sep | Q3 Inventory Change |
|---|---|---|---|---|---|---|---|---|---|---|---|---|---|---|---|
| NTCD06 | NT Yankee Hotel Foxtrot CD | 744 | 1,579 | 3,017 | 4,690 | 4,158 | 3,724 | 3,316 | 2,051 | 4,232 | 3,944 | 3,550 | 2,998 | 2,571 | 1,827 |
| NTCH01TBBK | NT Black Toboggan Hat | 242 | 70 | (144) | 641 | 457 | 241 | 527 | 365 | 260 | 718 | 682 | 645 | 605 | 363 |
| NTCT08SXWH | NT Moon Buggy T-shirt SS White | 326 | (78) | 1,595 | 1,147 | 760 | 405 | 2 | 1,664 | 1,376 | 1,246 | 1,135 | 1,003 | 812 | 486 |
| NTCT10SXWH | NT Farm Wheel Ringer T-shirt SS White | 890 | 700 | 524 | 364 | 161 | (30) | 301 | 127 | 32 | (24) | 393 | 346 | 271 | (619) |
| NTCD12 | NT Farm Wheel Rolls CD | 1,301 | 576 | 847 | (5) | 218 | 605 | (56) | 4,234 | 3,781 | 3,516 | 3,169 | 3,010 | 2,713 | 1,412 |
| NTCT26SXGT | NT Old School Logo T-shirt SS Granite | 532 | 702 | 809 | 929 | 583 | 223 | 384 | 88 | 333 | 219 | 112 | (6) | 353 | (179) |

**Figure 14.3  (continued) Third quarter 2003 sales, receipts, and inventory data for Night Train merchandise.**

Demand for Night Train Products in 2003

| Item Number | Item Description | 5-Oct | 12-Oct | 19-Oct | 26-Oct | 2-Nov | 9-Nov | 16-Nov | 23-Nov | 30-Nov | 7-Dec | 14-Dec | 21-Dec | 28-Dec | Q4 2003 Sales |
|---|---|---|---|---|---|---|---|---|---|---|---|---|---|---|---|
| NTCD06 | NT Yankee Hotel Foxtrot CD | 535 | 407 | 429 | 481 | 559 | 343 | 1,066 | 1,413 | 1,699 | 2,131 | 2,713 | 2,125 | 1,948 | 15,849 |
| NTCH01TBBK | NT Black Toboggan Hat | 64 | 45 | 44 | 51 | 88 | 80 | 123 | 175 | 233 | 337 | 348 | 314 | 239 | 2,141 |
| NTCT08SXWH | NT Moon Buggy T-shirt SS White | 195 | 139 | 168 | 160 | 80 | 184 | 224 | 442 | 580 | 647 | 723 | 618 | 544 | 4,704 |
| NTCT10SXWH | NT Farm Wheel Ringer T-shirt SS White | 74 | 46 | 31 | 82 | 36 | 60 | 116 | 202 | 218 | 283 | 372 | 294 | 237 | 2,051 |
| NTCD12 | NT Farm Wheel Rolls CD | 193 | 155 | 168 | 142 | 286 | 215 | 542 | 662 | 1,090 | 1,330 | 1,539 | 1,255 | 901 | 8,478 |
| NTCT26SXGT | NT Old School Logo T-shirt SS Granite | 113 | 114 | 137 | 142 | 110 | 158 | 256 | 324 | 424 | 521 | 713 | 604 | 416 | 4,032 |

Receipts of Night Train Products in 2003

| Item Number | Item Description | 5-Oct | 12-Oct | 19-Oct | 26-Oct | 2-Nov | 9-Nov | 16-Nov | 23-Nov | 30-Nov | 7-Dec | 14-Dec | 21-Dec | 28-Dec | Q4 2003 Receipts |
|---|---|---|---|---|---|---|---|---|---|---|---|---|---|---|---|
| NTCD06 | NT Yankee Hotel Foxtrot CD | | 5,000 | | | 3,000 | 3,000 | 3,000 | 3,000 | | | | | | 17,000 |
| NTCH01TBBK | NT Black Toboggan Hat | 250 | | | | 500 | | | | 500 | | | 500 | 500 | 2,250 |
| NTCT08SXWH | NT Moon Buggy T-shirt SS White | | | | | | 2,000 | | | | 2,000 | | | | 4,000 |
| NTCT10SXWH | NT Farm Wheel Ringer T-shirt SS White | 500 | | | 500 | | | | | | 250 | 500 | 500 | 500 | 2,750 |
| NTCD12 | NT Farm Wheel Rolls CD | | | | | | | | | 1,000 | 1,000 | 2,000 | 2,000 | 4,000 | 10,000 |

| Item Number | Item Description | 5-Oct | 12-Oct | 19-Oct | 26-Oct | 2-Nov | 9-Nov | 16-Nov | 23-Nov | 30-Nov | 7-Dec | 14-Dec | 21-Dec | 28-Dec | Q4 Inventory Change |
|---|---|---|---|---|---|---|---|---|---|---|---|---|---|---|---|
| NTCT26SXGT | NT Old School Logo T-shirt SS Granite | | | 500 | | | | 500 | 500 | | 500 | 1,000 | 2,000 | 1,000 | 6,000 |

Week Ending Inventory of Night Train Products in 2003

| Item Number | Item Description | 5-Oct | 12-Oct | 19-Oct | 26-Oct | 2-Nov | 9-Nov | 16-Nov | 23-Nov | 30-Nov | 7-Dec | 14-Dec | 21-Dec | 28-Dec | Q4 Inventory Change |
|---|---|---|---|---|---|---|---|---|---|---|---|---|---|---|---|
| NTCD06 | NT Yankee Hotel Foxtrot CD | 2,036 | 6,629 | 6,200 | 5,719 | 8,160 | 10,817 | 12,751 | 14,338 | 12,639 | 10,508 | 7,795 | 5,670 | 3,722 | 1,686 |
| NTCH01TBBK | NT Black Toboggan Hat | 791 | 746 | 702 | 651 | 1,063 | 983 | 860 | 685 | 952 | 615 | 267 | 453 | 714 | (77) |
| NTCT08SXWH | NT Moon Buggy T-shirt SS White | 617 | 478 | 310 | 150 | 70 | 1,886 | 1,662 | 1,220 | 640 | 1,993 | 1,270 | 652 | 108 | (509) |
| NTCT10SXWH | NT Farm Wheel Ringer T-shirt SS White | 697 | 651 | 620 | 1,038 | 1,002 | 942 | 826 | 624 | 406 | 373 | 501 | 707 | 970 | 273 |
| NTCD12 | NT Farm Wheel Rolls CD | 2,520 | 2,365 | 2,197 | 2,055 | 1,769 | 1,554 | 1,012 | 350 | 260 | (70) | 391 | 1,136 | 4,235 | 1,715 |
| NTCT26SXGT | NT Old School Logo T-shirt SS Granite | 240 | 126 | 489 | 347 | 237 | 79 | 323 | 499 | 75 | 54 | 341 | 1,737 | 2,321 | 2,081 |

**Figure 14.3   (continued) Fourth quarter 2003 sales, receipts, and inventory data for Night Train merchandise.**

data showed that sales varied somewhat randomly from week to week but also picked up during the summer when college students were out of school, and the bands were on tour. Sales dropped in the fall but really picked up again before Christmas. Murphy expected to see a similar pattern in the coming year.

Currently, Musictoday had no formal order-cycle process. Whenever a warehouse employee noticed that they were running low on certain items, a report would be run on that band's inventory, and Musictoday would send out the appropriate purchase orders either to the artist or directly to the supplier. Upon looking at the pattern of receipts and inventory for Night Train, it became clear that Musictoday had been largely reactive in placing orders. The buyers each covered many items and did their best to avoid stock-outs, but they lacked any real tools for deciding how much or when to order. A CD that retailed for $14.95 cost about $9 and came in case quantities of 100. The T-shirts and hats also offered on the Night Train website retailed at various price points with different margins and case quantities (see Table 14.1). Partial cases could be ordered but incurred a "broken case" charge that was usually prohibitive, so the buyers generally ordered everything in multiples of full cases.

**Table 14.1  Product Cost, Shipping Pack Quantity, and Retail Selling Prices**

| Item Number | Item Description | Cost | Case Quantity | Retail Price |
|---|---|---|---|---|
| NTCD06 | NT Yankee Hotel Foxtrot CD | $9.18 | 100 | $14.95 |
| NTCH01TBBK | NT Black Toboggan hat | $12.23 | 25 | $29.95 |
| NTCT08SXWH | NT Moon Buggy T-shirt SS white | $8.75 | 50 | $24.95 |
| NTCT10SXWH | NT Farm Wheel Ringer T-shirt SS white | $8.75 | 50 | $24.95 |
| NTCD12 | NT Farm Wheel rolls CD | $9.18 | 100 | $14.95 |
| NTCT26SXGT | NT Old School logo T-shirt SS granite | $8.75 | 50 | $24.95 |

Night Train CDs were supplied by Alliance Entertainment Corporation (AEC), headquartered in Coral Springs, Florida. To replenish its stock of Night Train CDs, Musictoday would submit a purchase order first to the band, who would forward it on to AEC, usually within two business days. Upon receiving an order, AEC would have the products shipped within five business days, and transit time was approximately three business days. All other Night Train merchandise came from a promotional-products company and would arrive, on average, 4 weeks after Musictoday issued a purchase order.

Murphy realized that in order to improve the level of service Musictoday provided to its clients, his division would need to formalize its ordering procedures. First, he thought that there must be an optimal order quantity. Murphy estimated that it cost $100 to receive a shipment regardless of the size of the order (ignoring the cost of putting items away, which would vary depending on the number of items). He estimated the carrying cost of Musictoday inventory at 15% per year—10% for the cost of capital, 3% for facility operating costs, and 2% for obsolescence. Of course, when the inventory was held on consignment, Musictoday only incurred the variable facility cost.

## Train at the Crossing

Armed with greater insight into the factors driving inventory economics, Murphy felt that he could begin a pilot program to improve the service levels provided to Night Train. He knew that this was going to be a big year for Night Train as the band prepared for the release of a major album and an extensive summer tour. Holding on to this client was critical to Musictoday's long-term success, and the best insurance policy against losing Night Train would be to take control of the stock-out situation. Murphy, however, wanted his department to understand that improving their inventory-planning process would not eliminate stock-outs altogether, and it would not suffice as an end goal. Instead, Murphy realized that an improved inventory-planning process simply went one step toward improving the overall operations effectiveness of Musictoday.

# Chapter 15

# Better World Books*

"The Online Bookstore with a Soul," Better World Books collects and sells books online to fund literacy initiatives worldwide. With more than two million new and used titles in stock, we're a self-sustaining, triple-bottom-line company that creates social, economic and environmental value for all our stakeholders.

—**www.betterworldbooks.com**

As the day wound down, Floyd Lynch, facility and safety manager for Better World Books (BWB), looked out the window of his office and thought about the question that Chris Fuchs, co-founder and VP of operations, had posed to him in a meeting earlier that day: "Should BWB expand their current warehouse facility or should they consider opening a new facility?" Lynch, an MBA graduate of the Darden School, reflected upon BWB's recent growth and the criticality of tackling warehouse capacity to sustain their anticipated future growth.

---

* With permission, this chapter presents the case "Better World Books" (Case Number UVA-OM-1432) prepared by Timothy M. Laseter and Elliot Rabinovich drawing upon a paper written by Alejandro Sanchez Abarca, Julio Serna Molina, Niraj Nath, Hector de los Rios, and Siddhartha Sinha, published by the University of Virginia Darden Graduate School of Business.

## Company Background

In 2002, three friends from the University of Notre Dame, who at that time were struggling with lack of liquidity, came up with the idea of selling used books via the Internet to earn some money. At the same time, they wanted their commitment to social and environmental responsibility to be at the core of their business. With this in mind they founded BWB, and an idea spawned from their own economic problems turned into a company considered a pioneer in social enterprise, a company with the mission of promoting literacy.

They understood that some campus bookstores were not interested in purchasing used textbooks because the local faculty would not commit to reusing them in the following academic year. But a greater reach online allowed them to resell the books on campuses that did seek those texts, allowing them to both make money and serve the local community. BWB would collect unwanted textbooks, sell them online, and pass profits over to literacy and education charities.

BWB acquired its first 2000 books in a 2002 book drive at the University of Notre Dame in support of a local nonprofit literacy group and also helped fund a local reading program. In the spring of 2003, BWB's founders were working in the business full time without taking a salary. The fledgling company received a big boost by winning the McCloskey Social Venture Business Plan Competition at the University of Notre Dame. The award of $7500 was immediately invested back into the business. The first full-time employee was hired in August 2003. Soon they were expanding operations to colleges and universities around the country.

In September 2004, BWB started its Library and Thrift Store Division to expand its inventory beyond college textbooks. Increased revenues and cash flow brought on more talent to the pricing, sales, and operations teams and allowed the company to rapidly increase inventory levels.

The year 2007 was the first profitable year for BWB. During this year, BWB implemented substantial operations improvements that led to greater profitability. For instance, they installed handheld accept/reject technology to expedite the process of screening and taking out unmarketable books from their catalog. They also launched www.BetterWorld.com as a consumer brand.

By 2008, www.BetterWorld.com had grown to become a powerful sales channel, drawing rental, publishing, and arbitrage business revenue that could provide explosive growth in future years. Annual revenues had grown from $20,000 in 2003 to $800,000 in 2004, $4 million in 2005, $9.4 million in 2006, $16.8 million in 2007, $21.5 million in 2008, and $30 million in 2009. This compelled BWB to round out its core management team by bringing in experienced individuals for the roles of chief financial officer and vice president of marketing.

## Company Culture

BWB may be defined as a for-profit "social business venture." The BWB mission statement is "to capitalize on the value of the book, to fund and support literacy initiatives locally, nationally, and around the world." To that end, BWB is deeply committed to its performance in its "triple bottom line," which measures sustainable environmental, social, and economic value. This has allowed BWB to incorporate ecological and social performance into their financial reports.

By 2009, BWB had raised $2.3 million for more than 80 nonprofit literacy programs and had created more than 230 full-time jobs. The company has consistently aimed to "benefit all stakeholders, not just shareholders." Certified as a "B Corp" (a designation representing a for-benefit corporation), BWB has been hailed as one of the leaders in the emerging field of for-profit social enterprises. From winning a Fast Company/Monitor Group Social Capitalist Award as one of ten "Profits with a Purpose" to securing significant equity funding from Good Capital due to its potential to create substantial and sustainable social impact, BWB has established itself as a model for successfully blending profit and social purpose. BWB is committed to breaking the cycle of poverty and dependency through promoting literacy and education around the globe "one book at a time."

## Used-Books Industry

Various sales channels, ranging from local book stores to the Internet to book fairs, participate in the used-book market. Most used-book sales occur informally between owners and buyers of books without any formal records, making it hard to define actual sales figures and estimate the overall size of the used-book market (Anirvan 2004). The sparse available data come mostly from major online book retailers such as Amazon who keep records of categorized sales, from students who have been surveyed, and from a few hundred bookstores. A report of the U.S. used-book market published in 2004 mentioned that there are 8,000–10,000 used-book dealers selling books ranging from a few hundred to 3.5 million through a variety of sales channels.

Over the past two decades, the used-book market has expanded rapidly, which could be attributed to a multitude of factors:

a. Higher cost of new books
b. An increase in the number of book collectors
c. A greater penetration of the Internet, which has made search for used books easier by readers

The different channels available for selling used books include open shops, mail order/Internet, private appointments, antique malls, local and regional book fairs, print catalogs, dealers, flea markets, not-for-profit book sales, garage sales, and auctions. According to a survey done by Book Hunter Press in 2002, open shops constituted 57% of the used-book market followed by the Internet at 19%, private appointments at 18%, and antique malls at 6%.

## Trends

A study conducted by the Book Industry Study Group (BISG) showed that the sales from used books increased 11% between 2003 and 2004 and represented 8.4% of the total customer spending on books (Book Industry Study Group, 2005). Another customer survey done by Ipsos-Insight showed a 5% increase in the used-book category from 2002 to 2003. Figures 15.1 and 15.2 show the revenue from and growth of book sales across channels in 2003 and 2004, respectively.

The used-book category can be further subdivided into two broad segments—educational and noneducational. The educational segment, which includes college textbooks and educational titles, dominated the used-book market with sales of $1.6 billion in 2004. However, trends in 2004 also indicated that sales in the noneducational category, which includes titles pertaining to trade, professional, and religious subject areas, is growing at a much faster rate than sales at the educational category. While sales in the educational category

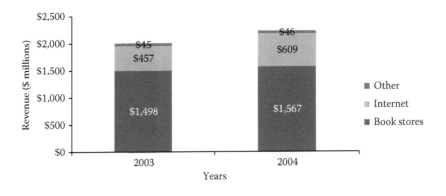

**Figure 15.1    Sales revenue by the sales channels. (From Book Industry Study Group (BISG). Rapid growth in used book market driven by the Internet. September 29, 2005. http://www.bisg.org/news-5-23-rapid-growth-in-used-book-market-driven-by-the-internet.php.)**

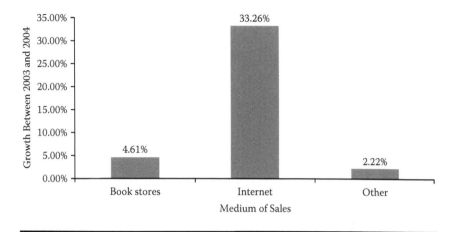

**Figure 15.2  Growth of sales channels. (From Book Industry Study Group (BISG). Rapid growth in used book market driven by the Internet. September 29, 2005. http://www.bisg.org/news-5-23-rapid-growth-in-used-book-market-driven-by-the-internet.php.)**

increased only 7% from 2003, there was an increase of 25% in sales in the non-educational category. Based on the empirical growth rate of AbeBooks.com, an Internet seller specialized in used and rare books, BISG estimated that the used-book sales would reach $1.5 billion in 2009, assuming a 20% year-after- year growth rate.

## The Internet as Vehicle for Books Sales

The Internet has created a shift in the book-buying process. In the past, buyers had to visit physical stores to search for a specific book that might not be in stock. Internet bookselling has increased price competition, lowering book prices and eliminating the frustration of driving to a physical store. The centralized Internet-based stores offer easy-to-search databases connecting thousands of booksellers and buyers to carry out transactions involving millions of books. According to the BISG, used-book sales through the Internet showed an increase of 33% while sales through traditional stores increased by only 4.6% between 2003 and 2004. Furthermore, the top four Internet book retailers for used books in 2003 were AbeBooks (with 39.2% of the online market share), Amazon (with 17.3%), Alibris (with 12.7%), and eBay (with 9%). Moreover, AbeBooks, Amazon, and Alibris received significant support among seller preferences. A total of 78.8% of used-book customers surveyed expressed their preference for AbeBooks, while 58.1%, 50.7%, and 44.4% did so for Amazon, Alibris, and Barnes and Noble, respectively.

## Supply Chain of Internet Book Retailing

The ability to quickly supply what customers request ranks among the most important factors for success at online bookstores. For this reason, many Internet book retailers, such as Amazon.com, use advanced systems for managing the shipping dates to customers. Based on the type of book, title, and availability, delivery dates are determined to ensure that customers get the books when promised. Despite this common focus, various online retailers employ a mix of supply and distribution strategies. Amazon, for example, employs the strategy of keeping only the best-selling titles in stock and fulfilling the remaining orders through wholesalers such as Baker & Taylor who have the capability of shipping directly to customers, enabling Amazon to sell books without even touching them in some cases. On the other hand, multichannel booksellers such as Barnes and Noble have distribution centers that stock more titles than any wholesaler, but that strategy creates a trade-off by consuming precious shelf space, which limit their ability to stock more books of same title.

## Value Proposition

How do you create value out of used book? How do your stakeholders identify with that value? The founders of BWB, David Murphy, Chris "Kreece" Fuchs, and F. Xavier Helgesen, sat around a pile of books in a small room at the community center in South Bend, Indiana, wondering what would differentiate them from the local bookstore across the Notre Dame campus.

The founders contemplated the role of the Internet and how it would change the book industry in the years to come, envisioning a business plan around online sales and reuse of second-hand books with a social impact. Directing a portion of their revenues to literacy programs would differentiate the company from the traditional players and allow them to partner with libraries and campuses. Student groups could help them find ways to raise funds for their initiatives and participate in literacy campaigns and support their book drives on campuses to collect books. Selling the collected books online would generate revenues for nonprofit literacy partners, and the older, unsellable books could also support the literacy mission if redirected to schools in Africa.

As a result of the founders' vision, BWB has been able to create value out of discarded books by matching supply with demand and directing unusable books in libraries and campuses to countries where book availability has been scarce. This was crucial to link the value propositions for different stakeholders: by selling a product and generating revenue they provided an outlet to libraries and campus students, books to students in Africa, and funds to nonprofit literacy partners with no covenants on use of funds. While some books are then donated directly to a particular partner, the majority of the books are resold online to generate direct funding for groups like Books for Africa, the National Center for Family Literacy, Room to Read, Worldfund, and Invisible Children.

BWB also creates value for its customers—students—by creating a platform to buy and sell secondhand books and by reducing the financial impact of book expenditures in their academic pursuits. Partnering with bookstores on campus, they have also given students an outlet to dispose of excess books. Moreover, by building a sustainable competitive advantage while creating value for shareholders, employees, literacy programs, and the environment, BWB is able to appeal to the segment of stakeholders that value corporate social responsibility. Today the company has more than 19,000 Facebook fans and more than 6700 Twitter followers some of whom buy books only from them.

## Operations

BWB has been able to mesh together the best of offline collection/distribution and online retailing to create value. The company employs a high level of operational expertise and leverages an in-house technical support system, including proprietary software developed by the company engineers. In 2009, the company systematically consolidated shipping information from more than 1500 campuses and 1000 libraries, and began directing cartons to consolidation points across the country to drive inbound shipping cost savings. Smaller consignments are directly shipped to the warehouse using a client-based mailing system accessed through the company's online portal. Student groups and librarians can request packaging material online, print UPS labels, and ship the cartons directly to the warehouse with limited involvement by BWB staff. This significantly reduces handling costs for the company, allowing the company to direct more effort toward optimizing shipping costs to the warehouse.

Upon arrival at BWB, books are scanned and traced back to the originator using client-unique barcodes and stacked in a warehouse sized to hold 2.8 million books. The stacking system, developed in-house, also identifies stacking space on shelves and, through a labeling system, directs the books to specific locations. On the receipt of a sale order, a picking employee identifies the book, using the locator code, and readies the book for shipment in less than 20 minutes. The company developed highly efficient processing capabilities, allowing it to ship up to 50,000 books a day. The shipping and processing labor works round the clock in three shifts, prioritizing international, emergency orders.

The warehouse also acts as a fulfillment center for new book orders from partner publishers who offer their books on the site as well. For orders involving both new book purchases and used inventory, the warehouse maintains a fulfillment rack to receive and repackage new books with used ones to reduce multiple shipping costs.

BWB is able to map potential sales month to month as it fluctuates significantly with semester cycles each year and, using proprietary software system, is able to match sales with warehouse processes. This has further resulted in continuous improvements in reducing inventory turns, inventory flow times, and space utilization. High-density shelving and automated machinery for sorting/selecting incoming books has also improved productivity and shortened processing time, which has led to lower labor costs and improved customer service.

Working with UPS as its sole preferred shipping partner at its warehouse location, BWB has become the largest UPS customer in South Bend, Indiana. Leveraging this volume commitment for both inbound and outbound sales, BWB has been able to negotiate rates that match those available to other leaders in the online book retailing industry.

All outbound shipping by BWB to its U.S. destinations is offered to customers free of charge and for international locations at a flat rate of $3.95 worldwide. The company has recently expanded into the United Kingdom with a local warehouse and is further looking at expanding into local operations in Australia to minimize shipping cost in these two critical English-speaking countries.

## The South Bend Facility

BWB's founders moved their warehousing operations into the current South Bend facility in 2004, 2 years after BWB's founding, to allow them to grow their business without having to rent additional space for at least some years. The longer-term perspective led them to invest in a facility that, at the time, seemed to be overspecified for their needs. Five years later and given the growth of the company, the founders were exploring an expansion of the South Bend facility (see Figure 15.3 for the layout of the facility and the current expansion). Lynch wondered what this expansion would do to the economics of the

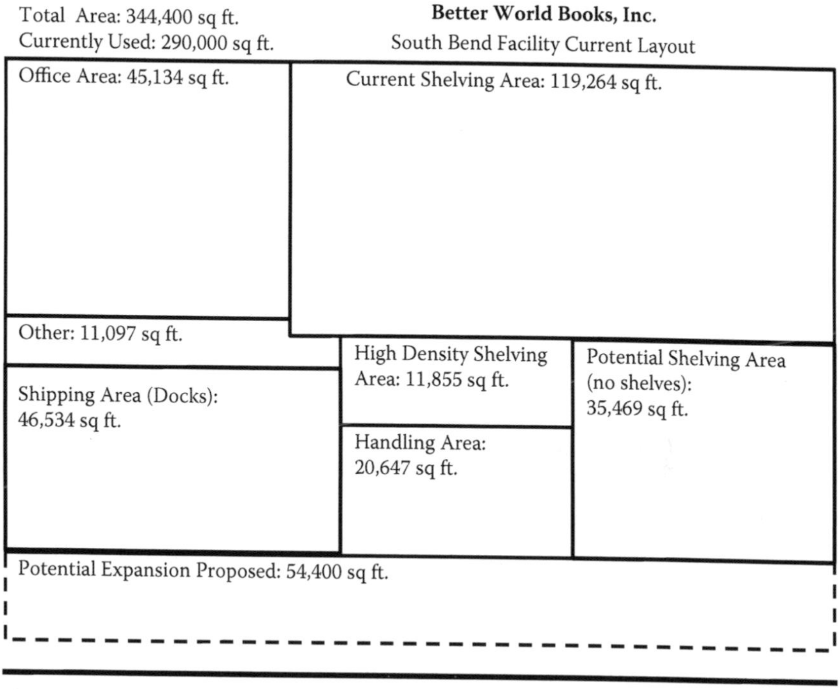

Total Area: 344,400 sq ft.
Currently Used: 290,000 sq ft.

**Better World Books, Inc.**
South Bend Facility Current Layout

Office Area: 45,134 sq ft.

Current Shelving Area: 119,264 sq ft.

Other: 11,097 sq ft.

Shipping Area (Docks):
46,534 sq ft.

High Density Shelving
Area: 11,855 sq ft.

Potential Shelving Area
(no shelves):
35,469 sq ft.

Handling Area:
20,647 sq ft.

Potential Expansion Proposed: 54,400 sq ft.

**Figure 15.3** *Source:* **Better World Books.**

facility (see Table 15.1 for the income statement of the facility). After talking to Chris Fuchs and other members of BWB, Lynch collected potential cost and capacity information associated with the expanded South Bend facility (see Table 15.2)

Lynch also knew that the current fixed costs were $1,057,000 for rent, repair, and utilities and $285,380 for other costs. Lynch's calculations assumed that the expanded facility would be working at full capacity. Therefore, Lynch wondered how realistic this full-capacity assumption was.

If the full capacity utilization assumption was not realistic, it would certainly affect the unit costs associated with shipment processing in the South Bend facility. Lynch knew that the utilization of the South Bend facility as it stood right now had a significant effect on the cost of processing an ordered book (see Figure 15.4 for information on utilization rates and costs of the facility). Finally, Lynch thought about scale curves and other proposals that he had on the table. Could he somehow use what he knew about the current and expanded facility to estimate the cost of other facilities?

**Table 15.1 Income Statement for South Bend Facility**

| Better World Books, Inc. Income statement for South Bend facility (in thousands) | | |
|---|---|---|
| | *2010 (E)* | *2009* |
| Net sales/revenue | $9,854 | $8,456 |
| Costs of goods sold | 3,879 | 3,13 |
| Inventory | 2,534 | 2,153 |
| Direct labor | 1,345 | 1,160 |
| Gross profit | 5,975 | 5,143 |
| Admin. and sales expense | 335 | 285 |
| Rent, repair, and utilities | 1,134 | 1,057 |
| Deprec. and amort. | 289 | 247 |
| Other income | (2,356) | (1,945) |
| EBIT | 1,861 | 1,609 |
| Interest expense | 904 | 865 |
| Taxable income | 957 | 744 |
| Taxes | 574 | 446 |
| Net income | 383 | 298 |

*Source:* Better World Books webpage <http://www.betterworldbooks.com>.

**Table 15.2 Expanded Facility Estimated Costs and Capacity**

| *Capacity (monthly books held)* | *Variable Cost ($/book)* | *Total Fixed Costs* | *Total Unit Cost ($/book)* |
|---|---|---|---|
| 5.5 Million books | $1.20 | $1,542,380 | $1.48 |

*Source:* Better World Books webpage <http://www.betterworldbooks.com>.

| Monthly Avg. Unit Volume | Implied Capacity Utilization | Variable Unit Cost | Fixed Facility Cost | Total Cost | Avg. Unit Cost |
|---|---|---|---|---|---|
| 643,188 | 20% | $1.20 | $1,342,380.00 | $2,114,205.60 | $3.29 |
| 1,286,376 | 40% | $1.20 | $1,342,380.00 | $2,886,031.20 | $2.24 |
| 1,929,564 | 60% | $1.20 | $1,342,380.00 | $3,657,856.80 | $1.90 |
| 2,572,752 | 80% | $1.20 | $1,342,380.00 | $4,429,682.40 | $1.72 |
| 3,215,939 | 100% | $1.20 | $1,342,380.00 | $5,201,506.80 | $1.62 |

**Figure 15.4a   Current utilization table for South Bend Facility.**

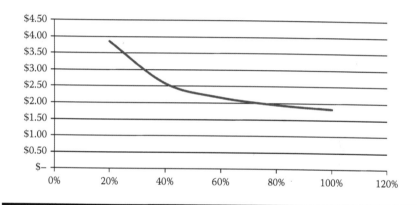

**Figure 15.4b** *Source:* Author developed based upon conversations with Better World Books.

# Expansion Options

In order to try to reduce costs and to increase efficiency and flexibility, Lynch was considering three different facility options for BWB:

1. **Expand South Bend facility**

   This alternative would allow BWB to keep all of the current employees and would not need to train new ones. BWB would now have 340,400 square feet that will allow them to store about 4.5 million books. However, it may be risky to continue investing more money in this facility.

2. **Open multiple facilities in different locations**

   Instead of having only one facility, BWB may also analyze the option of having multiple facilities in multiple locations. Even though this could be the most capital intensive option, it could also have the best impact on cost reductions by lowering transportation cost.

3. **Do nothing**

   BWB would keep its 290,000-square-foot facility in South Bend and squeeze in 3.2 million books.

# References

Anirvan. Publishers question used books. July 13, 2004 <http://journal.bookfinder.com/2004/07/publishers-question-used-books.html>.

B Corp. website <http://www.bcorporation.net/betterworldbooks>.

Better World Books webpage <http://www.betterworldbooks.com>.

Bole, Angela. Used-book sales: A study of the behavior, structure, size and growth of the U.S. used-book market. February 27, 2006 <http://www.bisg.org/news-5-28-the-first-comprehensive-report-on-used-book-sales.php>.

Book Industry Study Group (BISG). Rapid growth in used book market driven by the Internet. September 29, 2005 <http://www.bisg.org/news-5-23-rapid-growth-in-used-book-market-driven-by-the-internet.php>.

Huang, Tzu-Chen and Yang, Li-Ying. The growing market in used books. <http://are.berkeley.edu/~sberto/UsedBooks.pdf>.

Italie, Hillel. Study: Used books are $2 billion industry. September 28, 2005 <http://www.highbeam.com/doc/1P1-113615085.html>.

Rayner, Richard. An actual Internet success story. June 9, 2002 <http://www.nytimes.com/2002/06/09/magazine/an-actual-internet-success-story.html?pagewanted=all>.

Shatzkin, Mike. Supply chain impact of internet book selling. March 14, 2003 <http://www.idealog.com/supply-chain-impact-of-internet-bookselling>.

Siegel, Susan and David S. A portrait of the U.S. used book market. 2004 <http://www.bookhunterpress.com/index.cgi/survey.html>.

Wikipedia <http://en.wikipedia.org/wiki/Better_World_Books>.

# Chapter 16

# Cooking.com*

Tracy Randall, president and founder of Cooking.com, finished reading the article "The Hidden Cost of Clicks" and laid down the copy of *strategy+business* magazine on her desk. She reflected on the advice in the article and her recent efforts to develop a deeper "cost-to-serve" understanding in her company. The need for continued sales growth, coupled with the necessity of keeping costs down, put pressure on Randall to make sure that the company's capacity-constrained fulfillment center carried products that offered the greatest profit potential, not just the highest gross margins. The company was already operating with a variety of fulfillment models, but she was not sure whether Cooking.com had the optimal mix.

The company already offered cookbooks through an outsourced fulfillment model in partnership with Jessica's Biscuits, an online retailer focused exclusively on cookbooks. Some suppliers also provided direct customer shipment of certain items, saving the company the cost of handling and storing product inventory. Although Cooking.com already offered 35,000 products and 8,000 recipes, the largest selection among Internet retailers, Randall knew that the company had to continue expanding its offerings to customers in a profitable way. Even though the Internet retailing model theoretically offered unlimited shelf space in its virtual store, inventory had to be held somewhere in the system, and doing so was certainly not free.

---

* With permission, this chapter presents the case "Cooking.com" (Case number UVA-OM-1321) written by Timoty M. Laseter and Elliot Rabinovich and published by the University of Virginia Darden Graduate School of Business.

# Company History

Founded in 1998, Cooking.com emerged from a collaboration among coworkers at the Disney Store in Glendale, California, and Idealab!, an incubator in Los Angeles. On the heels of a few successful e-commerce start-ups, Idealab! was focused on funding several vertical e-commerce businesses. Excited about the promise of Internet retailing, the founders and Idealab! settled on the idea of kitchenware products for cooks. The retail category offered strong margins, a healthy average order size, and only a few focused competitors. Consumers seemed to have a strong connection to content, which would drive down marketing costs over time.

The founders established four goals for the company that continued to guide its strategies:

- To offer a complete assortment of products, including every top brand
- To create a shopping experience that was extremely intuitive and simple
- To provide dependable and affordable delivery
- To assist customers quickly and efficiently by offering highly responsive customer service

The company grew quickly, aggressively pursuing the opportunities offered by the Internet boom and raising several million dollars in 1999 and 2000. As the Internet hype began to subside in 2001, Cooking.com, like most Internet retailers, shifted its focus from revenue growth to profits. Unlike many competitors that folded after the bubble burst, Cooking.com successfully restructured its business to eliminate the need for further cash infusions and survived the crash. In 2004, the company realized a small profit, but its sales growth was stagnant. Nevertheless, having established a stable base, the management team returned its focus to expansion during 2005 and projected further growth for 2006. (See Table 16.1 for key financial metrics.)

**Table 16.1 Cooking.com Key Financial Metrics**

| Items | Fiscal 2004 | Fiscal 2005 | Fiscal 2006 (projected) |
|---|---|---|---|
| Average order | $86 | $80 | $85 |
| Annual orders | 372,100 | 462,500 | 529,400 |
| Revenues | $32 million | $36 million | $45 million |
| Gross margin | 37% | 36% | 40% |

By the end of 2005, Cooking.com had cemented its position as a leading Internet retailer of kitchenware. With sales of $40 million, Cooking.com was ranked 176 in the *2006 Internet Retailing Top 500 Guide.* Though much smaller than most of its online and traditional retailing competitors, its clear focus on kitchenware made it a substantial player in a fragmented industry.

## Overview of Kitchenware Industry

The eight product categories offered by Cooking.com—table and barware, small appliances, cookware, cooking tools, storage, bakeware, cookbooks, and cutlery—constituted a $15.4-billion market in the United States. As of 2005, the Internet accounted for about 5% of sales of these products. As shown in Table 16.2, Cooking.com accounted for a measurable but variable share of these online sales.

Historically, such department stores as Macy's, Rich's, and Hecht dominated the retail market for kitchenware. Over time, the department-store channel declined in the face of growing competition from such mass merchants as Wal-Mart and Target. Specialty retailers, such as the $3.5-billion Williams-Sonoma, also played an important role in this market; 43% of Williams-Sonoma's sales were direct to the consumer via catalog and web operations. Online, Amazon .com also played a major role, with kitchen and housewares ranking as one of the larger of its 34 product categories. As shown in Table 16.3, Cooking.com garnered a significant level of online sales of cooking products relative to other retailers, but was dwarfed by larger retailers with broader product lines and by those with traditional retail stores.

The manufacturers of cookware, also known as "food-preparation product," included such global giants as Korea's $133-billion Samsung and Japan's $81-billion Matsushita, both significant producers of microwave ovens. Large U.S.-based companies included the $14-billion Whirlpool Corporation, which sold a variety of small appliances and cookware under the KitchenAid brand, and the $6-billion Newell Rubbermaid, with 25% of its sales in cleaning and organizing products often used in the kitchen. Smaller domestic companies, such as the $609-million World Kitchen, manufacturer of cooking and bakeware products under the Revere, Corelle, Chicago Cutlery, and EKCO brands, operated at the other extreme, with a broad nonappliance product offering and focus on the U.S. market. Other American companies, such as Sunbeam (a subsidiary of American Household), with 2005 sales of $444 million, and Hamilton Beach/Proctor-Silex (a subsidiary of $3.2-billion NACCO) focused on small appliances such as mixers and toaster ovens. No company produced products for all segments of the industry, leading to relative fragmentation, as

**Table 16.2  Cooking.com Market Size and Share (2005)**

| Product Category | U.S. Retail Market ($/billions) | Online U.S. Market ($/millions) | Cooking.com Sales ($/millions) | Cooking.com Market Share |
|---|---|---|---|---|
| Table and barware | 4.2 | 210 | 9.5 | 4.5% |
| Small appliances | 4.2 | 210 | 6.3 | 3.0% |
| Cookware | 3.2 | 160 | 4.5 | 2.8% |
| Cooking tools | 1.5 | 75 | 1.5 | 2.0% |
| Storage | 0.8 | 40 | 3.1 | 7.8% |
| Bakeware | 0.6 | 30 | 1.4 | 4.7% |
| Cookbooks | 0.5 | 25 | 0.4 | 1.6% |
| Cutlery | 0.4 | 20 | 5.0 | 25.0% |
| Subtotal | 15.4 | 770 | 31.7 | 4.1% |
| Other categories[a] | | | 3.8 | |
| Total | | | 35.5 | |

*Source: Internet Retailer; Home World Housewares Census; Cooking.com estimates.*

[a] Specialty foods, large appliances, outdoor entertainment, and kitchen furnishings.

shown in Figure 16.1. Regardless of the headquarters location of the company or the particular segment of focus, most food-preparation product companies produced or sourced a large proportion of their goods in or from Asia.

## Cost-to-Serve Drivers

Cooking.com stocked more than 5,000 of the 35,000 items offered on its site in its own fulfillment center in Ontario, California. As shown in Table 16.4, the average prices and gross margins varied significantly across the seven product segments. Small appliances generated the second-highest average price per unit at $78, but the lowest gross margin at 34%. Cooking tools and storage were priced much lower, at $18 and $23, respectively, but produced a higher gross margin at 50% and 49%, respectively.

**Table 16.3  Competitor Profiles and Cooking Product Market Share (2005)**

| Cooking Products Web Retailers | Cooking U.S. Web Sales ($/millions) | Total U.S. Retail Sales ($/millions) | Total Web Sales ($/millions) | Internet Retailer Sales Rank | Monthly Visits (thousands) | Customer Conversion Rate | Average ticket ($) |
|---|---|---|---|---|---|---|---|
| Williams-Sonoma | 200 | 3,539 | 766.3 | 19 | 5,500 | 10.5% | 110 |
| Amazon | 90 | 8,490 | 8,490.0 | 1 | 120,236 | 3.2% | 184 |
| Sears Holding | 70 | 49,124 | 2,160.0 | 7 | 36,000 | 5.0% | 100 |
| Target | 60 | 52,620 | 896.6 | 16 | 41,509 | 2.0% | 90 |
| Crate & Barrel | 50 | 929 | 173.1 | 59 | 3,679 | 5.6% | 70 |
| *Cooking.com* | *40* | *40* | *40.0* | *176* | *1,500* | *3.0%* | *86* |
| Wal-Mart | 40 | 312,400 | 1,050.0 | 12 | 41,667 | 2.8% | 75 |
| JCPenney | 30 | 18,781 | 1,039.3 | 13 | 20,057 | 2.9% | 150 |
| QVC | 20 | 6,501 | 1,017.0 | 14 | 20,243 | 6.9% | 70 |
| Costco | 20 | 51,900 | 534.0 | 27 | 8,500 | 1.3% | 400 |
| Federated | 10 | 22,390 | 450.0 | 29 | 13,733 | 2.2% | 125 |
| Subtotal | 630 | 526,714 | 16,616.3 | | | | |
| Others | 430 | | 92,758.7 | | | | |
| Total | 1,060 | | 109,375.0 | | | | |

*Source: Internet Retailer estimates; Home World Housewares Census; Cooking.com estimates.*

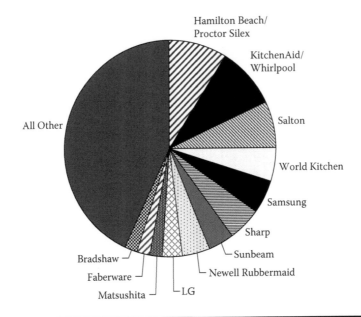

**Figure 16.1 Food-preparation manufacturers by share. (From Food Preparation Products, 2002. Reidel Marketing Group.)**

However prices and gross margins did not tell the whole story. Although the company generated 42% gross margin on the $27.8 million in sales channeled through its fulfillment center, operating costs for the facility ran around $2.8 million, leaving an operating margin of about 32%. Cooking.com also offered several shipping options, with charges based on the order value. The shipping fee generally exceeded the out-of-pocket cost paid to the carrier, which helped to offset the costs of the facility and also funded the occasional free-shipping offer.

Randall realized that continued profitable growth required fully understanding the true profitability of the offered products, based on a deeper understanding of the operational cost drivers. To tackle this issue, she formed a task force spearheaded by Laura Shaff, vice president of finance, with the blessing of Bryan Handlen, the chief operating officer. Working with some outside experts, the team identified six major operational cost categories and developed some insight into the drivers of each.

**Table 16.4  Cooking.com Metrics for In-House Stockkeeping Units (SKUs) by Product Category**

| Product Category | 2005 Annual Sales | Average Price Per Unit | Gross Margin | SKUs Carried | Inventory Turns (per year) | Avg. Weight (lbs) | Inbound Ship Cost | Average Size (cu ft) | Special Handle SKUs | Return Rate |
|---|---|---|---|---|---|---|---|---|---|---|
| Table and barware | $8,631,000 | $32 | 44% | 1,979 | 6.3 | 6.9 | $224,000 | 0.42 | 60% | 3.2% |
| Small appliances | $5,928,000 | $78 | 34% | 882 | 6.1 | 8.4 | $176,900 | 0.86 | 26% | 4.2% |
| Cookware | $4,252,000 | $80 | 42% | 815 | 7.5 | 6.6 | $97,100 | 0.61 | 12% | 3.1% |
| Cooking tools | $1,168,000 | $18 | 50% | 330 | 5.1 | 1.3 | $17,200 | 0.10 | 2% | 1.7% |
| Storage | $2,419,000 | $23 | 49% | 296 | 7.8 | 3.7 | $44,100 | 0.35 | 19% | 3.0% |
| Bakeware | $1,488,000 | $19 | 46% | 474 | 5.6 | 2.6 | $26,000 | 0.16 | 13% | 1.8% |
| Cutlery | $3,921,000 | $56 | 43% | 406 | 8.3 | 2.5 | $39,700 | 0.12 | 0% | 2.5% |
| Total | $27,807,000 | $44 | 42% | 5,182 | 6.5 | 4.7 | $625,000 | 0.40 | 19% | 1.2% |

*Source:* Cooking.com data: casewriter analysis.

## Inbound Shipping

Inbound shipping costs to the Ontario facility ran $625,000 a year based on receipts of nearly 3 million pounds of product. All suppliers shipped from a facility—a manufacturing plant or, more typically, a distribution center—located within the United States. Most Asian-produced goods came from distribution centers located near a West Coast port, but shipments were received from the Midwest and East Coast as well. One of Cooking.com's largest suppliers, Calphalon, a producer of pots and pans, shipped in full-truckload quantities at a cost of 9.8 cents/pound Suppliers of such bulky, high-unit-volume products as microwave ovens shipped in less-than-truckload (LTL) quantities at a cost ranging from 24 cents/pound from the West Coast to 38 cents/pound from the Midwest to 43 cents/pound from the East Coast. The remaining suppliers—those selling small goods like cooking tools or bulkier products with lower unit sales—shipped goods via parcel post. Those rates varied from 29 cents/pound from the West Coast to 47 cents/pound from the Midwest to 56 cents/pound from the East Coast. A few suppliers—such as KitchenAid, a producer of small appliances, and Le Creuset, a supplier of cookware and bakeware—shipped their goods prepaid to Cooking.com, with the freight cost buried in their pricing. Table 16.4 provides the breakdown of the total inbound shipping costs by product category.

## Receiving and Put-Away

Upon receipt, products were put away in various storage locations throughout the facility. Large goods, such as small appliances and large cookware sets, came in pallet quantities and were put away by forklift into tall racks in the main aisles of the facility. Some of the more expensive items that did not come in pallet quantities, such as cutlery, were put on racks within an access-controlled area of the building to minimize "shrinkage," the term used for the difference between expected and actual inventory in a distribution facility due to stocking errors, damage, and pilferage. Some smaller items were stocked by hand in bins for easier access later. Figure 16.2 provides images of these three basic types of shelving systems. The receiving and put-away operations employed an average of 21 full-time-equivalent employees (including salaried management) at a cost of $475,000 a year (fully loaded).

## Inventory-Carrying Cost

As shown in Table 16.4, inventory turns varied significantly across the product segments as well. Cooking-tools inventory only turned five times a year, while

**Figure 16.2a Pallet storage. Cooking.com options for inventory storage. (From Cooking.com.) (continued)**

cutlery turned more than eight times a year. Of course, inventory value was not the only consideration. Bulkier items with a low unit cost (e.g., storage products) took up more space "per inventory dollar" than did higher-priced goods like cookware, which had an average price nearly four times higher than that of an average storage product but a cubic volume less than twice that of storage products.

On average, Cooking.com turned inventory every 8 weeks. Based on annual sales of $27.8 million from the fulfillment center products and a 42% average gross margin, it held about $2.6 million in inventory, on average, across the year. The company had access to bank loans at prime rate, but its overall cost of capital was significantly higher considering its funding from private venture-capital investors who tended to expect returns in excess of 30% annually.

**Figure 16.2b    (continued) Cutlery storage. Cooking.com options for inventory storage. (From Cooking.com.)**

Cooking.com ensured critical inventory accuracy through ongoing cycle counting by several hourly employees under the guidance of a full-time salaried supervisor. Records suggested that the equivalent of eight full-time workers focused on inventory issues at a fully loaded labor cost of $235,000 a year. Inventory also incurred costs for taxes and inventory obsolescence equal to 2% of the value of inventory annually. The fixed costs of the facility, including rent, depreciation, and utilities, ran $425,000 a year; 75% of the building space was for inventory storage, 10% for receiving, and 15% for packing and shipping.

## Pick, Pack, and Ship

Cooking.com employed 24 full-time equivalents, including a full-time supervisor, in its "pick, pack, and ship" operation at a cost of $650,400 a year, and

**Figure 16.2c (continued) Small-unit storage. Cooking.com options for inventory storage. (From Cooking.com.)**

consumed $331,800 in corrugated boxes and packing supplies annually. Even though many items came in shippable boxes, Cooking.com repackaged all its items in boxes featuring its own brand name. Because most packaging also served as visual displays of the product, the typical cookware product featured pictures of the contents of the box. Thus, the repacking avoided spoiling the surprise if the purchase was a gift. Furthermore, repacking reinforced brand awareness with the recipient. Unfortunately, many products required special handling. Glassware required additional packing supplies, and certain products were designated "ship alone" because they tended to damage other goods when placed in the same box. Management of the fulfillment center estimated that "special handling" increased the labor cost by 5% and the cost of packing materials by 30%.

## Outbound Shipping

As noted previously, Cooking.com charged a shipping fee for each customer order, based on the value of the order. Orders of less than $49 were charged a flat rate of $7.99 for standard shipping and handling, while orders between $49 and $99 incurred a charge of $9.99 for shipping and handling. Items between $99 and $150 required a shipping-and-handling fee of $10.99, and those between $150 and $250 were charged a fee of $12.99. Orders above $250 incurred a fee of $14.99. Overall shipping revenues totaled $2.3 million a year, or 8.1% of sales. The weight of the package and the distance shipped drove actual shipping costs, however, and ran about 76 cents/pound, on average.

## Returns

Although overall returns averaged less than 2%, Cooking.com discovered that the return rate varied by product category, as shown in Table 16.4. In most cases, the customer paid for return shipping and simply received credit for the product cost, but for one-third of the returns, Cooking.com credited the customer for the product, the original shipping, and the cost of return shipping, resulting in incremental shipping costs of around $27,600 a year. Typically, the product returned to the fulfillment center could be restocked or returned to the vendor for full credit, but in about one-third of the cases, Cooking.com had to discard the product or sell it to employees. On average, the company captured about 15% of the product cost in those cases and wrote off 85% of the original product cost, which produced a write-off of about $48,000 a year. The equivalent of one full-time employee handled returns during slow periods at a fully loaded labor cost of $28,800 a year.

# Conclusion

As she thought about her upcoming meeting with the board of directors, Randall wondered whether the work to date on understanding the cost-to-serve drivers could shed light on the best product categories for further investment. On the one hand, with the fulfillment center running at capacity, she knew that additional SKUs could be carried only if other items were dropped. On the other hand, many manufacturers had expressed a willingness to offer products on a drop-ship basis directly to the end consumer for fees ranging from 60 cents to $15, plus actual shipping costs. Maybe it was time to check back with Laura Shaff and see what conclusions the team had reached.

# Chapter 17

# RelayFoods.com*

Zach Buckner, the founder and the CEO of RelayFoods.com hung up the phone after a brief thank-you call with his lead investor. Though he and Arnie Katz, president and COO, had come within weeks of running out of cash, they had now successfully closed a round of equity financing that would fund the company through the end of the following year at current projections. Buckner's innovative model for addressing the last-mile challenge in Internet grocery retailing seemed to be working. After less than 2 years, the Charlottesville, Virginia, pilot was generating annualized revenues at a rate in excess of a million dollars. More critically, projections indicated that it would be cash flow positive before the end of the next year. The three-month-old pilot expansion into Richmond, Virginia, was generating three-digit monthly sales growth but still consuming cash. However, with a market seven times larger, Richmond should soon outperform Charlottesville.

The RelayFoods.com business model, built around partnerships with local retailers, farmers, and employers, supported the growing "localvore" movement and minimized the need for capital for inventory and distribution facilities. However, it also demanded coordination of significant logistical complexity. The company now offered more than 15,000 stockkeeping units from 90 plus supplier-partners and an evolving set of more than 25 pickup locations across the two cities. The hub-and-spoke model worked, but the management team was

---

* With permission, this chapter presents the case "RelayFoods.com" (Case Number UVA-OM-1431) prepared by Timothy M. Laseter and Elliot Rabinovich, drawing upon a paper written by Eli Yoffe, Fabio Costa, Parker Garrett, and Anshul Sharma, and published by the University of Virginia Darden Graduate School of Business.

not convinced it was optimal. To date, the company had employed a philosophy of low-cost experimentation as it explored terrain that had proved inhospitable to predecessors. It now appeared time to make some bigger bets on the company's operations strategy.

## RelayFoods.com's History

Graduating in electrical engineering from University of Virginia in 2002, Zach Buckner started his career in consulting at Elder Research, most recently serving as its vice president of technology. The entrepreneurial spirit led Buckner into several small ventures during high school and into founding and selling a document management start-up while studying at UVA.

As a consultant and especially as a family man, Buckner learned to appreciate his free time. Whenever he shopped at Wal-Mart, Kroger, or any other store, he reflected upon the host of inconveniences from finding a parking space to wandering the aisles searching for a product to standing in the checkout line and driving back home with his purchases. He knew there had to be a way to do it more efficiently.

Following his entrepreneurial desire, Buckner started researching the last-mile challenge and found that many Internet era start-ups, including Webvan, NetGrocer, and FreshDirect, had explored alternative models for getting goods to consumers with less hassle. While the first two failed, FreshDirect still operated successfully in New York City, where the density of population and supplier direct sourcing methods favorability contributed to the company's bottom line.

Despite the history of failures within the industry, Buckner still believed that a sustainable economic model could be replicated in specific cities across the United States. Speaking with various advisors and analyzing the reasons behind the failures, Buckner realized that one of the major reasons was the inherent inefficiency of the to-your-door delivery system.

Buckner concluded that the solution was to eliminate the consumer need to drive to a store but still avoid home delivery. Rather than suffer the last mile, he wanted customers to meet him halfway—at pickup points convenient to their homes or offices. After a year of reflecting on the problem and developing a business plan, he secured a first round of financing and founded Retail Relay Inc., which later evolved to RelayFoods.com.

Several interns from engineering and IT backgrounds helped Buckner develop an Internet site and organize the launch of the service in late 2008. Families and friends became the first customers during the beta stage. Though he almost abandoned the business in early 2009, a few small but critical cash infusions kept the company alive through the winter. Infusion of some fresh talent, including current president and COO Arnie Katz, in the summer of 2009 spurred double-digit monthly growth and renewed confidence in the business model. Investments from several sophisticated angel investors built further confidence and allowed Buckner to redesign the web interface, rebrand the business as RelayFoods.com, and expand the concept into Richmond.

## U.S. Grocery Stores and Supermarkets

With 70,000 grocery stores nationwide, the U.S. retail grocery industry generates almost $500 billion in annual revenue.* Relatively concentrated, the 50 largest grocery store chains, such as Kroger, Safeway, and Supervalu, generate about 70% of industry revenue. The mix of sales in a typical grocery store included 50% perishable foods, 30% nonperishable foods, and 20% nonfood items. Nonfood items include health and beauty products, cleaning products, and medication.

Two factors drive demand and shape the competitive landscape: population growth and changing formats. U.S. population growth of 1% per year limited overall industry growth. Traditional grocery stores also faced competition from other retail formats; wholesale clubs, convenience stores, drugstores, dollar stores, and restaurants all sought to capture a share of the consumer wallet for food and household supplies. Though 90% of groceries were purchased through traditional grocery stores in 1988, by 2010 the share had dropped below 50%.

With notoriously thin margins, grocery store profitability depends on high-volume sales and efficient operations. Large companies gain advantages through their ability to carry a wide selection of products and by scale economies in centralized purchasing, distribution, marketing, and financing. Small companies can compete by selling niche products and brands that the larger retailers eschew due to insufficient volume, and by providing more intimate customer service based upon rich insight into customer needs in local markets.

## Alternative Online Grocery Retailing Models

Given the vast size of the grocery retail industry, a variety of companies had targeted the market during the heyday of the Internet era in the late 1990s. Unfortunately, most had failed to produce a profitable alternative to the traditional formats.

---

* IBISWorld Industry Report: U.S. Supermarkets & Grocery Stores Industry Report.

## *Webvan*

Founded in 1996 during the dot-com bubble by Louis Borders and initially funded by Benchmark Capital, Webvan offers the most spectacular case example of the excessive hype of the Internet bubble. Borders, a successful entrepreneur and the creator of the inventory system used to manage the vast book inventory of The Borders Group, believed that online retailers would never make it into the consumer's home unless there could be a faster, less expensive, and more efficient way of delivering.* He believed that Webvan could be the bridge between the disadvantages of driving to the store for instant gratification and the convenience of shopping on the Internet.† Webvan raised more than $800 million and achieved a valuation of $7.9 billion on the opening day of its initial public offering (IPO)—a valuation equal to about half that of the industry-leading Kroger despite having sales of less than half a single grocery store at the time. Despite the valuation and massive cash infusion, Webvan declared bankruptcy in 2001, leaving a wake of empty distribution assets. Although a failure, this business offered a great case for studying the economics of grocery delivery.

Webvan's business model centered on owning the last mile of e-commerce. The company created large distribution centers (DC) at 336,000 square foot with capacity equal to 20 grocery stores but far less labor intensive and with lower industrial versus retail real-estate cost. The highly automated distribution centers contained more than 5 miles of conveyor belts and more than 40 specially designed carousels to minimize the walking distance for the order picker. Each DC cost around $35 million and would require more than 500 people to process orders at full capacity.‡

After a customer placed an order through the company's website, it was electronically transmitted to the relevant DC. The sophisticated software system created the optimal plan to assemble the order according to specific parameters such as weight, crushability, size, and so forth. Pickers at the various carousel stations pulled items for multiple orders simultaneously using a "pick to light" system to indicate the proper tote for each item. In other areas, order pickers pulled high-volume items such as soft drinks from simple flow-through racks with limited technology. Conveyors routed the completed totes from all of the areas including frozen zone and a kitchen for preparing fresh meals to the shipping dock for aggregation onto trucks assigned to each transfer station.§

The large central DC fed 10 to 12 smaller cross-dock stations within a 50-mile radius of the DC where drivers transferred the orders into 60 smaller

* Linda Himelstein, "Can You Sell Groceries Like Books?" *Business Week*, August 26, 1999.
† Andrew McAfee and Mona Ashiya, "Webvan," *Harvard Business School*, March 13, 2003.
‡ Ibid.
§ Ibid.

delivery trucks with multiple temperature zones for dry, perishable, and frozen goods for delivery directly to the customer's door.* To minimize customer time waiting for a delivery, Webvan committed to a 30-minute shopper-specified delivery window between 7 a.m. and 10 p.m.[†] Drivers used a wireless device to check the order and to print a receipt—and also provide immediate credit to a customer account for returns or other problems.

Webvan claimed that their proprietary DC automation allowed them to reduce the average total touches on a grocery item from 14 times for the conventional supermarket supply chain to 8 times.[‡] The company also planned to turn over inventory 24 times a year compared to 12 for a regular supermarket. The target pick rate per worker was more than 400 items an hour—far faster than a person shopping among the aisles of a grocery store. At their height, Webvan had facilities in operation or under construction in 10 U.S. cities: Atlanta, Chicago, Dallas, Denver, Newark, Philadelphia, Sacramento, San Francisco, Seattle, and Washington, D.C.

Each DC in the Webvan model was designed to hold 50,000 items and handle 8,000 orders per day.[§] Because of the intense investment in technology of a DC, Webvan needed around 4000 orders a day in a DC at the average order size of $103 in order to break even.[¶] Webvan estimated that 8000 orders would bring them to between a 10%–12% operating margin—a remarkable figure compared to 2%–3% for a conventional supermarket.** Unfortunately, the company never achieved breakeven volume in any market, and instead lost almost $160 per order across all of its DCs.

## FreshDirect

Founded in 1999 by Joe Fedele, a seasoned veteran of the grocery industry, and Jason Ackerman, a former grocery industry-focused investment banker,[††] FreshDirect launched operations in the New York City metropolitan area in September 2002, slightly more than a year after Webvan filed for bankruptcy. Offering next-day delivery to most of Manhattan and parts of Brooklyn, Queens, the Bronx, Staten Island, Nassau County, Westchester County, Hoboken, and

---

* Ibid.

[†] Laseter, Houston, Chung, Byrne, Turner, Devendran, "The Last Mile to Nowhere: Flaws and Fallacies in Internet Home-Delivery Schemes," *Strategy+Business*, July 1, 2000.

[‡] The Webvan Group, Prospectus filed with SEC, November 5, 1999.

[§] IBID.

[¶] Jean Murphy, "Webvan: Rewriting the Rules on 'Last-Mile' Delivery," Global Logistics & Supply Chain Strategies, August 2000.

** Henry Blodget, Webvan Report, Merill Lynch & Company, January 26, 2001.

[††] O+F (Ops and Fullfillment), July 2003, pp. 34.

Jersey City, FreshDirect has avoided the fate of Webvan thanks to higher delivery density of the market and by vertically integrating into preparation of higher-margin fresh products.

FreshDirect uses SAP software to process thousands of orders for groceries and meals placed on their website each day. The company buys directly from farms, fisheries, and dairies, and as long as a customer places his or her order by midnight, he or she can get those fresh groceries the next evening during a 2-hour delivery slot of the customer's choice. Orders are dispatched to the kitchen, bakery, and deli, as well as fresh storage rooms, produce-ripening rooms, and production areas within the company's refrigerated facility. All fresh items are custom-cut, packaged, weighed, and priced. In the case of dry goods or frozen foods, items are picked from storage before being placed inside bins that travel along conveyors to the sorting area to be scanned and gathered in corrugated fiberboard boxes. The boxes are labeled, recorded, and loaded into refrigerated delivery trucks.* See Figure 17.1 for select photographs drawn from the FreshDirect website photographic tour.

FreshDirect generated an estimated $240 million in sales in 2009 by filling 230,000 orders a week. The privately owned company does not release financial figures but claims to have turned profitable 16 months after opening its doors. FreshDirect attributes its success to giving customers less expensive food and more flexibility in arranging deliveries. Operating for nearly a decade, the firm has certainly impacted the NYC grocery market: In 2008 there were one-third fewer supermarkets in New York City than when FreshDirect first opened for business.†

FreshDirect operates out of a fully refrigerated processing facility the size of five football fields located just across the river from Manhattan. Equipped with multiple Wi-Fi access points to keep the multitude of technical equipment and hand scanners in constant communication, FreshDirect uses tools from SAP for inventory control and order processing, each customized by the German tech giant.‡ Thanks to a combination of location near the docks and its real-time order processing, FreshDirect achieves unusually quick seafood stock turns; while the average grocer may have 7 to 9 days of seafood inventory, FreshDirect's turns every day.§ (See Figure 17.2.)

As customers place orders, the inventory system tracks product availability in real time to mark an item as unavailable if the supply falls too low. A light

---

* Jennifer Harsani, *PC Magazine*, 18 May 2004, p. 76.
† 2008 Shulman, R., "Groceries Grow Elusive for Many in New York City," *Washington Post*, February 18, 2008.
‡ SAP Customer Success Story 2009 FreshDirect, SAP website.
§ Kevin Coupe, *Chain Store Age*, April 2004, p. 38.

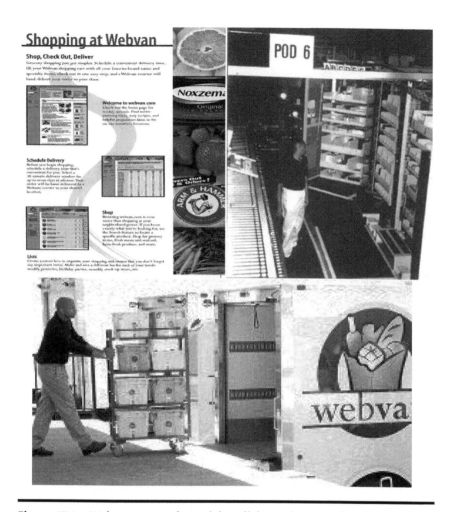

**Figure 17.1** Webvan screenshot, pick-to-light pod carousel, and cross dock. (From Webvan website directions page; IE Solutions, September 2000.)

shows the worker the bin containing the product and how many to grab to fill an order. After all the items in an order are placed in a packing box in the various departments, another worker repacks and sort items in one of 10 delivery bays and loads orders on a temperature-controlled FreshDirect truck. In order to complete this logistically intensive process, the company employs about 1400 manufacturing workers and 600 delivery drivers.

Buying direct from suppliers, paying them in days rather than weeks, and avoiding the "slotting fees" (payments by suppliers for prime shelf space) common in traditional retail all help FreshDirect to negotiate highly favorable terms

**Figure 17.2 FreshDirect vertically integrated processing facility. (From FreshDirect Photographic Tour, FreshDirect.com.)**

with suppliers. Add all these advantages together, and the firm's fresh selection is offered at prices that can undercut the competition by as much as 35%.* And FreshDirect does it all with operating margins in the range of 20%, easily dwarfing the razor-thin 2% margins earned by traditional grocers. Interestingly,

---

* Strategy & Technology, www.gallaugher.com/Strategy%20&%20Technology.pdf, September 2008.

a uniquely high cost of FreshDirect's business model is a heavy load of parking tickets: they add up to about $600,000 annually.*

## *RelayFoods.com*

RelayFoods.com has developed a unique business model, drawing upon the lessons of previous "last-mile" failures. Like FreshDirect, RelayFoods.com focuses on higher-margin perishables but with a local twist. The company sources from small local farms and retailers to avoid the massive capital investment required by its predecessors, and it uses pickup points to transfer goods to the customer to avoid the high last-mile costs. (See Figure 17.3)

A normal day at RelayFoods.com's original Charlottesville pilot starts the evening before the delivery. Customer orders submitted by midnight are sent to a network of supplier partners, including 17 local farms, 14 local prepared-food purveyors, 5 local produce providers, 4 local butchers/fishmongers, 4 specialty grocery stores, and 2 anchor grocery stores. The suppliers pull the requested items—in some cases sorted by the end customer—for pick up by RelayFoods .com each morning. After completing the collection loop, the driver returns to the fulfillment center where drivers team with other employees to sort the items of food into totes organized by dry, perishable, and frozen for each individual customer. In some cases, the farmer delivers directly to the fulfillment center, and in other cases, Relay holds select inventory on premises so it can be delivered less frequently. Relay currently aims to sort about $500 worth of product per person per hour at the fulfillment center during a 4-hour window, using drivers and part-time sorting laborers.

After redistributing the food into labeled order bins, the drivers reload the trucks to one of a dozen different pickup locations throughout the city. The driver serves customers from the truck between 3 p.m. and 7 p.m.; some walk up to a neighborhood location, others drop by on their way home from work, or the gym, and others simply swing by a convenient location along their commuting route home.

Unlike its competitors, Relay does not source direct from manufacturers nor does it set the pricing. Each supplier partner determines the product mix and price with Relay taking a prenegotiated percentage of the margin generally equal to one-third of the gross margin the retailer would normally capture. Accordingly, customers pay the same prices as they would at the individual retail shops supporting Relay. As of summer 2010, Relay offered about 15,000 SKUs on the Charlottesville site, the vast majority of which was held by the supplier

---

* Baseline, "Is Online Grocer FreshDirect about to Succeed Where Webvan Failed Miserably?" February 2004, Larry Dignan, pp. 60.

**Figure 17.3** RelayFoods.com local farm network and pickup location. (From RelayFoods.com, Inc.)

partners, allowing Relay to have a positive cash cycle by immediately collecting charges from customer credit cards but paying suppliers monthly.

## Operations Strategy for RelayFoods.com

The initial pilot in Charlottesville, Virginia, had proved the basic concept. Revenues had grown at a double-digit monthly compounded rate for 21 consecutive months with sales running at a million dollars per year by fall of 2010. The company had just launched a second pilot in Richmond, Virginia—a market seven times larger. Buckner felt confident that the basic Relay model offered a superior approach for addressing the challenges of the last mile in comparison to its two larger predecessors (see Table 17.1.)

The company had also established strategic partnerships with two large companies—Whole Foods Market and SUPERVALU—which could allow it to serve customers more profitably. Whole Foods offered access to its 365 brand of private-label goods, which provided a great value to the consumer with simultaneously higher gross margins for Relay. Branded, nonperishable case goods, such as cereal, juice, and canned soup, were supplied by local SUPERVALU retailers in both Charlottesville and Richmond, and the parent company was prepared to offer bulk delivery of high volume items directly to the Relay fulfillment center once the company reached sufficient scale for such a mixed model. Products delivered directly to the fulfillment center would produce significantly higher

**Table 17.1  Comparative Cost Structure for "Last Mile"**

|  | Webvan | FreshDirect | RelayFoods.com |
|---|---|---|---|
| Compensation for delay | $3.00 | $5.00 | N/A |
| Orders delivered per day per truck | Up to 20 | Up to 40 | Up to 70 |
| People per truck | 1 | 2 | 1 |
| Daily travel per truck | 100 miles | 40 miles | 50 miles |
| Average order size | $103 | $100 | $80 |
| Gross margin | 20% | 30% | 15% |
| Average delivery fee | Free | $6.00 | Free |

*Source:* Case writer estimates from various sources.

gross margins but would require an investment in inventory and might entail more handling cost.

The company had also experimented with home delivery in select neighborhoods in the Charlottesville market at a price of $8 per delivery but at a discount down to $5 per delivery for a subscription using the maximum of weekly deliveries. While not part of the original model, RelayFoods.com had launched home delivery as a low-cost experiment. Findings to date showed that home delivery customers tended to place larger orders and more frequently. Interestingly, customers who experimented with home delivery had a higher reorder rate, even if they ultimately chose the pickup option most frequently. The company had not offered home delivery in Richmond as it continued to contemplate the appropriate degree of vertical integration—both forward and backward.

Buckner wanted to continue to conduct small-scale experiments but also recognized it might be time to place a few big bets on the company's operations strategy. A clear comparison of the Relay operations strategy against Webvan and FreshDirect would help inform those bets.

## Chapter 18

# eBags: Managing Growth*

In early 2004, Jon Nordmark and his management team (Figure 18.1) sat down to review the most recent sales numbers for the holiday season with much anticipation. Thus far, it had been quite a ride for eBags management. The company had survived the "tech bust" of 2000 to 2002 relatively unscathed and was one of the few Internet retailers to turn a profit. In December they had been named one of *Internet Retailer* magazine's top 50 websites. Now, the financial statements before them indicated their company could boast of a seventh consecutive quarter with a positive cash flow and second consecutive quarter of profits.

While Nordmark and his team felt optimistic about the current state of eBags, they realized that e-commerce was evolving quickly, and the strategic choices they made over the next few months would determine the future growth of their company. Thus far, the management team had concentrated its efforts on marketing and merchandising but realized that expansion would require a more holistic view of the business.

The team concluded that eBags would have to seek out additional revenue streams to sustain its high level of growth. Two proposals for expansion were

---

\* With permission, this chapter presents the case "eBags: Managing Growth" (Case number UVA-OM-1179) written by Tim Laseter, Elliot Rabinovich, and Manus Rungtusanatham, with the assistance of Todd Lappi and Ken Heckel, and published by the Darden Graduate School of Business.

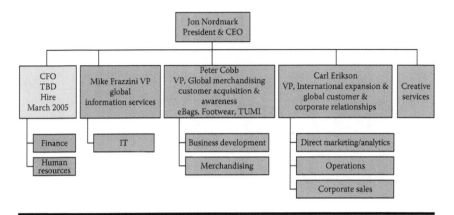

**Figure 18.1  Organizational chart.**

under consideration. One involved expanding the current business model to Europe, while the other involved adding shoes to the eBags product portfolio. While both options looked promising, Nordmark knew that there would be challenges from an operations standpoint and wanted to make sure that he thoroughly understood the implications of each option.

# eBags History

In the spring of 1998, Jon Nordmark convinced four other people, Peter and Eliot Cobb, Frank Steed, and Andy Youngs, to join forces with him to build an online luggage- and travel-products store. The choice of a business that provided a wide variety of luggage, bags, backpacks, and travel accessories was not surprising since Nordmark, Peter Cobb, Youngs, and Steed were all top executives with Samsonite USA and American Tourister. Together, they saw the Internet as an opportunity to take their experience and build a major retail company.

It was a risky move for each of them. To get the company started, each contributed $50,000 and agreed to work for free until the company could establish funding from outside sources. As they struggled to find the initial funding, Nordmark took cash advances on his credit cards, borrowed money from his family, and took a second mortgage on his home to keep the company afloat. At one point in late 1998, both Nordmark and eBags were completely broke.

In January 1999, Benchmark Capital, a leading Silicon Valley venture capital firm, stepped up to the plate with funding. Robert Kagle, a partner with Benchmark, praised Nordmark as both a visionary and pragmatic businessman.

Soon after the initial investment, other venture capitalists "smelled blood" and began to contribute capital, with investments totaling $6.8 million.

In March 1999, eBags.com was officially launched. More venture capital money followed, and by November 1999, eBags had received more than $30 million in funding. With plenty of capital, Nordmark and his team focused on driving sales growth and boosting brand offerings. By the end of the first year of operations, eBags had achieved an average monthly sales growth of 98% and had broadened their product offering from 6 to 56 brands. The year 2001 marked the turning point for eBags as it was named "website of the Year" by *Catalog Age*, and had its first profitable month in December. Numerous marketing and merchandising awards followed in the ensuing years.

By early 2004, eBags was the largest online provider of bags and accessories, carrying more than 200 brands and 8000 products. eBags had sold more than 2.5 million bags and had been a consistently profitable company, one of the few dot-coms to survive, let alone thrive.

## The Luggage Industry*

Like most U.S. industries, the luggage industry experienced significant growth and innovation as a result of the nation's transformation after World War II. Materials such as rip-stop nylon, fiberglass, plastics, aluminum, leather, and simulated fabric that had been developed for wartime were now put to use in the industry. Manufacturers designed products that were durable yet light enough to meet federal air travel requirements. During the 1970s, utility yielded to fashion as designer luggage became the vogue. Also, as air travel became more efficient, the emphasis was on speed, and manufacturers began to produce carry-on luggage that allowed travelers to avoid check-in lines and baggage claim areas. In the 1980s, luggage became a status symbol. Consumers demanded that their luggage demonstrate their wealth, status, and fashion taste. In response, manufacturers produced luggage in a wide range of styles, colors, sizes, and fabrics, which led to a surge in the breadth and fragmentation of the industry. While fashion remained a key determinant, the 1990s and early 2000s saw a return to emphasis on utility, as international business travel exploded in the new global economy.

The domestic luggage market, a $1.28 billion market in 2000, was fragmented with a wide range of products that were distinguished primarily by

---

* "Luggage," *Encyclopedia of American Industries*, online edition. Gale, 2004. Reproduced in Business and Company Resource Center. Farmington Hills, MI: Gale Group, 2005. http://galenet.galegroup.com/servlet/BCRC.

product quality, product usage, and price. The luggage market included traditional travel bags, suitcases, briefcases, backpacks, handbags, computer cases, and other travel accessories. The high end of the market consisted of high-quality, full-featured products with prestigious brand names. These items carried high price tags and were selectively distributed to specialty stores and a few major retailers. The middle portion of the market held a vast number of products that were differentiated by features, brand name, and price. Distribution was wide in this portion of the market, with products reaching specialty stores, large retailers, and discount stores. The low end of the market consisted of private-label and unbranded products. These products had few differentiating features and were sold in significant volume at low prices, which resulted in low margins for retailers and manufacturers.

Because of the fragmentation of the marketplace, there were only a few major competitors with significant national market shares, namely, Samsonite, American Tourister, JanSport, and Eastpak. The rest of the market was divided into smaller national or regional brands that served a specific niche. Brands such as the North Face, kate spade, Totes, Eagle Creek, and Liz Claiborne were just a few of the many recognizable names found in the market.

Manufacturing was managed through global sourcing with a focus on the lowest cost processes that met the quality standards and specifications of the product. For example, Samsonite, the only truly global luggage producer, operated 11 manufacturing facilities worldwide, 2 in the United States, 3 in Western Europe, and the remainder in the developing regions of Eastern Europe, Mexico, India, and China. JanSport listed more than 20 contract manufacturers on its website, including 5 in the United States, 4 in China, 3 in El Salvador, and 2 in Mexico. Other locations included Vietnam, Madagascar, Indonesia, Singapore, Malaysia, Honduras, Macau, and Jakarta.

The fragmented base of luggage producers and the wide range of quality/price segments led to a broad and fragmented retail market as well. Luggage and travel accessories could be acquired through retailers ranging from department stores, luggage specialty stores, discount stores and, in some cases, manufacturer-owned outlets. Marketing programs focused on brand advertising that reinforced the unique qualities of the product. In-store point-of-sale programs and promotional activities supported the marketing strategy as well.

It was the fragmented nature of the luggage market and his experience with Samsonite that led Jon Nordmark to launch eBags as an innovative business solution.

## eBags Business Model

Nordmark and his team's experience in the luggage industry provided a strong foundation for success, but the eBags business model represented a major departure from the traditional one. It sought to reduce industry fragmentation and bring the customer closer to the manufacturer by bringing a diverse collection of brand-name products into one online store location.

eBags began by developing strong relationships with major manufacturers and by marketing four different product lines: bags, business cases, handbags, and backpacks. The company sought products in these categories that covered the three segments of the market (high end, middle, and low end). eBags sold its concept to manufacturers by stressing the value added by bringing a wide range of customer segments into closer contact. Furthermore, the online storefront shortened the supply chain, thereby offering the opportunity for significant inventory cost savings. In exchange for bringing the customers closer to the manufacturer, eBags pushed the drop-ship inventory model (see Figure 18.2) onto the manufacturers. In this model, inventory was managed at the manufacturer or distributor level. In serving as the intermediary for the customer, eBags placed daily orders to the vendor, who then shipped the item directly to the customer. This model eliminated eBags' risk of inventory obsolescence, which was a significant consideration in a market being driven more by style than by functionality.

With most products sold in shippable cartons, the drop-ship model was not a large departure for the major luggage providers, and it gave them more

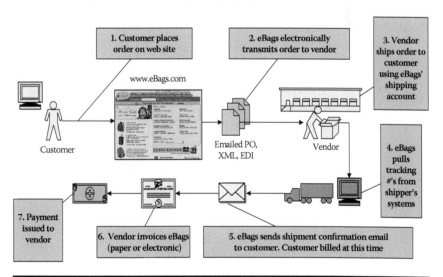

**Figure 18.2  Drop-ship order-fulfillment process.**

immediate feedback from the customers than the traditional retail model. For eBags, the drop-ship model practically eliminated the need for inventory, thereby reducing holding costs below those of traditional retailers. Furthermore, eBags could offer a much wider "virtual" assortment than a traditional luggage retailer facing physical space constraints and/or needing costly floor space to expand.

To effectively reach all potential customers, eBags built an engaging website storefront that marketed products based on demand and availability. The main selling point to the customer was eBags' ability to bring a wide variety of products to one location. Without the storefront, customers had to spend time and money traveling to different specialty shops or department stores in search of the perfect product. With the eBags site, customers could search by type, brand, product line, and price. eBags made a conscious decision not to compete on price. Rather, they chose to compete on product breadth, selection, and convenience. Products on the eBags site, therefore, showed the manufacturer's suggested retail price (MSRP). Since the ability to comparison shop in such a fragmented market was important to the customer, the eBags site was judged successful in reaching the target market.

eBags' challenges stemmed from having to disrupt the traditional value chain that existed between manufacturers and retailers. Department stores and specialty shops presented significant friction to the online system. When eBags initially launched its site in 1999, online retail accounted for only 1% of market sales, but based on the success of Amazon.com and eBay, the handwriting was on the wall. The retailers argued that they provided manufacturers with consistent demand and an inventory cushion, advantages that eBags could not provide. eBags countered with the argument that its business model brought more customers to the manufacturers at a faster pace and that these advantages outweighed inventory-holding costs. In time, the online market data would be available to manufacturers to better estimate demand and handle inventory. Additionally, eBags argued, this business model allowed them to focus extensively on product promotion and marketing activities that would increase sales levels. eBags assumed the responsibility of maintaining the website, photographing products, and marketing and promoting products and brand names.

As the initial products and brands experienced sales success, eBags was able to build up its supplier network from 10 to 300 suppliers, with product lines increasing from 1000 stockkeeping units (SKUs) to more than 15,000 SKUs. In order to build awareness, eBags developed an affiliate program that encouraged nonretail websites to promote eBags. In return for setting up a link to eBags on their independent website, the affiliate earned a commission as high as 20% for every eBags sale that resulted from the customer clicking on the eBags link. This served as a low-cost way to market eBags and promote sales in previously untapped market segments.

As the supplier base expanded, eBags saw a need to better serve the low-end, cost-conscious portion of the market. Feedback from the website indicated that customers were looking for generic travel products that were reliable but low in cost. In response, eBags launched its own private label that was sourced through low-cost Asian manufacturers. In this manner, eBags was able to satisfy the low end of the market with decent margins. The drawback came when eBags was forced to maintain an inventory for the private label, as the drop-ship model could not be applied efficiently with its Asian contract manufacturers.

# eBags Operations Model

In order to eliminate the high inventory-holding costs associated with over 8000 different luggage items and 15,000 individual SKUs, eBags employed the drop-ship model (Figure 18.2),* which accounted for 85% of the shipments for eBags. Trade-offs existed, however, in earning lower profit margins than traditional retailers and the inability to control the shipping schedules of the manufacturers.

With the development of the private label, eBags incorporated the traditional speculative inventory model. The private label consisted of 15% of shipments, with roughly 1000 SKUs maintained in an eBags warehouse in Dallas, Texas. In line with its strategy of limited inventory-holding costs, eBags strived to maintain an estimated 2-month sales level of private-label inventory and to minimize production runs while maintaining the same timeliness and accuracy targets that it held for drop-ship products. By global-sourcing the manufacture of the private label through a network of low-cost Asian manufacturers and tight inventory management, eBags could satisfy the cost-conscious customer—while still enjoying a healthy profit margin.

Data management was critical to eBags' operational efficiency, and the company built strong vendor relationships by maintaining a high degree of transparency. eBags exchanged data with vendors on a daily basis through a system called the eBags Partner Network (EPN). This web-based interface constituted 60% of the data exchange, while traditional file transfer protocol (FTP) and electronic data interchange (EDI) constituted the remaining 40%. The EPN allowed vendors to update inventory status for individual SKUs on a real-time basis, identifying them as in stock, out of stock, or discontinued (Figure 18.3). In turn, this enabled eBags to more effectively market the product lines to the

---

* "Looking Big: How Can On-line Retailers Carry So Many Products?" *Wall Street Journal*, April 28, 2003.

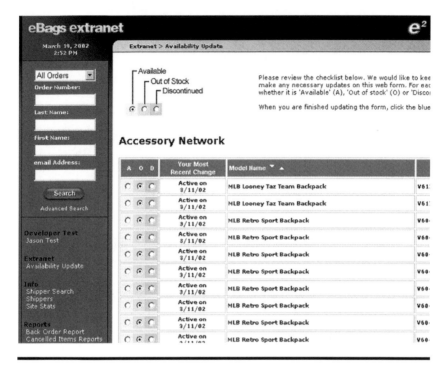

**Figure 18.3    EPN screen sample—vendor inventory update.**

customer, ensuring that customers did not request items that the manufacturer could not deliver.

eBags incorporated a vendor scorecard system into the EPN that enabled vendors to track key metrics such as product sales, product returns, customer ratings, and testimonials (Figure 18.4). The information on the vendor scorecard served as a motivational tool for vendors to improve operational performance on such operational elements as back-order rates, delivery time, and processing rates. eBags set stringent goals for its vendors and strived to achieve overall objectives of maintaining an on-time delivery rate of 95%, a shipping accuracy of 99.995%, a back-order rate of less than 1%, and an order-process time of fewer than 2 days. The vendor scorecard was a valuable tool in enabling eBags to maintain the visibility of vendors and reinforce positive performance that increased customer satisfaction and led to strong sales growth.

Shipping was handled through one primary carrier—United Postal Service (UPS). Products were sent directly from the manufacturer or from eBags' own warehouse to the customer. eBags and the customer could track the product shipment status via UPS's online system. eBags was responsible for the cost of

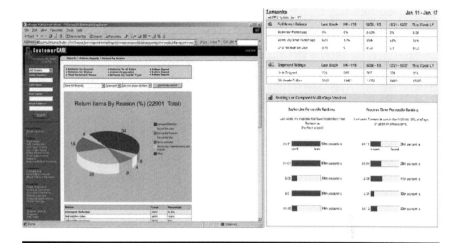

**Figure 18.4    EPN screen sample—vendor sales data and vendor scorecard.**

shipping to the customer, as well as the cost of return shipping for any product that did not meet the customer's expectations. It sent a prepaid UPS shipping label directly to the customer, who simply mailed the package back to the manufacturer or eBags, depending on the agreement with the individual vendor.

The return policy was liberal but consistent with that of other Internet retailers. eBags offered a 30-day grace period for free returns. Return rates for luggage averaged 6% to 7% of the bags sold, a relatively low rate. This was believed to be primarily due to the ability of the customer to evaluate and understand the product prior to purchase. The key determinants of size, fabric/material, color, and purpose were easy to communicate via a product photo on the website.

# The Footwear Industry*

In 2003, the domestic footwear industry was a $40.7 billion market, making it nearly three times larger than the luggage and travel accessory market currently served by eBags. As with the luggage industry, the footwear industry was highly competitive and extremely fragmented. The top-five U.S. footwear manufacturers were Nike, Inc., Jones Apparel Group, Reebok International Ltd., Timberland Company, and Brown Shoe Company, Inc., with none of the competitors holding more than 8% market share. The competitive nature of the industry led to fragmentation, as shoes were distinguished by performance,

---

* "Footwear in the USA," http://www.euromonitor.com/mrm/scripts (assessed June 2004).

design, product quality, fashion awareness, styling, and—finally—price. With nearly 30% of domestic consumers demonstrating strong brand loyalty, it was imperative for manufacturers to develop consistent and reliable products that met the target market's demand.

The consumer market was divided into three segments: women's (50.4% of sales), men's (40.3%), and children's (9.3%). Personal consumption of footwear accounted for 15% of overall apparel spending, with women spending on average 80% more than men. As discount retailers entered the market, the average price paid for shoes decreased such that shoes priced under $100 currently accounted for 36% of total shoe sales in the United States. The market was also seasonal, with peaks occurring during the back-to-school, Christmas, and Easter periods.

Distribution was managed primarily through specialty outlets (47% of the market), department stores (20.6%), and mass merchandisers (16.7%). Specialty outlets focused on a specific type of footwear, such as Foot Locker's athletic shoes. Typically smaller than a mass merchandiser, specialty outlets offered fewer brands and styles than a mass merchandiser. Unlike a discount retailer such as Wal-Mart, mass merchandisers sold only footwear and offered a wide variety of types because offering multiple brand names gave them a broad range of low-priced products to offer customers.

In the early 2000s, consumer price sensitivity increased significantly, and mass merchandisers such as Famous Footwear, DSW, and Payless Shoes increased their focus on a low-price strategy, which continued to bring price-conscious customers into their channel. As a result, specialty stores experienced a decrease in importance as a retail channel in the domestic footwear market. eBags hoped to exploit this price sensitivity in the marketplace, coupled with the advantages of e-tailing.

In many ways, the product extension into footwear seemed like a logical one to eBags. By leveraging its strengths in marketing and merchandising, eBags felt confident that it could exploit the similarly fragmented footwear industry by providing one-stop shopping for consumers. The breadth of products and consumer behavior was similar to the luggage industry although shoes did present some unique challenges versus luggage and travel accessories. Shoes needed to be tried on by customers before they were satisfied with the product, and online buying behavior suggested that customers often purchased multiple pairs of shoes simultaneously, fully intending to return ones that did not fit correctly or otherwise failed to meet their expectations.

Another challenge for eBags stemmed from having to increase consumer awareness. The name eBags did not suggest to the average consumer that footwear could be purchased on the website. eBags needed an approach to overcome this barrier, either through website acquisitions/mergers, affiliate programs, or advertising and marketing. By 2004, more than 36 online footwear retailers existed in the marketplace. Each one was viewed as a potential acquisition/ merger for eBags. Affiliate programs would consist of agreements between eBags and other nonretail websites. In promoting eBags on their own websites, these affiliates would receive a commission for every sale that occurred as a result of the customer navigating through the affiliate's website.

A comparison with a potential acquisition candidate, Shoedini, highlighted many differences between footwear and the current eBags product lines (Table 18.1). If successful in the footwear market, eBags saw future potential for additional product extension in the clothing and apparel market, which was the largest online retail market.

## The European Market

The European luggage market was considered to be just as highly fragmented as the domestic market that eBags currently faced. Most European luggage retailers were small, family-run stores that operated with limited selling hours and offered a less diverse product line. As international travel increased, these retailers did not meet the demands of their customers adequately. Customers were looking for wider selection and variety along with breadth of style and utility, and, even more important, those in one country had different priorities from people in a neighboring country. For example, German customers placed a high value on functionality, while French and Italian customers valued style, color, and seasonality. British customers looked for a balance in their luggage selection; they preferred a mix of function, value, and quality.

A key motivation for developing the European luggage market was the high level of Internet usage that Europe had reached by 2002. An estimated population of 190 million Internet users spread across Europe and surpassed the 165 million Internet users in the United States. Additionally, the Internet penetration rate (percent of population with Internet access) averaged nearly 50% among the top-12 nations in Europe (Figure 18.5). And, finally, the levels of online retail sales in the two largest regions (Germany and the United Kingdom) had risen dramatically from 1997, reaching a total of $1.94 billion in 2002 (Figure 18.6). eBags estimated that the reachable European market could expand up to $17 billion by 2004, an estimate supported by projected annual European electronic commerce market growth of 33%.* The recent success of online retailers Amazon.com and eBay in European markets provided encouragement for eBags.

---

* "On-line Retailers Look Overseas," *New York Times*, January 10, 2005.

**Table 18.1  Comparative Data by Category**

| Product Category | Purchase Frequency | Return Cost % | Model Count | SKU Count | Average Selling Price | Average Gross Margin | Product Lifecycle | Product Return Rate |
|---|---|---|---|---|---|---|---|---|
| Backpacks | 1.08 | 15.1 | 621 | 1,486 | $53.00 | 46% | 2 years | 7% |
| Business cases | 1.05 | 12.3 | 330 | 557 | $55.00 | 49% | 5 years | 6% |
| Business accessories | 1.06 | 20.2 | 383 | 873 | $25.00 | 48% | 4 years | 6% |
| Handbags | 1.23 | 12.9 | 1,913 | 4,571 | $55.00 | 52% | 3 months | 10% |
| Luggage | 1.14 | 10.8 | 832 | 1,818 | $90.00 | 47% | 6 years | 6% |
| Shoes (Shoedini) | 1.16 | 9.87 | 3,123 | 92,218 | $68.00 | 48% | 3–6 months | 25% |

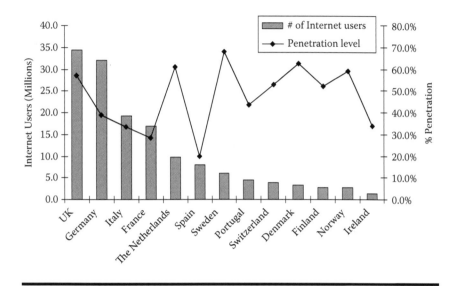

**Figure 18.5    European Internet usage.**

A significant void existed in the European market space that eBags intended to occupy. European vendors had yet to build significant relationships with online retailers, and eBags could capitalize on the opportunity to consolidate the distribution channel and reduce fragmentation. Establishing a one-stop shopping experience for customers in the European marketplace could provide the same level of success that eBags had achieved in the United States.

Nonetheless, challenges existed in bringing the eBags business model overseas: language barriers associated with packaging and labeling, shipping requirements, brand awareness, maintaining the EPN interface, and webpage administration.

## Where Do We Go from Here?

Jon Nordmark leaned back in his chair and contemplated the decision in front of him. The success enjoyed by eBags was a result of innovative thinking and aggressive management that had created a unique opportunity to consolidate the fragmented luggage market. Now it was clear that eBags needed a strategy to project this success into the future.

Should eBags consider product extension into footwear, with the hopes of further extension into the online clothing retail market? Should the company consider business expansion into Europe? If so, what European markets should it enter, and

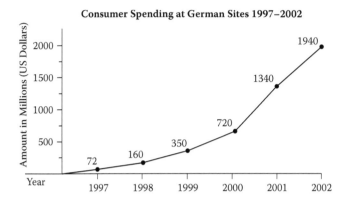

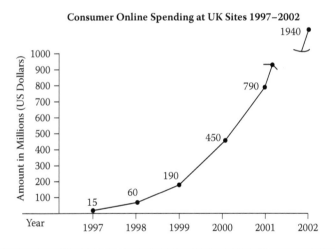

**Figure 18.6   European online consumer spending—UK and German sites.**

could the product expansion of footwear also be introduced in the European market? Each option presented its own set of unique advantages and challenges.

Clearly, the future of online retailing was on the rise. Consumers were enjoying convenience, variety, speed, and personal-tailoring that online markets brought to their shopping experience. This phenomenon was spreading beyond luggage into all retail market segments. What was the best way for eBags to leverage its strengths and profit from the continued growth of e-commerce?

# Index